SWEAR LIKE A TROOPER

A DICTIONARY OF MILITARY TERMS AND PHRASES

William L. Priest

Rockbridge Publishing
an imprint of
HOWELL PRESS, INC.
Charlottesville, Virginia

ABX- 2139

Published by
Rockbridge Publishing
an imprint of
HOWELL PRESS, INC.
1713–2D Allied Lane
Charlottesville, VA 22903
(804) 977-4006
http://www.howellpress.com

A Katherine Tennery Book

Library of Congress Cataloging-in-Publication Data

Priest, William L., 1949–
 Swear like a trooper : a dictionary of military terms and phrases / William L. Priest.
  p. cm.
 Includes bibliographical references.
 ISBN 1-883522-13-7
  1. Military art and science—Dictionaries. 2. United States—Armed
Forces—Terminology. 3. Soldiers—Terminology. I. Title.

U24 .P887 2000
355'.003—dc21   99-089486

10 9 8 7 6 5 4 3 2 1
Printed in the United States of America

CONTENTS

*In the loving memory of my parents, Ira Lee Priest
and Rita Marie Tresselt, who instilled in me
a deep and lasting love of history
and the languages of mankind.*

PREFACE

The English language is probably the most versatile language on earth. As it evolves, it absorbs and adopts words from other languages, and where there is no word, it creates one. One has only to listen to a person versed in computer technology for a few moments to realize that he or she is drawing vocabulary from the newest edition of the language. Adding color to the building blocks of the language are slang and jargon, which slide in and out of use, even changing meaning based upon the speaker's ethnic, social, political, and educational background. For those of us involved with teaching, research, or writing a historical novel, the correct use of such slang and jargon is not just important—it is vital.

My father and mother were avid readers who shared a deep love of history, although their points of view were very different. My father, who had seen combat with the First Marine Division in WWII, focused on the role of the military. My mother's history came from the historical novels that she devoured in great numbers. Historical events were dinner table conversation. My twin brother and I received great doses of history that piqued our own interests. For my part, I collect militaria and participate in living history programs, drawing from a repertoire of more than two dozen personas ranging from a 1750s privateer to a German soldier of WWII. Nearly thirty years of searching for the most accurate military portrayals gave rise to the compilation of this dictionary, triggered by a television mini-series, of all things.

Shogun, based on James Clavell's book by the same name about events in sixteenth century Japan, was a lavish production. I thoroughly enjoyed the program until the scene in which the sailors demand their grog. Everyone *knows* sailors drank a lot, but—there was no such thing as grog in the sixteenth century! A British sailor, until the late 1750s, would have demanded his spirits or beer ration. It was disappointing, to say the least. In that small but important detail, the validity of the production was shattered.

It was at that point that I decided to organize earlier informal research and compile a personal dictionary of military slang and jargon. I had already been collecting terms. My father provided some of the first—SNAFU, FUBAR, knucklehead, dog face, and many more—and I had long been jotting down terms I encountered in my reading. Now it was time to get organized. As the collection expanded, it became apparent that the meanings of many terms had evolved over the centuries, some having undergone drastic changes in usage. I believe this information is critical for the historians who interpret and edit military writings and the writers of military history or fiction, who, like the writers of the *Shogun* script, ought not to put themselves in a position from which they might be hoisted on their own petard. Thus began a labor of love of nearly twenty years that has become *Swear like a Trooper.* As the entries were added almost up to the press date, it became clear that this book can be offered only as a guide, not as the final word. Another edition is already under way.

EXPLANATORY NOTES

Within the pages of this book you will find more than fifty-six hundred entries, from AA to Zu Zu. The majority of the entries come from the armed forces of the United States, followed by Great Britain and her former commonwealth nations, France, the Netherlands, Vietnam, Japan, Imperial Germany, and the Third Reich.

Each entry is arranged as follows, although not every entry contains every one of these elements: term, pronunciation, military branches, date span, etymology, definition (which includes changes in usage), and a source code or codes.

The entries are, of course, alphabetical. Numbers are alphabetized by their word equivalents, so M79 is alphabetized as M seventy-nine. For phrases, especially those with more than one key word, there are usually at least two entries—one with the definition and one or more that direct the reader to the principal entry.

A rough pronunciation is provided where available for entries that might be difficult for English speakers to sound out. Foreign words and phrases are rendered as found in the source. Entries for acronyms indicate whether they are spoken letter by letter, as a word, or both; the reader should assume a letter-by-letter pronunciation if no other indication is made.

An attempt has been made to show the migration of entries from group to group. A [/] indicates shared usage at some point in time; a [>] indicates a migration from one group to another. For example, MM>BrN>USN/USA shows that a term arose in the merchant marine and was picked up by sailors in the British navy, who then passed it along to the sailors and soldiers of the United States. A list of abbreviations is provided on page *vii*.

The dates of usage are as accurate as possible. A specific time frame, such as 1768–1900, indicates that the entry was definitely in use in those years. But language is a slippery item, so the term may have been in use before or after that time frame in some military branches or geographic areas. The dates assigned to changes in meaning or usage are also subject to some give-and-take.

If there is more than one definition, the branch that used the term and the date span remain the same unless otherwise noted.

Some of the entries include an etymology, showing a term's evolution from ancient languages, in an attempt to trace the origins of each word geographically, ethnically, and militarily.

Where there is a clear source for a definition, it is noted by a three-letter code at the end of the entry. The table of source codes can be found on page *viii*. These are books that were particularly helpful in dating or defining entries.

A select bibliography is included.

ABBREVIATIONS

These abbreviations are used throughout the dictionary in an effort to save space. The abbreviation MM, which stands for Maritime or Merchant Marine, encompasses commercial shipping, a source of a great deal of colorful language that later worked its way into the military services. Words and phrases attributed to this source were generally in standard use by English-speaking sailors. Those terms particular to the British Merchant Marine or the U.S. Merchant Marine are so identified.

ANZAC . . Australia–New Zealand Army Corps
Arab . . . . Arabian
AusA . . . . Australian Army
AusN . . . . Australian Navy
Br . . . . . . British civilian
BrA . . . . British Army
BrAF . . . . British Air Force
BrMM . . . British Merchant Marine
BrN . . . . British Navy
CA . . . . . Canadian Army
CN . . . . . Canadian Navy
CSA . . . . Confederate States Army
CSN . . . . Confederate States Navy
Czech . . . Czech Republic
D . . . . . . Holland (Dutch)
DA . . . . . Dutch Army
DN . . . . . Dutch Navy
Fr . . . . . . French civilian
FrA . . . . . French Army
Gr . . . . . . German civilian
GrA . . . . German Army
GrAF . . . . German Air Force
GrAK . . . German Africa Korps
GrN . . . . German Navy
Hun . . . . . Hungarian civilian
It . . . . Italian civilian

ItA . . . . . . Italian Army
MM . . . . . Maritime, Merchant Marine (British and United States usage)
NatAm . . Native American
NZ . . . . . . New Zealand civilian
NZA . . . . New Zealand Army
NZN . . . . New Zealand Navy
Port . . . . . Portuguese civilian
Rus . . . . . Russian civilian
Sc . . . . . . Scottish civilian
Sp . . . . . . Spanish civilian
US . . . . . . United States civilian
USA . . . . United States Army
USAF . . . United States Air Force
USAAF . . United States Army Air Force
USCG . . . United States Coast Guard
USMC . . . United States Marine Corps
USMM . . United States Merchant Marine
USN . . . . United States Navy
USNA . . . United States Naval Air
Viet . . . . . Vietnamese Army
West Point United States Military Academy at West Point

SOURCE BOOK CODES

Following some entries in this dictionary are three-letter codes identifying sources that were particularly helpful in validating the definition. The codes and a short author/title identification are listed below. Please see the bibliography for more details.

ADW	Jewell, *Alamein and the Desert War*	MD	Scott, *Military Dictionary*
AET	Interview: Anthony E. Tresselt	MDB	*Military Dictionary* (1768)
AFR	Carlisle, *The Air Forces Reader*	MLS	*Military Symbols*
AFS	Weir, *The Answer Book*	MMD	Garber, *The Modern Military Dictionary*
AGE	Empey, *Over the Top*		
ANE	*Naval Encyclopedia, 1885*	MSH	*Basic Field Manual*
ARL	War Department, *Army Life*	NCT	Lovette, *Naval Customs and Traditions*
ASC	Weir, *Army Social Customs*		
ASL	Evans, *A Sailor's Log*	NSB	Macy, *The Nantucket Scrap Book*
AST	Shay, *An American Sailor's Treasury*	NTD	Soule, *Naval Terms and Definitions*
ATK	Colby, *Army Talk*	OFG	*The Officer's Guide*, 23rd ed.
BCD	Crocker, *Black Cats and Dumbos*	OST	Rodgers, *Origins of Sea Terms*
BJM	U.S. Naval Inst., *Bluejackets' Manual*	PAT	Interview: Ira "Pat" Lee Priest
BLO	Terry, *Bloods*	PWO	*Picturesque Word Origins*
BMO	Merrill, *Behold Me Once More*	RAS	Valle, *Rocks and Shoals*
BRC	Crisp, *Brazen Chariots*	RSC	Bell, *Room to Swing a Cat*
BWH	*The Merriam-Webster Book of Word Histories*	SAF	Caidin, *The Air Force: A Pictorial History*
CAM	Kilner, *The Cantonment Manual*	SAM	Interview: Samuel Cosman
CDA	Schwartz, *Complete Dictionary of Abbreviations*	SAW	Werstein, *1898: The Spanish American War Told with Pictures*
CWO	Funk, *2107 Curious Word Origins*	SEA	NAVPERS, *Seamanship*
DCA	Evans, *A Dictionary of Contemporary American Usage*	SFS	Hugill, *Shanties from the Seven Seas*
		SID	Kendall, *Still in the Draft*
DOC	Rogers, *Dictionary of Clichés*	SLA	Colcord, *Sea Language Comes Ashore*
DRA	Forty, *Desert Rats at War*		
DVT	Grose, *A Classical Dictionary of the Vulgar Tongue*	SSD	Partridge, *Small Slang Dictionary*
		TBS	Brereton, *The British Soldier*
DWO	Ayto, *Dictionary of Word Origins*	THN	Lenninger, *Time Heals No Wounds*
EMP	Empey, *First Call*	TLL	Grimshaw, *The Ladies' Lexicon*
FFF	Bairnsfather, *Fragments from France*	TNW	Pye, *The Navy Wife*
FOD	Carell, *The Foxes of the Desert*	TOC	Flower, *The Taste of Courage*
GFM	Marine Corps Assoc., *Guidebook for Marines*	TON	Windas, *Traditions of the Navy*
		TWW	Rodgers, *The Wooden World*
GWD	Kendall, *Gone with the Draft*	WEA	Johnson, *Welcome Aboard*
IHA	Flexner, *I Hear America Talking*	WID	Lucas, *War in the Desert*
LRY	Wiley, *The Life of Johnny Reb* or *The Life of Billy Yank*	WWW	*Wine, Women, and War*
		YSK	Whitehouse, *The Years of the Sky Kings*
MAN	Heinl, *Handbook for Marine NCOs*		
MCT	Boatner, *Military Customs and Traditions*		

A

AA USA/USAF (1918–present) antiaircraft fire. USAF (1950–60s) apprentice airman, a flier fresh from basic training. (ATK)

AAA (triple ay) USA (1960s–present) anti-aircraft artillery; also spelled triple–A.

AAA-0 (ay zero) BrA/ItA (1943) anything, anytime, anywhere—bar nothing (no exceptions). (TOC)

AAF US (1918–49) Army Air Force; American Air Force. (AFR)

AB *See* able seaman

aback *See* taken aback

abaft MM>USMC (12th c.–present) [Anglo-Saxon *beaften*, behind] behind, farther behind. (MAN OST)

abatage (ah•bay•TAJ) USA (20th c.) said of an artillery piece whose wheels are sitting on its brake shoes; a demolition caused by the detonation of a high explosive. (MMD)

abatis BrA>USA (1790s–WWII) an obstacle consisting of trees felled so that their interlocking branches impede advancing enemy troops. During WWI, barbed wire was added to the tangled branches. (*see also* live abatis)

Abdul (AHB•dool) BrA>USA (WWI– Korean War) a Turkish soldier or civilian.

abeam MM/USMC (16th c.–present) at a right angle to the centerline of a vessel; immediately beside someone or something. (MAN SLA)

able-bodied seaman *See* able seaman

able seaman MM (18th c.–present) rank earned by one who is thoroughly trained as a sailor; aka able-bodied seaman, AB. USN (18th–19th c.) a sailor at least eighteen years old who knew the ropes and had six years of experience before the mast as a common sailor. (SLA) (*see* know the ropes, rate, ship before the mast)

able-wackets BrN (18th–late 19th c.) a card game in which the loser had his hands soundly whacked with a knotted handkerchief or rope, once for each round lost; aka able-whackers. A play on the term able-bodied rating. (DVT) (*see also* able seaman)

able-whackers USN (19th c.) a variation of able-wackets. (ANE) (*see* able-wackets)

abnormal shot USA (1930s) a shot that hits six points or more away from the center of the target. (MMD)

aboard MM>USMC (14th c.–present) on board a vessel or in a room, building, or other location. (MAN OST)

abort GrA (WWI) a toilet. (*see also* latrine)

about-face USA/USN/USMC/USAF (20th c.–present) a marching order specifying a 180-degree turn to the right from the position of attention; in common/civilian usage, a complete reversal of opinion or action. (MMD) (*see also* about-face, right)

about-face, right CSA/USA (1860s–late 19th c.) a marching order for a 180-degree turn to the right. By the late nineteenth or early twentieth century, the phrase had been shortened to "about-face." (*see also* about-face)

aboveboard MM (17th c.–present) open, fair, and honest. From pirates' practice of hiding men and weapons below the boards (high sides) of their ships. Their prey saw no threat until it was too late. (TON)

abreast USA (19th c.–present) said of men who are advancing shoulder to shoulder, in line. (MMD)

abri (ah•BREE) FrA (WWI) a dugout. (WWW)

absent without leave USA (1860s–present) absent from the service or one's unit without official permission; aka AWOL, dickey leave. (MMD) (*see also* adrift, AOL, AWL, AWOL, French leave, leave)

absentee USA (WWI–WWII) a man who is absent, with or without permission, for roll call or duty. (MMD)

absolute deviation USA (WWII) the smallest distance between the target and the actual point of impact of a bullet or shell. (MMD)

abstract USA (WWII) a detailed summary that was supposed to accompany returns of material and reports. (MMD)

abuses and disorders USA (WWII) a category of military offenses that included only those committed due to a lack of discipline (as opposed to malicious intent). (MMD)

abutment USA (WWI–WWII) the butt or stock of a shoulder- or hand-held firearm; the bridge support nearest the shore and the ramp that leads up to it. (MMD)

abutment bay USA (WWII) the part of a pontoon bridge nearest the shore. It was usually supported by a trestle. (MMD)

AC USA (1958–present) assistant commander; acting commander; army corps; air corps. (1960s) aircraft commander. (ASC)

academic board USA/USN/USMC/USAF (WWII) the heads of the academic departments at a military academy. The academic board determined the policy and curriculum of the academy. (MMD)

accelerator USA (WWII) a gun that uses multiple powder charges in split-second relays to increase the velocity of the shell being fired; a mechanism in a machine gun's recoil system that increases the speed with which the bolt of the gun moves and thus increases the rate of fire. (MMD)

accelerograph USA (WWII) a mechanism within the powder chamber of a cannon that measured the internal pressures at various points within the chamber as the gun was fired. (MMD)

accessory USA (WWI–WWII) an item that is needed for a weapon or machine to function but is not physically part of the weapon or machine. (MMD)

accessory defense USA (WWII) an artificial defense. (MMD)

accidental error USA (WWII) an error that occured at random, not as a result of a system failure. (MMD)

accompanying artillery USA (1920s–WWII) artillery, from single guns to battalion-size units, assigned temporarily to infantry units ranging in size from regiments to battalions; an artillery assigned to mobile, mounted cavalry or infantry units. (MMD)

accompanying battery USA (WWII) a light artillery unit assigned to a regiment for close support in an attack. (MMD) (*see* battery)

accompanying gun USA (WWI–WWII) a single field piece that was assigned to a battalion-size unit as a close-support weapon for assault or emergency defense. (MMD)

accompanying tanks USA (1920s–WWII) a detachment of tanks that was used in support of a battalion-size unit. The tanks either led or followed the attacking infantry. (MMD)

accompanying weapons USA (WWI–WWII) weapons that were not infantry or cavalry weapons but were assigned to those units to assist in their attack or defense of a position. (MMD)

ace[1] Fr>Br/Gr>US (WWI–present) a pilot who has shot down at least five enemy aircraft in one-to-one combat. German pilots needed ten kills to become aces. (ATK) (*see also* ace pilot)

ace[2] USMC (Vietnam) to kill: *Ace him!*

ace of spades US (1960s) a playing card that symbolized death to the Vietnamese. United States troops placed the cards on corpses to intimidate the enemy.

ace of the base USNA (WWII) a hot shot who would be or at least wanted to be a great pilot. (AFR) (*see* hot shot)

ace pilot USAAF (WWII) a well-trained pilot, though not necessarily a combat veteran. (MMD) (*see also* ace[1])

acey-ducey MM (19th c.) a variation of backgammon. USMC (WWII–Korean War) the company goofball. (TON) (*see also* clown)

ack-ack USA (WWI–WWII) antiaircraft fire, from the sound made by the .30- and .50-caliber machine guns often used against low-flying aircraft. (AFR BJM GWD)

ackers (AH•kers) BrA (WWI–WWII, Middle East) [Egyptian *piastres*, money] money, especially Egyptian money, from a mispronunciation of the Egyptian word; aka disasters, feloos. Also spelled akkers.

AC of S USA (1918) acting chief of staff.

(WWW)

Acorn Boys USA (1860s) soldiers of the XIVth Corps, from the acorn insignia on their hats. Alternatively, the name may have arisen during the Chattanooga campaign, when the troops ate roasted acorns to survive. (ASL)

acquire BrA>USA (WWII) to scrounge or steal. When the army's supply system failed, soldiers procured necessary supplies by other means. (ADW)

across the wire USA (1960s–70s) in Laos, Cambodia, or North Vietnam. A military force that crossed into these countries from South Vietnam was said to have gone across the wire.

ACSV USA/USMC (1960s–present) armored cavalry assault vehicle. In Vietnam, the M113 armored personnel carrier; aka green dragon.

acting gadget *See* gadget

acting Jack USA/USMC (WWI–1960s) a private first class given the temporary rank of corporal or sergeant. His pay rate did not increase accordingly. (*see* Pfc)

active Army USA (1950s) that part of the Army and Army Reserve that is on active duty. (ASC) (*see* active duty)

active duty USA (1950s) full-time service in the military. (ASC)

AD USA/USAF (1950s–60s) air division; accidental discharge of a weapon. USAF (1950s) active duty. (*see* active duty)

ADA USA (1970s) air defense artillery.

ADC BrA>USA/USAF (18th c.–present) aide-de-camp. (*see* aide-de-camp) USA (1941–45) Alaska Defense Command. USAF (1950s) Air Defense Command. USA (1950s) assistant division commander. (AFS ASC)

adjutant BrA/USA (17th c.–present) an administrative officer who acts as an aide or secretary. An adjutant usually is a lieutenant (on the company level) or a captain (on the regimental level) who handles routine paperwork and activities for the commanding officer. (ATK DWO) (*see also* aide-de-camp, base adjutant)

adjutant general *See* AG

adjutant's nightmare BrA (WWI) the *Army Telephone Code*, a book of complicated secret codes introduced in 1916 that changed frequently.

adjutant's post USA (WWII) the spot at which the adjutant stands during a parade review; a trick played on green recruits, who were sent to find and purchase the adjutant's post. (GWD) (*see* parade)

admiral BrN>USMM (ancient times–present) [Arabic *amir-al-bahr*] commander of the seas. The term was first used by Genoese and Sicilians. In 1297 Edward I of England made William de Leyburn "Admiral of the sea of the King of England"; the United States's first admiral was William Glasgow Farragut, promoted on July 16, 1862. (NCT TON)

admiral of the narrow sea MM (18th c.) a drunk who cast the contents of his stomach into the lap of the person sitting next to him. (DVT)

admiral's eighth BrN (18th c.) the admiral's share of what his fleet had seized. Under England's prize laws, the admiral was entitled to one-eighth of the value of the ships captured by his command, whether or not he had been present at the seizure. (TON)

admiralty BrN (14th c.) a generic reference to the high command of the British naval or maritime services.

admiralty ham BrN (ca. 1900) an irreverent name for canned fish. (TON)

adrift BrN>USMM (18th c.–present) said of an unanchored vessel not under the control of its crew, moved by wind and water; without control or guidance; cast or thrown away. BrA (WWI) absent from duty without permission. (*see also* absent without leave) (MAN SLA)

advance CSA/USA (1860s) a promotion; a part of a military force, such as an advance guard, in a position or in marching order ahead of the main force; aka avant-garde, van, vanguard. (MD)

advanced *See* advance

advance leave USA (ca. 1958–present) leave

3

granted in excess of leave that has been officially earned. (ASC) (*see* leave)

AEF USA/USMC/USN (WWI) American Expeditionary Force, American land forces serving in Europe during WWI. (AGE)

aerial torpedo USA/USMC (WWI) a shell fired by a heavy German trench mortar. In theory, such a shell could penetrate thirty feet of earth before exploding. The result was devastating to both men and emplacements. (AGE)

AF USAAF (WWII) audio frequencies. USAF (1960s) air force. (AFR AFS)

AFRTS (AY•fartz) USA/USMC/USN/USAF (1970s–present) Armed Forces Radio and Television System, the overseas radio and television service for military personnel. (1990s) name changed to Armed Forces Radio and Television Services.

AFAS (AY•fass) USAF (1950s) Air Force Aid Society. (AFS)

AFB USAF (1950s–present) air force base. (AFS)

AFFE (AF•ee) USA (1950s) Army Forces Far East. (ASC)

affichage FrA>USA (1917) [French *affiche*, a billboard or placard] laws posted on the bulletin board of the town hall. (WWW)

afloat MM (12th c.–present) [Anglo-Saxon *foletan*, to float] floating on the surface of the water; standing on one's feet and in fair condition, especially after a fight or drinking bout. (OST SLA)

AFNC USAF (1950s) Air Force Nurse Corps. (AFS)

afoul MM (12th c.–present) entangled, as two vessels that have collided and are snared in each other's rigging; to be in conflict with. (SLA) (*see* rigging)

AFR USAF (1950s) Air Force Regulations. (AFS)

AF Res. USAF (1950s) Air Force Reserves. (AFS)

African dominoes *See* African golf

African golf USA (WWII) craps, from the popularity of the dice game among black troops; aka African dominoes. (GWD)

AFSN USAF (1950s) Air Force service number, an identification number assigned to each individual. (AFS) (*see also* army service number)

aft MM/BrN>USN (15th c.–present) [Anglo-Saxon *aeft*, back or rear] toward the rear of a vessel, room, or enclosure. (OST)

afterguard MM/BrN>USN (17th–19th c.) ship's officers, whose traditional shipboard station was on the spar deck aft of the mizzen mast and near the wheel. In both British and American naval services, the term often included sailors assigned to guard the section of the deck aft of the mizzen mast. (SLA) (*see* aft, mizzen mast, spar deck)

AFV BrA>USA/USMC (WWII–present) armored fighting vehicle, including personnel carriers, armored cars, and tanks. (WID)

AG USA/USN/USMC/USAF (1900–present) adjutant general, the general who assists the commanding general. USA/USMC (1950s–present) assistant gunner, who feeds the ammunition belt into the machine gun and takes over the duties of the gunner if necessary. (AFS VET WWW) (*see also* A-gunner, TAG)

against the sun MM (18th c.) counterclockwise. (AST)

Agency USA/USMC/USN/USAF (1970s–present) the Central Intelligence Agency, or CIA.

AGO card USAF (1950s) an identification card permitting the travel of members of the military and authorized dependents within an area under military occupation. (AFS)

aground MM (19th c.–present) said of a vessel whose keel (bottom) is touching or resting on the bottom of a body of water; said of a person who is stranded. (BJM SLA)

AGS USA/USMC (1970s–present) a Soviet-made automatic grenade launcher.

A-gunner USA/USMC (1960s–present) assistant gunner, who feeds the ammunition belt into the machine gun and takes over the duties of the gunner if necessary; aka AG. (*see* AG)

AH USA/USMC (1960s–present) attack helicopter.

AHB USA (1970s–present) attack helicopter

battalion.

ahold (a•HOLT) BrN/USMM (18th c.–present) the act or the manner of holding: *He grabbed ahold of the line.* (SLA)

ahoy MM/BrN>USN (13th c.) a hail or call used between vessels; originally, a Viking war cry. BrN>USN (13th c.–present) a call used to summon sailors to their stations. (BJM OST)

AID USA/USMC/USAF (1960s) Agency for International Development.

aide USAF (1950s) an officer assigned to the commanding officer's staff. (AFS)

aide-de-camp FrA>BrA>USA (18th c.–present) an officer assigned to assist the commanding general in establishing and running a military post or camp. In practice, an aide-de-camp's duties include everything from delivering messages on the battlefield to helping the general's wife prepare for a gala. The title was adopted by the United States Army on March 2, 1821, by an act of Congress. In the twentieth century, the acronym ADC came into use. (AT EMP MD) (*see also* adjutant, base adjutant, personal staff)

aiguillette FrA>BrA> USA (1790s–present) a shoulder decoration in the form of a one- or three-strand braided cord. (AFS)

aiguillette

aiming stakes USA (WWII) stripes (one yellow for second lieutenant, one white for first lieutenant, and two white for captain) painted on the front and sometimes the back of an officer's helmet, intended to aid recognition by friendly troops in battle. The stripes presented easy targets for enemy snipers and so were covered with mud or paint whenever possible.

Air A *See* air attaché

air attaché USAF (1950s) a United States military warrant officer or commissioned officer assigned to an ambassador's diplomatic staff; aka Air A. (AFS) (*see* warrant officer)

air bear USAF (1950s–present) member of security or military police.

air blind USAAF (WWII) said of a pilot who relied more on his instruments than his natural senses when in flight. (MMD)

airborne copulation USA (1960s–70s) a flying fuck.

air cadet USAF (1950–present) one assigned to aviation school. (AFS)

Air Cav USA (1960s) Air Cavalry Division.

air chauffeur GrAF (WWII) a German fighter plane that provided protection for bomber formations and ground support for infantry. (FOD)

air combat maneuver USAF (1960s) general aerial combat; a pilot-versus-pilot aerial engagement; aka dog fight.

air corps chicken USAAF (WWII) chicken. (GWD SID) (*see also* albatross)

aircraft commander USAF (1950s) a pilot in command of an aircraft and its crew. (AFS)

aircrew USAF (1950s) the men and officers manning an aircraft. (AFS)

airdale USN (WWII–present) a disparaging name for a navy flier. (1970s) naval air personnel assigned to an aircraft carrier. (TON)

airdrome USAF (1950s) an area of an air base that included runways, hangars, landing and takeoff areas, waiting rooms, and taxiing areas. The airdrome did not include the base's workshops or supply maintenance sheds. (AFS)

airdrome officer USAF (1950s) a duty officer in charge of incoming aircraft and the comfort of their aircrews; the officer in charge of security and the ordinary business of the base; aka AO. (AFS) (*see* duty officer)

Air Force Aid Society USAF (1950s) an organization that provided emergency monetary assistance to Air Force members and their families. (AFS) (*see* AFAS)

Air Force blues USAF (1947–present) the blue class A uniform worn by members of the USAF since the USAAF ceased to exist in 1947. (AFS)

Air Force Establishment USAF (1950s–present) the name applied to all functions and facilities associated with the air force. (AFS)

air hog USAF (1950s) a pilot who never missed a chance to get in flight time, who ate up air time like a hog on an eating binge. (MMD)

air liaison officer *See* ALO

airlift[1] USA/USMC/USAF/USN (WWII–present) to move, as people or supplies, by aircraft, especially in times of crisis.

airlift[2] USAAF (1948) the movement of people and/or supplies by air transport.

airman USAF (1950s–present) one who holds enlisted rank in the air force. (AFS)

Air-Mattress *See* 82nd Airborne Division

air mile USAF (1950s) a nautical mile, or knot, which is equal to 6,076.1 ft. (AFS)

air mission USAF (1950s–present) a detail of both operational and technical military advisers sent overseas to aid in the development of a foreign nation's air force or air power. (AFS)

airplane USAAF>USA/USN/USMC/USAF (WWI–present) a motorized, fixed-wing aircraft; aka bus, crate, heap, job. (GWD MMD)

air staff USAF (1950s–present) a group of staff advisers assigned to the chief of staff, secretary, and undersecretary of the air force. (AFS) (*see* chief of staff)

air to mud USA/USMC/USN/USAF (1960s–70s) air-to-ground fire.

Air University USAF (1950s) the Air Force's education/research center at Maxwell Air Force Base, Alabama; aka AU. (AFS)

airy-fairy BrN>CN (1970s–present) BrN: said of naval air personnel. CN: said of an impractical or silly idea.

AIT USA/USMC (1960s–present) advanced individual training, received after basic training.

aiwa (AYE•wah) BrA (WWI–WWII) [Arabic *aiwa*, yes] yes. Acquired and widely used by British forces stationed in the Middle East and Egypt. (ADW)

ak dum BrA (19th c.–WWII) [Hindustani *ak dum*, instantly] instantly, used mainly by British soldiers who had seen service in India. (WWI) act dumb, a British soldier's pun on the German word *achtung*, meaning

attention. Tommies mocked German sentries in opposing trenches by calling out "Ak dum!" (*see* Tommy)

AK–47 *See* Kalishnikov AK–47

akkers (AH•kers) BrA (20th c., North Africa) the army paymaster in the field; money. Also spelled ackers. (DRA) (*see* ackers, feloos)

alarm ItA/BrA (17th c.–present) [Italian *all 'arme* (14th c.), contracted to *allarme*, to take up arms] originally, a call to take up arms; later, the fear felt when a traumatic event occurs; a warning signal given in time of impending crisis. (DWO)

alarm post CSA/USA (1860s) a designated place in every encampment where troops assembled in the event of a surprise alert. (MD)

albatross USA (WWII) chicken. (ATK) (*see also* air corps chicken)

alcoholic beverages *See* Anzac shandy, killdevil, lightning, panther blood, serum, stupor juice, swill, tiger piss, white lightning

Alcoholics Anonymous USA (WWII–present) an unkind name applied to the 82nd Airborne Division, which has back-to-back letter As as its insignia. (*see also* 82nd Airborne Division)

alee MM (14th c.–present) a vessel's leeward side, the side sheltered from the wind or weather. (AST NTD OST) (*see also* aweather, lee)

alert[1] ItA>FrA>BrA (16th c.–present) [Italian *all erta*, posted to the lookout] wakeful and in a keen state of mind. (DWO)

alert[2] ItA>FrA>BrA (WWI–WWII) an air raid warning. (DWO)

alibi USMC/USA (WWII–present) a round fired to make up for a round missed due to a misfire or stoppage. USMC (WWII) an excuse for a misfire or weapon jam during rapid fire on the rifle range when one was shooting "for the record." (SAM SID)

ALICE (A•liss) USA/USMC (1980s–90s) all-purpose, lightweight, individual carrying equipment, a standard field pack.

alk BrA (1940, North Africa) alcohol. (DRA)

All-African *See* 82nd Airborne Division

All-Afro *See* 82nd Airborne Division

All American Division *See* 82nd Airborne Division

all-a-taunto *See* all-a-taut

all-a-taut (all•a•TAWT) USN (19th c.) a call signalling that a vessel was completely rigged, prepared, and ship-shape; aka all-a-taunto (all•a•TON•to), all taut. (AST OST)

all clear USA/USMC/USN/USAF (WWII) a siren sounded to mark the end of an enemy air raid. (AFR)

allee-samee MM (late 18th c.) all the same, an even trade: *Small monkey for knife, allee-samee.* Pidgin English brought back from the Orient by United States and British sailors. (SLA)

Allemand (AH•leh•mahnd) Fr>BrA (WWI) [French *allemand*, a German] a German soldier. (AGE) (*see also* alleyman, German)

alles (AH•less) BrA (1940, North Africa) [German *alles*, everything or all] everything is all right. The term was picked up from German POWs. (DRA) (*see also* alles kaput, alles plunder)

alles kaput (AH•less kah•POOT) Gr>BrA (WWII) [German *alles kaput*, all gone, all done in, gone] an expression picked up from German POWs and used in the sense of "It's done for, nothing works, all is broken or useless—finished." (DRA) (*see also* alles, alles plunder, kaput)

alles plunder (AH•less PLUN•der) Gr>BrA (1940, North Africa) [German *alles,* all] an expression used in the sense of "All gone! Nothing left to plunder! No souvenirs left!" (DRA) (*see also* alles, alles kaput, kaput)

alleyman BrA (WWI) [French *allemand*, a German] a German soldier, from British soldiers' mispronunciation of the French word. (*see also* Allemand, German)

all hands MM (13th c.) [Old Anglo-Saxon, employed man] a traditional way to address a ship's crew members or call them to attention. (BJM OST)

all hands on deck USN (19th c.–present) an order for all personnel to man their stations and be ready for any situation.

Allied Forces (WWI) the nations that opposed Germany, primarily Great Britain and her possessions, the United States, Russia, France, Italy, and Belgium. (WWII) the nations that opposed the Axis forces (Germany, Japan, Italy, and their allies), primarily Great Britain and her possessions, the Union of Soviet Socialist Republics, and the United States.

all in the wind MM (19th c.) said of a wind-buffeted sailing ship with all of its sails shaking and shivering. (AST)

all night in USA/USN/USMC (early 19th c.–1970s) the status of one who did not have to stand a night watch and thus was able to sleep "all night in." In the navy, only the ship's captain and idlers regularly enjoyed this pleasure. It took an act of kindness on the part of the captain for a sailor to have all night in. USA (19th c.) the status of a member of a camp or fort's guard detail who did not have to walk a nighttime beat. He might act as an orderly for the officer of the detail or be posted in the guardhouse. (EMP MAN) (*see* idler, Jack, orderly)

allotment USA/USMC/USAF/USCG/USN (WWI–present) a sum of money deducted from one's pay for the use of specified persons, such as dependents, or for a specific purpose, such as an insurance premium or payment of a fine. (ASC BJM EMP)

allowance CSA/USA (1860s–present) funds granted to an officer for travel, food, a servant, and a horse. During the Civil War and through the end of the nineteenth century, for example, a company commander received an allowance of ten dollars per month. During WWI, enlisted men were entitled to an allowance for travel and family support. (MD) (*see also* allotment)

all packed up *See* packed up

all poshed up BrA (WWI) polished, spick and span. (*see also* posh, posh up)

all sails set MM (19th c.) said of a ship running at full speed; said of a person moving as fast as his legs can carry him; said of one who is dressed in his best finery and ready to go out on the town. (SLA)

all taut *See* all-a-taut

allume (ah•LOOM) FrA>BrA (WWI) [French

allumer, to light, to kindle] said of one who is partially drunk or pleasantly intoxicated. (WWW) (*see also* three sheets to the wind, half seas over)

Ally Slopper's Cavalry *See* ASC

Almost Airborne *See* 82nd Airborne Division

ALO USAF (1950s) air liaison officer, an officer-pilot assigned to a naval commander as an aide or adviser for air support. (AFS)

aloft MM (12th c.–present) at, on, or to the masthead or the higher rigging. Used metaphorically, as in *Poor Jack's slipped his cable an' gone aloft to Fiddler's Green.* (MAN OST) (*see* Fiddler's Green, rigging, slip the cable)

alongside MM (18th c.–present) next to a person or an object. (NTD)

aloof MM (16th c.–present) [Dutch *te loef*, to the windward] said of a sailing ship that has the wind in her favor and can, therefore, keep her distance from other ships. From this comes the civilian meaning: physically or emotionally distant from others, cold and indifferent. (DWO SLA)

alow MM (12th c.) downward, below, under. (SLA)

AM GrA/ItA/GrAK (WWII) Italian canned beef, which German soldiers called *alter Mann*, or old man, and Italians called *asino morte*, or dead donkey. (FOD)

a-main MM (16th c.) [Anglo-Saxon *maegen*, power or force] all at once, without warning. (AST OST)

ambulance FrA>BrA>USA (17th c.–present) [French *hôpital ambulant*, walking or mobile hospital] originally, a temporary field hospital, which spawned the idea of a wagon designed specifically for the transportation of the wounded. (1800) According to the language of the time, ambulances were "flying hospitals so organized [that they] can follow an army in all its movements . . . to succor the wounded as much as possible." (MD) The term was first used in the modern sense by the French in the eighteenth century. (MCT MD)

ambuscade FrA>BrA>USA/USN/USMC/

USAF (1860s–WWII) a unit of soldiers who lie in wait to attack the enemy from a hidden position, aka ambush. (MD MMD)

ambush[1] FrA>BrA>CSA/USA (1800–present) [French *embucher*, to move into the woods, and Italian *emboscata*, hidden in the woods>English *embush*] to attack from a hidden position, make a cowardly attack. (DWO MCT MMD) (*see also* ambuscade)

ambush[2] FrA/SpA>BrA>USA (WWII) the place where troops hid while waiting to make a surprise attack on an enemy force; the attack itself; the act of preparing a surprise attack; aka ambuscade. (DWO MCT MMD) (*see also* ambuscade)

AMC USA (1970s–present) air mission commander.

amen clerk BrA (17th–18th c.) parish clerk. (19th c.–WWII) chaplain's assistant; aka amen curler. (DVT) (*see also* amen wallah, chaplain)

amen curler *See* amen clerk

amen wallah BrA (WWI) an army chaplain or his clerk. (DVT SSD) (*see also* Amen clerk, Amen curler, chaplain, Holy Joe, wallah)

AMF USA (1960s–70s) Adios, motherfucker!

AMG BrA/USA/FrA (WWII) Allied Military Government. (TOC)

amidships MM (18th c.) halfway between the bow and stern of a vessel, in line with its keel; the human midsection. (BJM)

ammo dump USA/USMC/USN (WWII–present) a storage area for ammunition, both live and spent rounds. (*see* ammunition)

ammo humper USA/USMC (1960s) an infantryman; an artilleryman.

ammunition FrA>BrA>USA (17th c.–present) [French *la munition*, the supplies] gunpowder, shot, shells, and small arms cartridges. Originally used to refer to all military supplies, the term was acquired from the French by the English and mispronounced as l'ammunition. By the twentieth century it was commonly shortened to ammo. (DWO TON)

amok Port>BrA>USA (18th c.–present) [Malaysian *amoq*, to fight in a frenzy] in a wild, homicidal state. (18th c.) exhibiting a total lack of control: *he has run amok.* (CWO DWO MCT)

a month and a month USA (WWI–WWII) a punishment as a result of court-martial that consisted of a month in the guardhouse and a fine of one month's pay. (EMP)

ANC USA (1960s) Army Nurse Corps.

anchor[1] MM/BrN>USN (10th c. B.C.–present) [Greek *agkura*, a weight] a weight, traditionally hook-shaped, used to keep a vessel in place. The term originated with the Phoenicians and then passed to the Greeks, the Romans, and finally to Great Britain and Europe. United States Naval Academy (1960s) a midshipman with the lowest academic standing of his class. (DVT DWP NTD OST SAL) (*see also* mud hook)

anchor[2] MM (10th c. B.C.–present) [Greek *agkura*, a weight] to sit with the intention of staying for a length of time. The term originated with the Phoenicians and then passed to the Greeks, the Romans, and finally to Great Britain and Europe. (DVT OST)

anchor away *See* anchor aweigh

anchor aweigh MM/BrN>USN (19th c.–present) a traditional call or shout made when a vessel's anchor broke free of the bottom, allowing it to be weighed, or raised. Sometimes spelled incorrectly as anchor away. (NCT)

anchor clanker USMC (WWII–present) a derogatory name for a coastguardsman; aka anchorhead, deck ape, flatfoot, seaweed, squid, swab, swabbie, swab jockey. (PAT) BrN/USN (1950s–present) BrN: an ordinary seaman. USN: a boatswain's mate, probably because some of his shipboard duties involve the raising and lowering of the anchor. (*see also* popeye)

anchor-face BrN (1970s–present) a sailor who is overly enthusiastic or zealous about the service. (*see also* gung ho)

anchorhead *See* anchor clanker

anchor man USN (19th c.–present) a person assigned to watch the anchor cable as the anchor was raised and call "anchor aweigh" when it broke free of the bottom. (*see* anchor aweigh) (WWII) a civilian, especially a

draft dodger, from a comparison between an anchor lying safe and sound on the bottom of the ocean and the safety of staying at home in the states. (AFR BJM)

anchor to windward MM (18th c.) to keep within the law; to sit with the intention of staying for a length of time; aka anchor. (DVT OST)

anchor watch BrMM (17th c.) the men stationed on the spar deck and assigned to guard the ship during the night. (MAN OST) (*see* spar deck)

Andrew Miller BrN (18th c.–present) a ship noted for strict, often harsh, discipline. Tradition holds that Andrew Miller was the leader of a press gang noted for its efficiency in impressing sailors for the British navy. USN (19th–20th c.) a ship noted for its smartness; aka Andrew. Andrew Miller ships usually have very strict officers and tight discipline. (RAS) (*see* press gang)

ANG USAF (1950s) Air National Guard. (AFS)

angel USA/USN (WWII–1970s) one who bought alcoholic drinks. (1960s) a military nurse. USN (1960s) an aircraft carrier–based helicopter; a false radar image. (GWD)

angel cake and wine USA (WWII) bread and water served to a guardhouse prisoner in solitary confinement. (GWD)

angels USAF (1950s) a prefix used in radio communications to indicate altitude increments of a thousand feet. *Angels 15*, for example, indicated an altitude of 15,000 ft. (AFS)

angel's whisper USA (WWII) a bugle call. (ATK MMD)

ANGLICO (AN•glee•koh) USA/USN (1970s) air and naval gunfire liaison company.

animal USA (1960s) the instrument used to set off twelve to twenty claymore antipersonnel mines simultaneously; aka the monster. (*see* claymore, monster)

Annie-Laurie BrA (WWI) a mocking reference to any means of transportation away from the front. A pun on lorrie, the British word for truck.

annihilate Br>USA (16th c.–present) [Latin

annahiler, to reduce to nothing] to destroy totally. (DWO)

antebellum US (1847–present) [Latin *ante bellum*, before the war] before the war. Most often used to describe the period prior to the American Civil War, but in fact it was in use some fourteen years earlier. (IHA)

antifrostbite BrA (WWI) an evil-smelling lard composed mostly of pork fat and issued in 2-lb. metal cans with warning labels stating that it was "not to be issued to Indian troops due to religious reasons." According to regulations, the NCO in charge of each patrol was to have his men strip and rub down with the salve, but procedures of this sort were rarely followed. Later, Indian troops were issued ointment with a whale oil base. (*see also* crab fat)

antipersonnel mine BrA>USA/USMC (20th c.) a mine designed to maim or kill a person (as opposed to a vehicle). (*see also* AP)

Antonio BrA (WWI) a common Portuguese name applied indiscriminately to a Portuguese soldier or sailor serving with the British Expeditionary Forces in Europe.

ANZAC (AN•zak) BrA>USA (WWI–early WWII) Australian–New Zealand Army Corps. In 1915 the acronym was applied only to Australian and New Zealand forces serving at Gallipoli. By 1918, it applied to such forces serving in all theaters of the war. The term was dropped in 1940, when the Australians and New Zealanders formed separate corps.

ANZAC button AusA (1915–18) a pin or nail used to fasten clothing when a button was lost.

ANZAC shandy (AN•zak SHAN•dee) AusA/ NZA (WWI) a mixture of beer and champagne. (*see also* killdevil, lightning, panther blood, serum, stupor juice, swill, tiger piss, white lightning)

ANZAC soup AusA (1915–18) corpse-fouled water found in the bottom of a shell hole.

ANZAC stew AusA (1915–18) a stew with any kind of foraged meat and/or fat in it.

ANZAC wafer (AN•zac WAY•fer) AusA/NZA (WWI) a government-issue, hard cracker. (*see also* hardtack)

AO USAF (1950s) airdrome officer. (AFS) (*see* airdrome officer, AOD) USA (1960s–present) area of operation, a territory for which a specific unit has responsibility; artillery observer, responsible for observing enemy targets and calling in accurate artillery fire upon them. (AFS)

AOC BrA (WWI) Army Ordnance Corps, the military organization responsible for keeping troops supplied with weapons and ammunition.

AOD USAF (1950s) airdrome officer of the day. (AFS) (*see* airdrome officer)

AOL USA (WWI–present) absent over leave, away from one's base beyond the time permitted by orders. By WWII the term had been all but replaced by AWOL (absent without leave). (EMP) (*see* AWOL)

AP USAF (1950s) air police, comparable to the military police of the army and marine corps. (*see also* ape) BrA>USA (WWII–present) armor piercing, or any projectile designed to penetrate armor plate; antipersonnel, or a device, explosive, mine, or munition used against people (as opposed to vehicles). (AFS WID) (*see* antipersonnel mine)

APC USA/USMC (1960s–present) armored personnel carrier, an armored vehicle used to transport men into a battle area. Its main armament is usually a .50-caliber machine gun.

ape USAF (1950s) an air force military policeman, a pun on AP. (*see* AP)

APERS (AY•pers) USA (1970s) antipersonnel weapons, explosives, ammunition.

APM BrA (WWI) assistant provost marshal, in charge of military police. (AGE)

APO USA/USAF (1950s–present) army or air force post office. (AFS)

APOD USAF (1950s) aerial port of debarkation. (AFS)

APOE USAF (1950s) aerial port of embarkation. (AFS)

apoise (ah•POIZ) BrMM (18th c.) descriptive of a neat, well-trimmed ship under full sail.

Appell (ah•pell) GrA (WWII) roll call. (TOC)

apple knocker USA (WWII) a sarcastic name for a farm boy. (GWD)

apple polish USAF (1950s) to court favor with a superior in order to gain special considerations. (ASC)

applesauce enema USA (1960s–70s) a rebuke by a superior delivered in a tactful, semipleasant manner.

appropriate USA (WWII) to take or steal; to borrow.

après la guerre (ah•pray la GAIR) Fr>BrA (WWI) [French *après la guerre*, after the war] after the war, often said wistfully. (AGE)

apron USA (18th–20th c.) a felt-lined, lead sheet placed over the vent of a cannon to prevent moisture damage. (WWI–WWII) an incline with a barbed wire entanglement or lead sheet placed on top of it as a hindrance to the enemy; an incline protected by a layer of concrete, brush, or pavement. (MD MMD)

AR USA/USMC (1960s–present) automatic rifleman.

ARA USA/USMC (1960s–present) aerial rocket artillery, fired from a Cobra AGIH gunship.

ARAB BrA (late 18th c.–present) a regular army bastard. A less than complimentary term used by militiamen or conscripts to describe the soldiers of the regular army.

arab (AY•rab) Br>USA/USN (1800–WWII) a thief; a pirate; a bratty, mean, delinquent child; a derogatory term that, by extension, implied that all people from the Middle East were scoundrels. (SLA)

arsapeek AusA (1915–18) ass over head, upside down.

AR Cen USAF (1950s) Air Force Reserve Center. (AFS)

archer BrA (13th c.) [Latin /*arcus*, curved bow>Anglo-Norman *archer*] a warrior armed with and trained in the use of bow and arrows. (DWO)

Archies BrA>USA/USMC/USN (WWI–WWII) antiaircraft fire and antiaircraft guns. A mocking reference to a popular song of the era, entitled "Archibald, Certainly Not!" United States servicemen borrowed the term from the British during WWI. By WWII, the British and Americans more often used the German word for antiaircraft fire: flak. (ATK GWD MMD) (*see also* flak)

area bird West Point (1900–1950s) a cadet who was assigned to walk the yard as a punishment. (ASC) (*see* yard)

area command USA (1950s) a command assignment comprising a specific geographic area and one or more elements of the armed services. (ASC)

Are you writing a book? USA (WWII) a standard query put to one who asked too many questions. (GWD)

ARG USA/USMC (18th–20th c.) amphibious ready group.

Arkansas toothpick CSA/USA (1860s) a large-bladed, usually double-edged knife.

ARM USA/USMC (1960s) antiradiation missile.

arm *See* arms

armada Sp>BrA/BrN (1588–present) [Latin *armata*, to be armed] a large and powerful group of ships assembled for a specific mission. The name was first used by the Spanish to refer to the fleet of ships gathered for their 1588 invasion of England. (WFS)

arm bender USA (WWII) a drinking party. (GWD) (*see also* bender)

arm dropper USA (WWII) the section chief in the field artillery who, when a gun was loaded and ready, yelled "Fire!" and dropped his arm as a visual signal for the rest of the battery. (GWD)

armer Mussolini GrA (1940–43, North Africa) poor Mussolini; aka alter Mann (old man), a reference to Benito Mussolini, dictator of Italy. (FOD)

Arm in Tears BrA (WWI) [French *Armentières*, a town in France] a town in northern France, from British soldiers' mispronunciation of the French.

armistice CSA/USA (1860s–present) a temporary end to hostilities; a formal truce between governments of warring nations. (MD)

armor BrA (13th–15th c.) [Latin *armatura*, equipment or armor>English *armour* (14th c.) and *armature* (15th c.), weapons or armor] protective body covering, usually made of metal and leather; also spelled armour. USA (WWII) a tank or armored car, especially the former; an army-issue helmet, though not widely used with this connotation. (DWO GWD)

armored cow USA (WWII) canned milk. (AFR GWD)

Armored Fist *See* Panzerfaust

armored infantry USA (1950s) infantry troops that are part of an armored division. (ASC)

armory Br>USA (16th c.–present) [French *armoiries,* coat of arms>English *armory* (15th c.), protective suit of armor] a storage area for military arms and equipment. USA (20th c.) a storage area for the weapons and material of the National Guard and the place at which members of the guard meet for drill and training. (ATK DWO MD MMD) (*see also* arsenal, National Guard)

arms Roman>FrA>BrA>USA/USN (ancient times–present) [Latin *arma*, tools or weapons>Old French *armes* (13th c.)> English *armes* (13th c.)] personal weapons of war. The singular "arm" was first used in reference to a weapon in the nineteenth century. Prior use was always in the plural, as armes or arms. (DWO)

army BrA>USA (14th–18th c.) [Latin *armata*, armed>Spanish *armada*, armed force> French *armée*] seaborne armed forces as well as those confined to land. (19th–20th c.) an armed force confined to land. USA (18th c.–present) a country's military land force(s); a tactical administration unit made up of two or more corps and their supporting troops. (ASC DWO)

army attaché USA (1950s) an army officer who is a member of an ambassador's staff and represents the United States Army. (ASC)

army banjo AusA>USA (WWI–1960s) an entrenching tool. (ATK) (*see also* Irish banjo)

army bible *See* bible

army brat USA (WWI–present) an officer's child. (Korean War–present) a child of an armed services member, especially a career soldier. (AFR ATK)

Army Service Corps *See* ASC

army service cunts *See* ASC

army service number USA (WWI–present) an identification number assigned to each member of the army. (ASC) (*see also* AFSN)

army staff USA (1950s) members of the secretary of the army's staff assigned to duty in Washington, DC. (ASC)

army strawberries USA (WWII) prunes, a frequent but detested part of soldiers' diet. The United States Army of the WWII era was very concerned with the health, including the regularity, of its troops. (ATK MMD)

Army Telephone Code *See* adjutant's nightmare

Arnold, Benedict USA/USMC/USN/USAF (1770s–present) a traitor, from the name of the American officer in the Revolution who was first a hero, then a traitor to the cause.

around the corner BrA (WWI) a standard reply to the question "How far is it now?"

arrest CSA/USA (1860s–WWI) to relieve of duty and possibly confine. (AGE) (*see also* arrest in quarters)

arrest in quarters USA (1860s–present) to relieve from duty and confine to barracks, as an enlisted man; to relieve from duty and command and confine to quarters, as an officer. In both cases, the individual remains in quarters until the trial. (AGE) (*see also* arrest)

arrival USA (1917–18) a German shell coming in from the German side of the lines. (WWW)

arrive MM (13th c.–present) [Latin *arripare*, to come to land>Old French *ariver*, to land (on shore)>Old English *arrive*, to reach land (after sea voyage)] to land on shore after a sea voyage. (14th c.) to reach a destination. The word first appeared in print during this century and was used in this sense. (DWO)

arsenal ItA>BrA>USA (16th c.–present) [Arabic *dar-as-sina'ah*, house of manufacture>Venetian Italian *arzana*, dockyard in Venice>French *arsenal*, dockyard] a military storehouse in which weapons are manufactured, repaired, and stored; aka armory. (DWO MCT MD)

arse over Turkey BrA (WWI) head over

heels in love with someone, something, or some idea or notion. Used as a mild form of disrespect by British soldiers when speaking their minds about an officer's idea.

artie *See* arty

artificer CSA/USA (1860s–WWI) one assigned to repair artillery pieces and their associated vehicles. (WWII) a company mechanic. (MD MMD)

artillery Fr>Br>USA (14th c.–present) [Old French *artillerie*, to arm or equip] originally, munitions and supplies; a weapon that fires missiles or projectiles; a unit armed with such weapons. (DWO)

artillery bull USA/USAAF (WWII) a red flag waved on a rifle range to indicate a complete miss, from a reference to the red center or bull's-eye of a target; aka lingerie, Aunt Maggie's drawers, Aunt Nancy's pants, Maggie's drawers. (AFR MD MMD GWD)

arty USA/USMC (1960s–70s) artillery; aka artie.

ARVN (AR•van) USA/USMC (1960s–70s) Army of the Republic of Vietnam, the South Vietnamese army; a member of the armed forces of South Vietnam. (*see also* Viets)

ASAP (AY•sap) USA/USMC/USN/USAF (1950s–present) as soon as possible. (ASC)

ASC BrA (WWI) Army Service Corps, which built roads, cooked meals, and controlled supplies sent to the front lines. The ASC was very badly maligned by the poor bloody infantry (PBI), who felt that ASC boys had cushy rear-line jobs. Derogatory names for the ASC include Army Service Cunts, Charlie Chaplin's Corps, and Ally Slopper's Cavalry, after a prewar cartoon character. (*see* PBI)

ash and trash USA (1960s) a one-helicopter supply mission in Vietnam; aka ass and trash.

ash can USN (WWI–present) an antisubmarine depth charge, from the fifty-five-gallon metal drums used by civilians to hold ashes from home furnaces; also spelled ashcan. (BJM)

ashore MM/BrN (16th c.–present) USN/USMC (18th c.–present) on land. USMC (1980s–90s) not in boot camp. (SAM) (*see also* go ashore)

Asian two-step USA/USMC (1960s–70s) a krait, an Asian snake so deadly that once bitten, its victims supposedly took no more than two steps before falling dead.

asiatic USA/USMC/USN (1900–60s) said of one who developed odd and erratic behavior, supposedly from being too long on the Asian station. First used by Americans serving in the Philippines and China at the time of the Spanish-American War and the Boxer Rebellion, the term was applied only to those who had seen service in Asian or Pacific areas. (NCT)

Asiatic Ann BrA (WWI) a heavy Turkish gun that fired on Allied troops at Gallipoli, in 1915; aka Asiatic Annie. During WWI, British soldiers knew the Middle East as Asia Minor, a common geographical label of the era.

ASPB USA/USMC/USN (1960s) armored assault patrol boat.

Asquith BrA (WWI) an unreliable French match, which sometimes lighted and sometimes did not. It was named in "honor" of British government minister Herbert Asquith, who was often heard to say, "Wait and see."

ass and trash *See* ash and trash

assassin BrA>USA/USN/USMC (11th c.–present) [Arabic *hashshashin*, eaters or smokers of hashish] BrA (11th c.) a member of a sect of Muslim fanatics who, while under the influence of hashish, attacked European crusaders and specialized in the murder of individual crusaders. BrA (17th c.) USA (18th c.) the murderer of a politically important person. From the Arabic *Hashshashin*, members of a fanatical sect founded by Hassan ben Sabbah that carried out political murders, including the killing of European invaders of the Near East, under the influence of the drug hashish in order to create a singular, united empire of Islam. (DWO)

assault BrA>USA (1768–present) a sudden and violent attack without artillery support upon a breach in an enemy fortification; aka a storm. USA (WWII) a violent attack against an enemy position; a final rush with the intention of engaging in hand-to-hand combat; a concentrated attack made at a short distance from the enemy. (MD MDB MMD)

ass bandit BrN (WWII) an overt or active homosexual.

assembly BrA (1768–present) "Second beating of drum prior to march," sounded to gather the entire garrison in marching order. If only part of the garrison was being summoned, "first beat is then the Assembly." (MD MDB MMD) USA (1860s) a bugle call or drumroll used to gather troops prior to a march or combat. A drum summoned the infantry, while a bugle was used to assemble skirmishers. (WWI–WWII) a bugle call to assemble all troops to formations. (WWII) all the parts of a weapon. (MD MDB MMD)

A-staff USAF (1950s) air force general staff; a member of the general staff. (AFS) (*see* general staff)

Astower, Tom USN (19th c.) a happy-go-lucky sailor. (ANE)

ASVAB (AS•vab) USA/USMC (1960s–present) Armed Services Vocational Aptitude Test, intended to help place men in positions compatible with their skills. Its results were not always followed—one might score ninety-nine percent in administrative, yet be assigned to paint airplanes.

ASW USN (1970s) antisubmarine warfare. (MAN)

As you were! USA/USN/USMC/USAF (WWI–present) order to continue with activity that had been in progress prior to being called to attention. (ASC SAM)

AT USA/USMC (WWII–present) antitank, as shells, explosives, guns, and mines. (AFR)

ATA USAF (1950s) actual time of arrival. (AFS) (*see also* ATD, ETA)

a-taunto *See* all-a-taunto

ATC USAF (1950s) Air Force Training Command. USA/USMC/USN (1960s–70s) armored troop carrier, a river craft. (AFS)

ATD USAF (1950s) actual time of departure.

(AFS) (*see also* ATA, ETA)

A-team USA (1960s) a special forces, or Green Beret, unit of twelve soldiers. (*see also* Green Beret)

A-tent CSA/USA (1860s) a canvas tent with sloping sides that resembled the letter A and provided sleeping space for five to six men; aka wedge tent. (ASL)

ATGM USA (1960s–present) antitank guided missile.

athwart (a•THWART) Br (14th c.–present) USN (18th c.–present) [Old Icelandic *pwert*, across the vessel] across; across the deck of a vessel; aka athwartship. (OST TWW)

athwartship *See* athwart

Atkins, Tommy *See* Tommy

at loggerheads MM (16th–20th c.) engaged in a fight using loggerheads (pitch ladles) as weapons. Ashore: deadlocked, as in an argument. (NCT OST TON) (*see* loggerhead)

at sea MM (18th c.–present) on the ocean; aboard ship; uncertain or undecided. (SLA)

AU USAF (1950s) Air [Force] University. (AFS) (*see* Air University)

au Dela Fr>BrA>USA (WWI) God; the great beyond. (WWW)

au le feu (oh•luh•FOO) FrA (WWI) [French *au feu*, to or toward the fire, the light] the front, the battlefield; toward the front. (WWW)

Aunt Maggie's drawers *See* artillery bull

Aunt Nancy's pants *See* artillery bull

AUS USA (WWII) the Army of the United States; during WWII, used to designate something or someone with a temporary or nonregular army status. (ASC)

Aussie AusA>BrA>USA/USMC/USN/USAF (pre-WWI–present) Australian. (GWD)

Australian eleven AusA (1915–18) a very thin mustache, one that was said to consist of eleven hairs on each side of a man's upper lip. (*see also* eleven on a side)

avant-garde FrA>BrA>USA (15th c.–present) [French *avant-garde,* advance guard] a body of troops that marched ahead of the army's main body to clear obstacles and small groups of enemy soldiers from the path of the main column; aka van, vanguard.

By the nineteenth century, the term vanguard was more commonly used in the British and United States military. In 1900, "avant-garde" entered United States and British civilian speech to describe new and daring art styles. (MDB MMD FWS) (*see also* advance)

avast MM (17th c.) [Dutch *hound fast*, hold fast, or Portuguese *abasta*, enough] traditional command instructing sailors to cease their tasks immediately. Aboard ship, the term was often shortened to 'vast: *'Vast heavin'!* (SLA TON)

AVN USN (WWII) aviation volunteer, a civilian pilot trained by the navy and used for stateside flights. (AFR)

AVS USN (WWII) aviation volunteer specialist. AVSs were usually civilian, nonflying technical experts. (AFR)

AVT USN (WWII) aviation volunteer transport pilot, usually an experienced civilian flier commissioned by the navy. (AFR)

AW USA (WWI) the Articles of War. (WWW)

awash MM (15th–20th c.) said of a vessel that is barely afloat or flooded; said of one who is very ill, drunk, or unsteady. (OST SLA)

away off MM (19th–20th c.) at a far distance. (SLA)

aweather MM (14th c.–present) on or toward the weather or windward side.

awkward squad CSA/USA (1860s–Korean War) a group of soldiers very poor at performing drill and requiring extra hours of training. (GWD MMD)

AWL USA (WWI) absent with leave (permission) from one's post or camp. (EMP) (*see also* AWOL, leave)

awning BrA>USA/USMC/USN (17th c.–present) a cloth or canvas raised on four poles to provide shade.

AWOL CSA/USA/USMC/USN (1860s–present) absent without leave. In the 1860s, a returned offender wore a wooden sign bearing the letters around his neck for a period of time. (WWII) a wolf on the loose, someone after booze and broads. (AFR EMP IHA) (*see* absent without leave)

AWOL bag USA/USMC/USAF/USN (1960s–70s) a small overnight bag or piece of luggage sufficient to carry what was needed to go AWOL. (*see* AWOL)

AWS USAF (1950s) Air [Force] Weather Service. (AFS)

axle grease USA/USMC/USN (WWII) table butter, from its smell, taste, and sometimes color. (MMD) (*see also* grease[1])

aye MM/BrN>USN/USMC (16th c.–present) [Old English *yie*, yes] yes. In the United States and British navies, "aye, aye" is still the proper acknowledgment of a superior's order. (OST)

B

babe USA (1900) youngest man in unit, from "babe in arms"; good-looking female. (MMD)

babe in the woods BrA (18th–19th c.) a soldier or civilian placed in stocks as punishment. (19th c.) a new soldier in army, implying that he was at the mercy of wolves (experienced con artists among older soldiers). (DVT)

Baby[1] BrN/BrAF (WWI) a small model of a British Sopwith scout plane, or Sopwith camel; aka camel. (*see* camel)

baby[2] USA/USMC/USN (20th c.) term of affection for sweetheart; common table mustard, comparison between color of mustard and baby's bowel movement. During the Vietnam War, "baby shit" was more widely used to describe mustard than "baby." (AFR)

baby blimp USA (WWII) obese woman. (GWD)

baby carriage USA/USMC/USN (1910–WWII) a two-wheeled cart pulled by two men on which a machine gun was mounted;

it was unlikely to have seen serious use in actual combat. (GWD)

baby food USA (WWII) breakfast cereals, especially creamed cereals and oatmeal. (GWD)

baby hero USA (1960s) a mocking reference to someone who was brave or reckless.

baby navy USN (WWII–1960s) United States Coast Guard; aka bucket brigade, freshwater navy, hooligan navy, muddy water sailors.

baby shit *See* baby²

b-ache *See* bellyache

bachelor Br (13th c.–present) [Latin>Old French *bacheler*, young knight or squire> English *knight bachelor*] an unmarried man, possibly from the fact that many young knights or squires were without property and therefore unable to marry. (DWO)

bachelor's mess USA/USMC/USN (19th c.) living quarters on a military post for unmarried officers. USA (1860s–WWII) aka bachelor's quarters. (EMP)

back and fill MM (18th c.) tricky maneuver that required the handling of sail, tide, and current simultaneously in order to change a vessel's course; the action of one who is unsteady or undecided, wishy-washy. (SLA)

back-biter BrA>USA/USMC/USN (18th c.–present) a false friend who slanders another without victim's knowledge; someone who betrays a friend's confidence to benefit himself. (DVT MMD)

backen round MM (18th c.) said of the wind when it suddenly shifts counterclockwise. (SLA)

back scratching USA/USMC (1960s) using light-weapons fire to remove enemy infantrymen who have climbed aboard a friendly tank.

backtalk CSA/USA (1860s) an insolent reply to a superior, especially an officer.

back time USA/USMC (1960s) time and duty spent in rear (back) areas.

backyard soldier USA (WWII) a soldier stationed close enough to home to enable him to spend weekend leaves with his family. (GWD)

bad Indian USA (1840s) a common negative reference to Native Americans. (IHA) (*see* good Indian)

bad paper USA/USMC (1960s) a less than honorable military discharge.

bad time USA (WWII) an uncomfortable or dangerous situation; time spent in military jail or prison. (MCT MMD)

baffle paint USA (WWI) camouflage paint, intended to baffle or confuse enemy. (GWD)

bag USN (19th c.) sailor's seabag, bearing his ID number and kept in a locker on the orlop deck. USA (WWII) impolite term for a woman, usually preceded by old and/or ugly. (*see also* bag, seabag, what's the number of your; orlop deck)

bag drag USAF (1980s) method of carrying or dragging one's duffle bag when entering or leaving plane.

bagged and tagged USA/USMC (1960s–70s) to have been placed in a body bag with proper identification, said of friendly dead.

bag, hammock, and bird cage BrN (1750s) a sailor's full kit. The expression came from the fact that every sailor needed a seabag and a hammock, and many sailors had a pet parrot—hence, a bird cage. (*see* seabag)

bag of rations BrA (WWI) a fussy, zealous, and/or demanding person, especially an officer.

bag, what's the number of your USN (19th c.) a question often asked of a sailor embarking on a dangerous mission. If he were to die, the possessions in his bag would be auctioned off to his shipmates. The proceeds of the auction would be given to his next of kin or to the members of his watch, who would throw a party in his memory at the next liberty port. (ANE)

bahdin Arab>BrA (19th c.) [Arabic *bahdin*, later, not now] later, not now. Brought home by British soldiers serving in Egypt during the late 1800s.

bail¹ MM (17th c.–present) [French *bail*, bucket] to remove water from a vessel with a bucket. (OST SLA)

bail² MM (17th c.–present) [French *bail*, bucket] a container used to scoop contents

16

from a larger container; the act of emptying a larger container. (OST SLA)

bail out USN (18th c.) to bail water out of a sinking boat. USAAF (WWI) to jump out of an airplane with a parachute. USA (WWI) to abandon a vehicle, especially an armored vehicle. (AFR) USAF/USA/USMC (WWII–present) to exit hurriedly to escape impending disaster; to jump from an airplane in flight; to goof off in an attempt to avoid unpleasant work; to avoid the consequences of one's actions by making a hasty retreat from the scene. (AFR MMD)

bakshee BrA>USA (19th–20th c.) [Egyptian *bakshee*, gift, gratuity] a tip, a free, unexpected gift, borrowed by British soldiers serving in Egypt during the late nineteenth century; aka baksheen, baksheesh, buckshee, bucksish. USA (post-WWI) something extra, faked.

bakshee king BrA (19th–20th c.) army paymaster, who controlled soldiers' pay or gratuity.

baksheen *See* bakshee

baksheesh *See* bakshee

Balaclava helmet BrA>BrN (Crimean War, 1850s–70s) a pullover knit hat made by British soldiers from the heels of heavy woolen socks to protect their head and ears from the bitter cold of Balaclava. The British government officially adopted the hats, which by then had passed from soldiers to sailors offshore, and issued such knitted helmets to troops in wintertime. The helmet is a forerunner of the modern civilian ski mask. (1857–1870s) the full beards sported by many veterans of Crimea. (TON)

baldie USA (WWII) a regulation army haircut, which was very short and made many men appear to be bald. (MMD)

ballast MM (17th–20th c.) [Old Danish *barlest*, bare load] weights laid in the bottom of a vessel to aid its seaworthiness in heavy weather. Stones, bricks, pig iron, and sand are among the many types of ballast used over the years. (OST SLA) (*see* lose one's ballast)

ballgame USA/USMC (1960s–70s) an encounter with the enemy. (*see* firefight, skirmish)

ball of lead BrA (WWI) the human head, a comparison to the density or softness of lead shot.

balloonatic BrA (WWI) a sarcastic play on the word balloonist. Those who operated observation balloons for the army and Royal Navy were a gutsy lot; their crafts were filled with highly flammable hydrogen.

balloon goes up BrA (WWI) zero hour, the time the attack is to begin.

ballyhoo MM (19th c.) [*Ballahou*, two-masted, fast sailing vessel of West Indies, possibly the cry of African Dervishes *b'allah hoo*, "Through God it is!"] an uproar; a general disturbance; a description of a ship kept in a slovenly manner. (CWO)

Baltimore steak USA (WWII) beef liver. Baltimore was noted for its liver dishes, a dinner that a soldier of the 1930s to the early 1940s could afford. Privates made seventeen dollars per month in 1941. (GWD) (*see also* nigger steak)

BAM (bam) USMC (WWII) bad-assed Marine; broad-assed Marine, a nasty, impolite term for a female Marine. (PAT SAM)

Ba-ma-ba *See* Ba-moi-ba

Ba-me-ba *See* Ba-moi-ba

Ba-moi-ba (bah•moy•bah) USA/USMC/USN/USAF (1960s–70s) [Vietnamese *ba-moi-ba,* thirty-three] a Vietnamese beer with a trade name of "Thirty-three"; aka Ba-ma-ba (bah•mah•bah), Ba-me-ba (bah•mee•bah), Biere LaRue, Tiger Beer, Tiger piss.

bamboozle MM (18th c.) [possibly Scottish *bombaze*, to perplex; first used by dramatist Colly Cibber in 1703] to fly false colors to confuse one's prey. The goal was an easy capture. (DWO TON)

banana clip USA/USMC (1960s–present) a thirty-round, curved (banana-shaped) clip for a semiautomatic weapon.

band-aid USMC (1960s–70s) a corpsman or medic. (*see* corpsman)

B and B USA/USAF/USMC/USN (1950s–70s) broads and booze. (*see* R and R)

bandelier *See* bandoleer

B and G USA/USAF (1950s) the buildings and grounds of a military post. (ASC) an air base and its grounds. (AFS)

bandits USA/USMC/USN/USAF (WWII–present) enemy aircraft, especially fighter planes.

bandoleer BrA>USA/USMC/USN (1768–present) a belt with pouches for carrying ammunition; also spelled bandelier. The first bandoleers were small, leather-covered wooden cases that held cartridges for muskets. (MDB MMD)

banquette BrA (1768–WWII) a fire step or raised platform built on the floor of the forward face of a trench upon which its occupants stood in order to fire over the top of the parapet at the enemy. (MD MDB MMD)

bantam battalion BrA (WWI) a unit of British soldiers under 5'3", so named for the small but fierce bantam fighting cocks. (EMP)

Banyan Day BrA>USN (17th–20th c.) a meatless day, named for a tribe in the East Indies whose members ate no red meat. The British, and later the U.S., served meat to sailors six days a week and fish (much detested) one day a week, often a Wednesday. (DVT)

BAR *See* Browning automatic rifle

barbed wire gaiters USA (WWI–WWII) a phony award given to green recruits. (GWD)

barbette BrA>USA (1768) the positioning of artillery behind a parapet in such a way that guns could fire over the top of the protective earthwork rather than through an opening. USN (1880s) a circular metal gun shield mounted on an open deck. (1970s) an armored shell within which a turret moves. (MAN MD MDB MMD)

bare-ass USA (1960–1970s) barracks.

bare poles under MM (18th–20th c.) said of a vessel in foul weather with all of her sails furled (rolled up and secured to yards); said of a naked or nearly naked person. (NSB SLA)

barge MM (13th c.) [Greek *baris*, Egyptian boat>Latin *baria*, Egyptian boat>Old French *barge*, rowed vessel>English *barge*, cargo vessel] a large ornate vessel reserved for the use of royalty. (16th–20th c.) a ship's boat reserved for the use of high-ranking naval officers. (19th–20th c.) a large, slow-moving cargo vessel towed by another vessel. (20th c.–present) a power boat reserved for officers' use; a vessel that carries materials. (DWO MAN OST SLA)

bark *See* tar water

barker USA (WWII) a large-caliber, very loud piece of field artillery that barks like a large dog. (GWD)

barnacle back MM (19th c.) an old sailor who'd been at sea so long he was said to have grown barnacles, like the bottom of a ship that hasn't been scraped in a long while. (AST)

barndook BrA (18th c.–WWII) [Hindustani *banduk*, gun] an army-issued rifle or musket; aka bundook, brundook, bun doop, buntukk. The term was brought back to England by those who had seen service in India. (EMP)

barn door USA (WWI) [French *bonjour*] hello, to doughboys; aka bone jaw, bone jar. (WWW) (*see* doughboys)

baron BrA (WWI) a nickname for the commanding officer of a company, battalion, or regiment. Prior to and during WWI, many high-ranking British officers were sons of nobility and acted as if they still had the authority of their ancient ancestors. In the US Army during WWII, the term saw limited use.

barracks USA (18th c.–present) housing for enlisted men built and operated by the government, usually within a base or camp.

barracks bag USA (1900–WWII) the forerunner of the modern duffle bag, a large canvas satchel used to transport and store a soldier's personal belongings. (ATK) (*see* seabag)

barracks fatigue USA (WWII) rest and/or goof off time spent in the barracks. (GWD)

barracks lawyer USA (WWII) a soldier who was a self-proclaimed expert on military law; one who claimed to know all the rules and regulations. (MCT) (*see also* lower deck lawyer, sea lawyer)

barracks 13 USA (WWII) guardhouse. (ATK) (*see also* jail)

barracks wacky USA (WWII) applied to a victim of shell shock who "went off the deep end" while confined to the hospital or barracks. (*see* battle fatigue, PTSD, shell shock)

barrage BrA>USA/USMC (WWI–WWII) an excessive number, such as a barrage of questions, orders, or letters; a party where booze is as destructive as an artillery barrage. (GWD)

barricade BrA (1768) [English *bar*, to block or obstruct] a fence that forms an obstacle to the enemy. USA/USMC (1861–present) a hastily constructed obstacle made from any available materials. (MCT MD MDB MMD)

barrier CSA/USA (1861) temporary obstacle made of wood and within the confines of a fortification. USA>USMC (WWII) an obstacle used to impede the advance of the enemy; a border fortification used to block key highways into and out of a country. (MD MMD) (*see* stockade)

barrow jockey USA (WWII) a laborer who works with a wheelbarrow. (GWD)

BAS USAF (1950s) basic allowance for subsistence, money paid to an airman to offset the daily cost of living when food and/or housing was not provided by the government. (ASC)

base adjutant USAF (1950s) a staff officer who handled all administrative duties for his commanding officer, including official correspondence and records. (ASC) (*see also* adjutant, aide-de-camp)

base pay USAF (1950s) basic salary rate paid to an officer or enlisted man. Addi-tional payment was received for such items as flying status, overseas duty, and combat duty. (ASC) (*see* basic pay)

base wallah ANZAC (WWI) [Hindustani *wallah*, person] a soldier who worked in rear areas. The term was not a compliment; frontline troops considered such soldiers to have comparatively easy, safe jobs. (TBS)

bashed in BrA (WWI) utterly smashed or destroyed by an artillery barrage or aerial bomb.

basic allowance USA (WWII) payment made to servicemen who did not receive government-provided food and/or lodging. (ASC)

basic pay USA (WWII) the level of pay, based on rank, for all personnel. (ASC) (*see* base pay)

basket case USA (WWI) one who had been so seriously wounded that he had to be carried home in a "basket." (WWII–present) one in a state of severe mental disruption.

basket pay USAF (1950s) officers' customary yet unauthorized holiday or weekend leave. They covered themselves by placing a leave request in the base commander's basket, as if he were not present to handle their request in person. (ASC)

bastard USA (WWII) an inferior or unusual person or object; an item that is not of official issue or standard design. (MMD)

bastion ItA>FrA (15th c.) a small fortification at each point of a five-sided, star-shaped fort. Each bastion protected its neighbor. BrA (1768) a wedge-shaped fortification placed outside the walls of the main fort and in front of the main gate in order to protect that vital gate. USA/USMC (18th c.–present) a strong defensive position. (MD MDB MMD)

bat USA (WWII) a radar-guided bomb, named for the animal that uses a form of natural radar for navigation.

Bat' d'Af FrA (WWI) Battalions de Africa, or African Discipline Battalions. These units were raised from men who were given a choice between military jail or service with the trench mortars. Most of these men chose the mortars with joy, which resulted in their nickname: *les joyeux,* the joyful. (WWW) (*see* suicide squads)

bathmats BrA (WWI) wooden duckboards placed in the bottom of trenches to keep feet dry. They were not very effective.

bathroom stationery USA (WWII) government-issue toilet paper. (GWD)

bathtub USA (WWII) a motorcycle sidecar, named for its shape. (GWD)

batman BrA (18th c.) [French *bat*, burden, to carry>English *bat*, packhorse] teamster for packhorses; one who carried and tended officer's personal property. Items were carried on a bat (packhorse). (19th–20th c.) officer's servant. (AGE MCT) (*see also* bumbrusher, dingbat, orderly)

battalion USA (18th c.–present) generic name for a military unit made up of a headquarters company and three or more companies of infantry commanded by a lieutenant colonel or a major. In the artillery a battalion consisted of a headquarters company and at least two batteries of guns. (ASC)

batten down MM (17th c.) to close and/or make watertight a hatch or other opening on a vessel. (SLA)

batten your hatch MM (17th c.) an order to stop talking. (TON)

battery BrA>USA/USMC (16th c.–present) [Latin *batture*, to beat>French *batterie*, to beat>English *battle*, to beat>English *battery*, to beat with artillery] an artillery bombardment; an artillery unit; the artillery attack itself. USA (1861) a unit of two to six guns. (DWO MCT MD MMD)

battery acid USA/USMC/USN/USAF (WWII) coffee. (AFR GWD MMD) (*see also* blackout, blackstrap, coffee, ink, jamocha, java, joe, lifer juice, paint remover)

battery Q USA (WWII) artillery name for guardhouse. (ATK) (*see also* jail)

bat the breeze *See* shoot the breeze

battle FrA>BrA>USA/USMC/USN (13th c.–present) [Late Latin *battualia*, fencing exercise>French *bataille*, beating>English *battle*, to fight, to beat] a fight between warring factions. (DWO)

battle bowler BrA (WWI) a Model 1916 steel helmet, probably named for its round crown, which roughly resembled that of a derby hat; aka bowler.

battle fatigue USA/USMC/USN (WWII–Vietnam War) physical and/or psychological breakdown caused by stress of combat; aka combat fatigue. During WWI, the French and British at first considered the condition to be a sign of cowardice, and more than a few men suffering from it were executed. Before WWII, the condition was referred to as shell shock; after the Vietnam War, post-traumatic stress disorder (PTSD). (*see* PTSD)

battle group USA (1950s) unit consisting of a headquarters company, four rifle companies, and a mortar company under the command of a colonel. It was one step above a battalion and corresponded to the WWII regiment, which consisted of two or more battalions. (ASC)

battle pin USMC (WWII) collar pin. (SAM)

battle royal BrA (medieval era–18th c.) a brawl or fight in which opposing sides use clubs as well as fists. In the medieval era, opposing armies in a battle royal were commanded by their kings. (1721) a cockfight in which several birds fought at once. (DVT)

battleship BrN>USN (18th c.–WWII) a generic term for any large, heavily armed warship; aka man-of-war, warship. BrN (1890s–WWII) a ship with main batteries of ten- to fifteen-inch caliber guns. (1890–1906) a ship with a displacement of eleven to sixteen thousand tons that carried two to four twelve- or thirteen-inch caliber guns mounted in turrets, with a secondary battery of fourteen to forty guns of smaller calibers. (1906–1920s) a ship of twenty to thirty thousand tons displacement with eight to twelve guns of twelve- to fourteen-inch caliber, with a secondary battery of sixteen or more guns of five- or six-inch caliber. (1930s–50s) a ship that carried up to twelve fourteen- or sixteen-inch caliber guns mounted two or three per turret as the primary battery and three- and four-inch caliber guns, also mounted in turrets, as a secondary battery. In 1958, the USN took all of its battleships out of commission. The USS *New Jersey* was modernized and recommissioned in 1968. Since 1990, the USN has had on duty four *Iowa*-class battleships armed with sixteen-inch guns, Harpoon missiles, and Tomahawk cruise missiles. (*see also* dreadnaught, Harpoon missile, Tomahawk missile)

battle wagon USN (1900–WWII) a battleship. (PAT)

bayonet FrA>BrA>USA/USMC (15th–18th c.) [supposedly French *baionette*, named for town or port of Bayonne where Basques first used the weapon] a dagger inserted into the end of a musket barrel. Around 1700, these weapons were

1903 Springfield rifle bayonet

designed to fit onto the muzzle of the gun, permitting a soldier to fire without having to remove the bayonet first. (DWO MD MDB MMD) USA (1860–WWII) soldier. USA (WWII) more often called the cat stabber, cheese toaster, pig sticker, toad sticker, or toothpick. (GWD) USAAF (WWII) aka paring knife. (AFR)

bayonet strength BrA>USA (WWI) the number of men in an infantry unit.

bayou CSA/USA (1860s) a trench that ran to a specific position, such as a magazine, headquarters, or bomb-proof; aka bayou of communication. (MD) (*see* bomb-proof)

bay whore USAF (1980s) someone assigned to clean barracks; squadron bay orderly.

bazooka USA/USMC (WWII–1960s) [English *bazoo* (ca.1890), mouth] the first shoulder-fired antitank rocket, named for its resemblance to a musical instrument invented by comic Bob Burns in the 1930s.

B-Board USA (1900–WWII) board of officers assembled to determine if an officer with poor efficiency ratings should be permitted to stay in the service. (ATK)

BC USA/BrA (1900–WWI) battery commander in artillery. (WWW) USA/ USMC (1960s–70s) body count of both the enemy and friendly dead, taken after battle. (ATK) (*see* battery)

BCD USA/USMC/USAF/USN (WWII–present) bad conduct discharge. USMC (WWII–Korean War) big chicken dinner. (ASC MCT SAM)

BDR USMC (1980s–90s) basic daily routine, which in boot camp is spelled out in precise detail.

BDU USA/USMC (1970s–present) battle dress uniform, made of camouflage material.

beachcomber MM (19th c.–present) originally a whaler's term for a runaway sailor; later, one who searched the beach in hopes of finding salvage from shipwrecks. Pacific Islands: shiftless, unemployed white man who wandered from port to port.

beach USN/USMC (19th c.–present) a shore of an ocean, sea, or lake.

beached MM (19th–20th c.) said of a sailor who has been stranded ashore without a ship and precious little chance of finding one; aka on the beach. (1960s) on shore. (AST)

beachhead USA/USMC/USN (WWII–present) enemy shoreline that has been captured and fortified.

Beachy Bill BrA (WWI) a heavy Turkish gun that fired on Allied forces at Gallipoli in 1915.

beam MM (13th c.–present) a deck plank of a ship; the width of a ship at its widest point; the widest point of a person. (AST OST)

beam-ends MM (18th–20th c.) a ship or person that is top- or bottom-heavy, tilting in bow or stern. (AST)

beam, flying the iron *See* flying the iron beam

beam, flying the wet *See* flying the wet beam

beam, riding the *See* riding the beam

bean gun USA (WWII) mobile field kitchen, very likely a comparison between the rate of fire of a machine gun and the amount of beans prepared by such a kitchen. (GWD)

bean jockey MM (19th–20th c.) sailor assigned to help the cook serve food. (TON)

bean rag USN (19th–20th c.) a flag flown during mealtimes from ship's masthead; aka chow rag, meal flag. (TON)

Beans USA (19th c.–1960s) nickname for cook's helper, company cook, or commissary sergeant. (1960s) a meal.

beans and baby dicks USA/USMC (1960s–70s) beans and hot dogs; aka beans and dicks.

beans and motherfuckers USA/USMC (1960s–70s) C ration that consisted of ham and lima beans. (*see* C ration)

bean shooter USA (WWI–WWII) officer in charge of camp or field kitchen; aka Beans. (MMD)

Bear a hand! MM (18th–20th c.) traditional order to help with or speed up work in progress. (MAN OST)

bearded lady USA (WWII) a searchlight with a diffused beam (as opposed to a concentrated beam). (GWD MMD)

bear grease USA (WWII) government-issue lye soap, a mixture of lye, water, and animal fat. (SID)

beast USA/USAAF/USMC/USN (WWII–1960s) a new recruit or air cadet, one who recently entered training. USN (WWII) a cheap prostitute or B-girl. (1960s) a nasty term used by Caucasian soldiers to describe African-Americans or Hispanics, and vice versa. (*see* B-girl)

beast, mark of the *See* mark of the beast

beat CSA/USA (1860s) one who expertly dodged all kinds of work, but especially hard work. (*see also* deadbeat, galley stoker, goldbrick) USA (1833–WWII) the assigned area of a soldier on guard duty.

beating order BrA (1768) an order issued by the colonel of the regiment that authorized the activity of recruiting parties. The drummer who accompanied these parties "beat the drum" to signal their location to potential recruits. (MDB)

beat your chops USMC (WWII) to complain. (SAM) (*see* beat your gums, chip his molars)

beat your gums USN (WWII) to speak idly or excessively. (*see* chip his molars, shoot the breeze)

beaucoup (bow•KOO) Fr>USA/USMC (WWI–WWII, Vietnam War) [French *beaucoup*, very much, plenty] plenty or very much. (WWI) also spelled boco, boko, bokoo. (MCT)

beautify the post USA (WWII) a general order that covered all of the tasks necessary to keep the post neat and trim. (GWD)

becalmed MM (18th c.–present) said of a sailing craft that can make no headway due to lack of sufficent wind; used to describe a

person's attitude on hot day when clothes stick to a damp body, just as the limp sail clings to the mast and yards on a windless day. (DVT SLA)

become a landowner BrA (WWI) to die and be buried in France.

bed check USA (ca.1900–present) the point after lights-out at which the officer of the day makes rounds through the barracks to ascertain that everyone is in his or her bunk. (EMP)

Beddo BrA (WWII) a Bedouin tribesman of the Near East.

bedlam USA (ca. 1900) bachelors' quarters on an army post. The unruliness of the unmarried, off-duty officers was likened to the conditions of Bedlam, the popular name of St. Mary's of Bethlehem, a London insane asylum. Conventional wisdom held that a wife has a calming effect on an officer's behavior. (MCT) (*see* bachelor, bachelor's quarters)

bedpan commando *See* corpsman

bed sack BrA>USA (17th–19th c.) a cloth sack used to carry one's straw bedding. (AFR IHA MCT)

beef¹ USA (ca.1900) to complain, growl, or gripe. (MMD)

beef² MM (19th c.) manpower or muscle. An order for more beef demanded additional hands to finish a piece of heavy work. (SLA) USA (ca. 1900) a complaint. (MMD)

beef heart BrA (WWI) a fart.

been through the mill *See* go through the mill

beer *See* Ba-moi-ba, brew, bub, muddy water, swill, tiger piss

beetle BrA (1768) "Round piece of wood, of a foot and a half in length, and eight or ten inches in diameter, having a handle about four feet long" used to pack down earth in a field fortification or parapet. (MDB) USA (WWII) a girl, used only by troops stationed in Alaska. (MMD)

beetle cruncher USMC (1920s–WWII) an army man, especially an infantryman. (PAT)

beetle off BrA/BrAF (WWI) to fly straight, like a beetle, upon takeoff.

BEF BrA/BrN (WWI) British Expeditionary Force, the British land forces who served in Europe during WWI. (AGE)

before the mast *See* ship before the mast

behavior report USA (WWII) a letter written by a soldier to his girlfriend, supposedly a full report of his behavior while away from home. (MMD)

belay MM (16th c.–present) originally, an order to delay or temporarily halt the work at hand or to cancel a prior order; later, an order to secure a line. (OST)

belaying pin soup or hash MM (19th c.) the harsh treatment inflicted upon the sailors by the officers; a sound beating. (AST)

belay the last word USMC (WWI–WWII) an order to cease an activity, thus cancelling the last order received. (SAM) (*see* belay)

Belgeek BrA (WWI) [French *Belgique*, Belgian] a derogatory, generic term for a Belgian national.

Belgian pit *See* foxhole

Belgians, give it to the *See* give it to the Belgians

believer USA/USMC (1960s–70s) a dead enemy soldier, a mocking reference to one who has given up evil ways and become a true believer in Christ.

bella seenyoreena ItA>BrA (1940, North Africa) [Italian *bella Senorena*, beautiful lady] a beautiful and/or talented lady. (DRA) (*see* bint kwoyees)

bellhop, seagoing *See* seagoing bellhop

bellied USA (WWI) tankerman's description of a tank stuck high and dry on an obstacle or up to its belly in mud.

bellmare USA (19th c.–WWII) the lead pack animal of a baggage train, which wore a bell around its neck. The other animals were trained to follow the bell. (AGE)

bellyache[1] USA/USMC/USN (1860s–present) a stomach ache; a complaint. (MMD)

bellyache[2] USA/USMC/USN (1860s–present) to complain about a small matter or problem; aka b-ache. (MMD)

bellyful BrA (18th–20th c.) an excess, often of violence; said of someone who is beaten until he surrenders; said of a pregnant woman. (19th c.) enough food, problems, or headaches to last a lifetime. (DVT)

belly robber USA/USMC/USN (1860–early WWII) a company cook or mess sergeant who bore the brunt of the other enlisted men's anger if rations were short or of poor quality; one accused of robbing others of their food for his own benefit. (MCT)

belly up *See* tits up

belt, jerk a *See* jerk a belt

bend MM (17th c.–present) to secure two rope ends together; to secure line to a sail or another object. (MAN OST) USAAF (WWII) to damage aircraft. (MAN OST)

bender USA (1827) a drinking party, at which an arm is bent many times in the act of drinking; aka arm bender. (IHA) BrN> USN (18th c.–present) a drinking bout. (OST)

bending drill BrA (WWII) officially, the squatting drill included in daily calisthenics; unofficially, emptying one's bowels in full view of others. (GWD)

bends and motherfuckers USA/USMC (1960s–70s) physical drill that includes squat thrusts.

bend the throttle USAAF/USA (WWII) to fly a plane or drive a vehicle at faster-than-normal speeds. (AFR GWD)

bene bowse BrA (16th c.) [Italian *bene*, good, and Old English *bowse*, drink] good and/or strong spirits or alcohol. (DVT) (*see* booze)

Benedict Arnold *See* Arnold, Benedict

Benghazi cooker BrA (1940–43, North Africa) a makeshift campfire made by digging a hole in the sand and filling it with gasoline, named for a town on the coast of North Africa. The fire produced was hot and fairly long-lasting. (ADW)

benny USA (WWII) a short break or rest period; time in formation during which soldiers were allowed to talk, smoke, or drink from their canteens. (GWD)

benzine board USA (WWII) a board of officers who determined the punishment or penalties a soldier would receive for misconduct. The officers seemed to ration out punishment like gasoline or benzine was rationed. (GWD)

benzined USA (WWI) said of an officer who had been brought up on charges by a board of inquiry; said of an officer who had been retired or transferred as the result of a bad attitude. (WWW)

berloque FrA (WWI) the all-clear siren that sounded in Paris at the end of an air raid. (WWW)

berm CSA/USA (1861) a narrow path around the base of a fortification, between the parapet and the ditch below, which prevented the parapet from collapsing; also spelled berme. USA (WWII) shelf cut into the wall of a trench to keep it from caving in. (1960s–present) elevated perimeter of a fortification. (MD MMD)

Bermuda triangle USA (1993) the area north of the seaport in Mogadishu, Somalia, a rough place from which people tended to disappear.

berserk Br>CSA/USA/USMC/USN (19th c.–present) [Old Norse *berserk*, without a shirt or, depending on the translator, a bear or animal skin shirt; introduced into English by Sir Walter Scott (1822)] frenzied. Norse warriors, who often went into battle naked or wearing a bearskin shirt, tended to cut down both friend and foe in their wild fury. (DWO TON) (*see also* keep your shirt on)

berth MM (17th c.) sufficent space to maneuver a ship at sea. (18th c.–present) a ship's mooring place; a place to sleep, especially on a ship; the sleeping area aboard a ship. (DWO MAN)

best girl's on the tow rope BrN>USN (19th c.) sailor's phrase describing good weather and smooth sailing on the homeward bound cruise. (TON)

between the devil and the deep blue sea MM (17th c.) in a very difficult situation. (NCT) (*see* devil to pay and no hot pitch)

betwixt wind and water MM (18th–20th c.) the area just above the waterline of a ship where the surface of the waves (wind) and the ocean (water) meet; the status of one who is near death; the stomach or midsection; a ship hit at the waterline by shot in battle. (AST)

BFA USMC (1980s) blank firing apparatus, a small metal box that helps prevent powder burns while one is firing blank rounds. It fits over the end of a gun's flash suppressor.

B40 USA (Vietnam) a communist-made, rocket-propelled grenade launcher. (BLO)

BFV USA (1980s) Bradley fighting vehicle.

BG Br>USA (WWII–1960s) a brigadier general. (ASC)

B-girl USA/USMC/USN (WWII) a bar girl, not necessarily a prostitute, yet not a proper young lady in the eyes of society in general.

BHQ BrA (1940, North Africa) battalion headquarters. (BRC)

bible MM (18th–19th c.) a hand axe. BrN (18th c.–1867) a hand axe, the symbol on the sleeve patch of a boatswain, or deck boss, of a sailing ship. (18th c.) in most common usage, a large holystone. (DVT OST) (*see* holystone) USA (ca.1900–WWII) official army book of rules and regulations, hardbound with a blue cover until the 1940s; aka army bible. Soldiers were expected to follow its contents as fully as a Christian would follow the teachings of the Bible. It was standard issue to all soldiers from the late 1800s until after WWI. (AFR ATK GWD)

biddies CSA (1860s) vittles, food.

Biere LaRue *See* Ba-moi-ba

Big Bertha Br>USA (WWI–WWII) German artillery, especially heavy artillery, named for Frau Bertha Krupp, wife of the German arms manufacturer; a gun that shelled Paris at a range of twenty-five miles. (WWII) a big or heavy female. (GWD MMD)

Big Bill *See* Big Willy

big board USNA (WWII) a navy review board that consisted of all of the squadron commanders and senior flying officers under the direction of the superintendent of aviation training. (AFR)

big boot USA (WWII) commanding general. (SID)

big boys *See* big stuff

big brass USAF (1950s) high-ranking air force officers. (ASC)

big chow USN (WWII–present) a special

meal (a fancy one by sailor's standards) eaten just prior to entering into combat.

Big Dad USMC (1980s) boot camp term for senior drill instructor; aka boss or black belt. (*see* black belt, boss)

Big Dead One *See* Big Red One

Big Foot USA (WWII) the commanding general of a division, a comparison to the legendary hairy monster. (SID)

big friend USAF (1950s) a large bomber belonging to the United States or an allied nation. (ASC)

Big John USA (WWII) a new recruit, especially one from the country or fresh from the farm. (AFR GWD)

Bigot (BIG•ott) USA/USMC/USAF/USN (WWII) a code name that designated very top secret material. (WWW)

big pond USA/USMC (1960s–70s) the Pacific Ocean.

Big Portsmouth USN (1960s–present) a nickname for the naval prison at Portsmouth, New Hampshire.

big PX in the sky USA/USAF/USMC/USN (1960s–70s) heaven. (*see* PX)

big red USA (1991) used by troops in Desert Storm to refer to the sun over the Saudi Arabian desert. (*see* Desert Storm, Gulf War)

Big Red One USA (1960s–70s) the United States First Army Division; aka Big Dead One, Bloody One, Bloody Red One, BRO.

big stuff BrA (WWI) an artillery shell in excess of eight inches in diameter; an artillery shell that created massive damage upon impact; aka big buy. (AGE)

big-time operator USA (WWII) one who played politics to gain favor, a petty schemer or gangster in uniform.

big twenty USA (1960s–70s) reference to the twenty years of military service needed to retire with full benefits.

Big Willie USA/USMC (WWI) doughboys' name for Kaiser Wilhelm of Germany; aka Big Bill. (AGE) (*see* doughboys)

Big Willy *See* Mother

bilge[1] MM (15th c.–present) the lowest point of a ship's inner hull; the part of a ship that lies below the waterline. USN (1940s–present) poor-quality food; bad information. (MAN)

bilge[2] MM (15th c.–present) to cave in below the waterline. (AST) (15th c.) to complain or grumble. United States Naval Academy (19th c.–present) to fail an exam or be rejected for excessively poor grades. (*see* bilger)

bilger USN (WWII) a midshipman demoted for acquiring too many demerits at the U.S. Naval Academy. (AST) (*see* bilge)

bilge rat MM (15th c.) a large rodent that lived on the waste that fell into bilges; a person of low moral character, one who was not to be trusted. USN (WWII–present) a sailor assigned to duty below decks, especially in the engine room. USNA (WWII) a womanizing aviation cadet. (AFR) (*see* bilge[1], black gang)

bilge water USN (18th c.–present) a lie, unfounded rumor, or myth. (1960s) navy soup, its color, odor, and taste likened to the water in the bilges. (*see* bilge[1])

bilharzia *See* Bill Harris

bilk[1] BrA/BrN (17th c.) to cheat or swindle. (DVT)

bilk[2] BrA/BrN (17th c.) one who cheats or swindles; the act of cheating or swindling. (DVT)

billet FrA>BrA>USA/USMC (18th c.) [French *billet de logement*, ticket for lodgings> English *billet*, place to quarter soldiers] a paper given to each soldier with the location of his assigned quarters. At the time, the practice was to quarter soldiers among the civilian population. (WWI–1980) assigned quarters. USMC (1980s) a boot camp term for an assigned duty or job. (ASC MCT MD MMD) (*see* every bullet has its billet)

Bill Harris BrA (WWI) a nickname for bilharzia, a frequently occurring intestinal disease brought on by drinking bacteria-infested water from the Nile River.

bimbo *See* recruit

binnacle MM (15th–18th c.) [Latin *habitaculum*, to inhabit>French *habitacle*, where something lives or dwells>Spanish *bitacula*>English *bittacle*, compass housing] the cupboard near a ship's rudder or wheel that held the navigation instruments. (18th c.) the stand located near the ship's wheel that held the compass. (DWO OST)

binnacle list USN (18th–20th c.) the roster of men who were unable to report for duty due to illness or injury. The list was tacked to ship's binnacle, where it could be easily seen and read by the officer of the deck. (BJM) (*see* sick call)

binnacle word USN (18th–20th c.) a refined or pretentious word that was not part of an ordinary sailor's vocabulary. Such words were used by gentlemen officers who often stood their duty at the ship's wheel, near the binnacle. (DVT) (*see also* binnacle)

bint BrA (WWI–present) [Egyptian *bint*, girl] an Egyptian or Arabian girl; a man who plays the part of a woman in a play. (WID) (*see also* frat, skirt)

bint kwoyees BrA (1940, North Africa) [Arabic *bint*, woman, and *kwoyees*, pretty] a pretty woman, a talented woman. (DRA) (*see also* bella seenyorenna, bint, frat)

BIO BrA (WWI) the British Intelligence Office and/or its officers. (WWW)

bird USA (1950s–90s) an aircraft, especially a helicopter. (1950s) a missile.

bird cage BrA>USN (WWI–WWII) a sniper's concealed firing platform, usually located high in a tree; a prisoner-of-war compound. USN (WWII) the flight officer's station on the "island" of an aircraft carrier. (TON) (*see* island)

bird colonel USA/USAF/USMC (WWII–present) a full colonel, for the eagle worn on his or her uniform shoulder straps as insignia of rank. (ASC)

bird-dog USAF (1950s) to use a radio direction finder that tracks its prey like a hunting dog; to track aircraft with radar. USA/USAF (WWII–1960s) to dance with a superior's wife or girlfriend; to become friendly with such a lady; to follow someone closely. (1960s) to work diligently at a difficult problem. (ASC)

birdfarm USN (1960s–70s) aircraft carrier.

birdfarms USN (1960s–70s) a cluster of air-

craft carriers off the coast of Vietnam.

bird-hatch USN (1960s–present) to have more than one child, supposedly coined by Admiral Hyman Rickover.

birdland USA (1960s) a soldier's reference to the living quarters of senior army officers, those with rank of full (bird) colonel and above. (*see also* bird colonel)

birdman BrA/USAAF (WWI) aviator. (ASC)

birdshit USA (1960s) paratroopers, who drop from aircraft.

birthday suit BrA (ca.1771–present) nakedness, the suit one was born wearing. (DVT)

biscuit BrA>USA/USN/USMC (14th–20th c.) [Medieval Latin *biscoctus*, twice cooked> Old French *biscut*>English *biscuit*, twice cooked] twice-baked foodstuff, especially bread. The first baking cooked the ingredients, and the second dried the product. Aka ship's biscuit, brown George, brown wig, jug, munition bread. Military biscuits were very dry and hard. BrA (1750s) a hammock mattress said to be the size and hardness of a ship's biscuit. BrA (WWI) an army-issue mattress so undersized that it took three of them to make a bed for one average-size person. It was hard and very durable. (DWO) (*see also* brown George, hardtack)

biscuit bitches USA (1960s–70s) the women volunteers of the Red Cross or USO who entertained men near the front lines in a socially acceptable manner. USA/USMC (1960s, Vietnam) the Red Cross workers who provided coffee and donuts to those in the field; aka donut dollies.

biscuit flipping range USN (18th–19th c.) twenty-five yards or less, the average distance that one could throw a ship's biscuit. (*see* biscuit)

biscuit gun USAAF (WWII) a fictitious weapon that supposedly could shoot food up to a pilot while in flight. A common prank involved sending a new recruit to the cook with a request for the weapon. (GWD)

biscuit shooter USA (1890s–1940s)) an officer's cook; in peacetime, a female cook employed by the post. (EMP)

Bish' BrN (1750s) the Bishop, a sailor's

name for the ship's chaplain. (*see* chaplain)

bitch[1] BrA>USA BrA (16th–19th c.) one who was lewd or went whoring. (19th c.) one who played the role of a woman in a tea ceremony. (DVT)

bitch[2] BrA>USA (18th c.) to quit or surrender from fear. (19th c.) to spoil or ruin. USA (20th c.) to complain constantly and loudly. (DVT)

bitch box USA/USN (WWII–present) a public address system.

bite butts USA (WWII) to smoke partially smoked or broken cigarettes.

bitter end MM (15th–18th c.) the section of the anchor cable that is inboard and secured to the bitts; the last link of an anchor chain. (18th c.) the position of one who struggles in a hopeless cause, from an anchor cable that has slipped from the bitts and cannot be saved or secured. (OST) (*see* slip the cable)

bivouac[1] GrA>FrA>BrA>USA (18th c.–present) [Swiss-German *beiwacht*, to post additional guard>French *bivac*>English *bivouac*, to remain on alert at night] to remain on the alert at night. The term originally applied only to the night watch of Zurich, then to any unit standing watch. (AGE ATK MDB)

bivouac[2] GrA>FrA>BrA>USA (18th c.–present) [Swiss-German *beiwacht*, to post additional guard>French *bivac*>English *bivouac*, to remain on alert at night] a temporary camp. (AGE ATK MDB)

bivvy BrA (WWI–WWII) a British soldier's term for bivouac. (WID) (*see* bivouac[2])

bivvy sheet BrA (WWI) a poor quality, rubberized, army-issue groundsheet. (AGE)

BK USA (1960s–70s)) a below-the-knee amputation. (BLO)

blab off USA (WWII) to talk out of turn, to reveal a secret or confidence, to say too much, especially when the subject should not have been mentioned at all. (GWD)

Black Belt USMC (1980s) boot camp term for senior drill instructor, from the black, patent leather belt that was part of his uniform. (*see also* Big Dad)

Black Bess *See* Brown Bess

blackbird MM (18th c.) an African-American, freed or slave. (IHA)

blackbirder MM (1838) a ship owner or captain who was part of the slave trade. The term sometimes applied to the sailors who manned the slave brigs. (IHA)

black death Vietminh (1960s–70s) American M16 rifle, for its color. (*see also* black magic)

black eagle USA (WWII) one who could be trusted to relay the most accurate information via the latrine. (*see* latrine rumor)

black gang USN (mid-19th c.) sailors who worked in the engine rooms of old coalburning ships. Coal dust covered them with black, gritty film. (TON) (*see* bilge rat)

blackguard BrA (1535) a cleaner of pots and pans. (18th c.) one who was dirty and untidy; one who did dirty work for the Horse Guard of the Royal Palace, including bootpolishing and cleaning up after troopers and their horses. (DVT)

black hand gang BrA (WWI) trench raiders, who often were not expected to return from a raid on enemy trenches. Later, bombers and stretcher bearers were included in this group, as they were special targets of German snipers. (*see* bomber)

blackhawk USA (WWII) a regulation black necktie. Summer neckties were khaki colored. (GWD) (*see* khaki)

"Black Jack" *See* Pershing, John J. "Black Jack"

blackjack BrA (18th c.) a drinking jug or cup made of leather. (DVT) USA/USN (19th c.) to soldiers, a strong laxative; to sailors, a pirate flag bearing a skull and crossbones insignia; an evil-looking scoundrel.

blacklist USA/USMC/USN (19th c.) an unofficial record of errors and misdeeds committed by enlisted men and used by an officer to keep the men in line; a list of men designated to receive extra duty as punishment for offenses.

black magic USA (1960s–70s) M16 rifle; aka widow maker. (*see also* black death)

black market GrA>BrA>USA/USMC/USAF/USN (WWI–present) [German *Schwartz-*

markt, black market or illegal sale of rationed materials and foodstuffs] originally, the illicit sale of stolen government property; now the illicit sale of any illegally obtained property.

Black Monday BrN (17th c.) a Monday on which a flogging was scheduled. Floggings were customarily executed immediately after breakfast, usually on a Monday. (DVT) (*see also* blue Monday, boy's cat, earn your stripes, flog, gunner's daughter, man's cat, thieves' cat)

blackout USA/USN/USMC/USAF (WWII) coffee. (AFR GWD MMD) (*see also* battery acid, blackstrap, coffee, ink, jamocha, java, joe, lifer juice, paint remover)

blackout, pass the *See* pass the blackout

blackshoe USN (1960s–70s) a member of the seagoing navy who wore regulation black leather shoes. Aviators were permitted to wear brown shoes.

blacksnake USA (1860s) the long leather whip used by mule skinners to enforce orders given to their stubborn charges. (ASL)

blackstrap BrA (17th c.) hard labor given to soldiers stationed at Gibraltar. (18th c.) USA/USMC/USN (18th–20th c.) molasses. USN (19th c.) any of the strong wines of the Mediterranean region. USA/USAAF/USN (1900–WWII) strong coffee. (AFR GWD MMD) (*see also* battery acid, blackout, coffee, ink, jamocha, java, joe, lifer juice, paint remover) (AGE AST DVT) (*see* coffee)

Black Wednesday USAAF (WWII) a Wednesday on which was scheduled mandatory calisthenics with rifles. (AFR)

blade time USA (1960s–70s) time spent airborne in a helicopter.

blanco BrA>USA (19th c.) a white polish used on white leather belts.

blanked BrA (WWI) [French *vin blanc*, white wine] tipsy, slightly drunk.

blanket USA (WWII) a pancake. USAF (1950s) the cloud cover that lies above aircraft in flight. (ASC GWD) (*see* fuzziewuzzies)

blanket bay BrN (1750s) a sailor's hammock.

blanket drill BrA (WWI) an afternoon nap, much favored by men who had served in India. USA/USMC/USN (WWI–WWII) sleep. (SAM) (*see* bunk fatigue, pressing blankets, sack drill, sack time)

blanket party USMC/USN (1960s–present) a beating by one's shipmates. The victim is wrapped in a blanket to prevent identification of his attackers.

blanko water USA (WWII) army coffee. (GWD) (*see* blackstrap, battery acid, coffee)

blast BrA (18th c.) to bawl out with curses and oaths. (DVT)

blazer USN (19th c.) a bomb ketch or a mortar vessel, from the amount of fire and smoke that issued from its gun. (ANE) (*see* bomb, bomb ketch)

blessés, les FrA (WWI) [French *blesser*, to hurt, wound] wounded soldiers. (WWW)

blessures FrA (WWI) battle wounds. (WWW) (*see also* blessés, les)

bletherhead USN (19th c.) a dense, unthinking person. (ANE)

blethering USN (19th c.) incoherent, silly, or insolent. (ANE)

Blighty BrA (20th c.) [Hindu *bilayati*, over the seas, foreign] home, meaning England. (AGE WID)

blighty bag BrA (WWI) a small kit bag used by a British soldier on home leave. (*see* kit bag)

blighty hut BrA (WWI) a soldier's home in England.

blighty one BrA (WWI) a wound serious enough to require a return to England, hopefully for the duration of the war.

blind[1] BrA (17th c.) totally drunk. (GWD IHA) (*see* blind drunk)

blind[2] USA (ca.1900–WWII) a monetary fine imposed by court-martial; a curse delivered strongly and with full intent, supposedly powerfully enough to cause blindness. (GWD IHA)

blind drunk USA (1830) totally intoxicated. (IHA)

blind flying USAAF (WWII) on a blind date. (AFR)

blip BrAF>USAAF (WWII) the spot of light

that appears on a radar screen to indicate an approaching aircraft. (TOC)

blister bandits USMC (1980s) a boot camp name for recruits who develop such severe cases of foot blisters that they are relieved from heavy duty.

blitz[1] GrAF>BrAF>USAAF (1939–45) [German *blitzen*, lightning, bright] to shine, from a metal polish trade named Blitz. (MCT MMD)

blitz[2] GrAF>BrAF>USAAF (1939–45) [German *blitzen*, lightning, bright] bombardment, especially by enemy planes. (MCT MMD)

blitzbuggy *See* jeep

blitzes BrAF>USAAF (1939–45) combat patrols made up of fighter planes and scout planes. (AFR MMD)

blitzkrieg Gr>Br>USA (1939–45) [German *Blitzkrieg*, lightning war] the use of a lightning-fast line of talk to gain sympathy from a female; sometimes, one who had ready cash to spend. (GWD)

blitzkrieg promotion USA (WWII) a quick promotion in rank due to wartime pressures placed on the army by its rapid expansion. (GWD)

blitz wagon USAAF (WWII) a staff car, usually driven at lightning speed. (AFR)

blizzard CSA/USA (1860s) a very heavy musket volley. (LRY)

blob-stick USA (WWII) a wooden rifle and bayonet used for bayonet practice. (AFR)

block MM (14th c.) [Old French *bloc*, pulley] a pulley. (OST TWW)

blockade mutton Gr (WWII) dog meat. By 1940, the British blockade had caused beef to become a rare commodity in Germany, and the German government had declared dog meat a legal foodstuff for civilians and soldiers alike.

blockbuster GrAF>BrAF (WWII) an aerial bomb with enough explosive force to destroy an entire city block.

blockhouse GrA>BrA (16th–17th c.) [German *Blockhaus*, house that guards or blocks specific area] a structure designed to guard jails and prisons. BrA>USA (18th c.–present) a structure especially designed and constructed to deny the enemy access to important targets, such as bridges, towns, and gates. (DVT)

Bloe, Joe *See* Joe Bloe

b'longee MM (18th–20th c.) to belong to or be owned by, pidgin English brought back to the West by sailors who had been to the Far East. (SLA)

blood USA/USMC/USN (ca.1910–70s) tomato catsup; aka redeye or red lead. USA/USMC (1960s–70s) an African-American soldier or Marine; a name applied to and used by black servicemen when speaking of or to one other. (GWD)

blooded USA (WWI) said of a unit or person who has seen combat.

blood ship MM (19th c.) a ship whose officers were mean, cruel, and abusive to the sailors they commanded. (AST) (*see also* thieves' cat)

blood stripe USA/USMC (1960s–70s) a promotion (stripe) gained as a result of the death or serious wounding of a senior ranking man.

bloody hooker *See* slung his hammock in a bloody hooker

Bloody One *See* Big Red One

Bloody Red One *See* Big Red One

blooper *See* M79 grenade launcher

blouse USA/USMC (1860s–present) a service uniform coat; any coat or jacket. (ASC SAM) USA (WWII–present) the class A uniform coat. (ASC)

blow MM (18th c.–present) a wind of gale force, or thirty-five to sixty-five knots, capable of knocking a man down.

blow away USA/USMC (1960s–present) to kill. (SLA)

blow-boy USA (WWII) an army bugler.

blow buggy USAF (1950s) a single-engine jet fighter plane of the 1950s; aka blow pipe, blow torch. (ASC)

blowhard MM (ca. 1860) a loud, boisterous person who is all talk and no action. (ANE) CSA/USA (1860s) a braggart, loudmouth, bore. (LRY)

blow job USA/USN/USMC (WWII–present) oral sex.

Blow, Joe *See* Joe Blow

blow one's stack USA/USMC/USN (19th c.–1960s) to lose one's temper in a sudden, violent manner; to get angry; aka blow one's top. (SAM WEA)

blowout USN (19th c.) a wild run ashore during liberty; enjoyment to the fullest. (ANE)

blow pipe *See* blow buggy

blow smoke USA/USMC (1960s–70s) to con or confuse someone.

blow the grampus USN (19th c.) to awaken a sleeping man by throwing water on him. (ANE)

blow torch *See* blow buggy

blowup USN (19th c.) a sudden or violent eruption of anger. (ANE)

blubber BrA (15th c.) to cry or wail uncontrollably. (DVT)

blubber cheeks MM (18th c.) fat facial cheeks. (DVT)

blubber hunter USN (19th c.) a sailor who served aboard a whaling ship, a term of contempt used by merchant sailors and navy men, who considered a whaler to be a fisherman rather than a true sailor. (AST)

blue[1] USA/USMC/USAF/USN (1960s–70s) a body of water, from the color used to mark waterways and bodies of water on military maps.

blue[2] BrA (18th c.–present) sad, disappointed, or upset. (DVT) USN (19th c.) sad or depressed, from the practice of flying a blue flag and/or painting a blue band around the hull of a ship prior to returning to home port when the captain or one of the officers had died during a cruise. (TON)

Blue, the BrA (1940, North Africa) the North African desert; aka the Ghot (gote). (DRA)

Blue and Gray Division USA (1917) the 29th Division. Established in July 1917 of National Guard units from Virginia, Maryland, Pennsylvania, and New Jersey, the division's patch was a circular blue and gray (ying and yang) design.

bluebacks *See* Federals

bluebellies *See* Federals

bluecoat USA (1833–1900) a soldier, so named for the blue uniforms issued by the government. (1861) a Southern term for a Northern soldier. (IHA)

blue-cross gas BrA (WWI) a sneezing gas employed by the Germans. The projectiles that contained the gas were marked with blue crosses.

bluejacket BrN>USN (18th–20th c.) an ordinary enlisted sailor, from the short-waisted blue wool jacket that became popular in the eighteenth century and was standard until the early twentieth century. (BJM MAN) (*see also* gob, swab, swabbie)

Blue Max USA (1960s) a nickname for the Medal of Honor, which hangs from a blue ribbon. Possibly a mocking reference to a German WWI medal, the Pour de Merit (aka Blue Max), Germany's highest military award. (*see* Medal of Honor)

blue Monday BrN>USN (18th–20th c.) traditionally, the day that floggings ordered by the captain's mast of the previous week were held. Officers wore their dress blues. This sad occasion was also known as the Monday blues. (*see also* black Monday, boy's cat, captain's mast, earn your stripes, flog, gunner's daughter, man's cat, thieves' cat)

blue murder, go like *See* go like blue murder

blue on blue USA/USN/USMC/USAF (1980s–present) a death resulting from friendly fire.

blue peter BrN>USN (ca. 1777) a blue-and-white pennant flown from the main mast to signal shore parties to return to ship. Usually flown just before the ship weighed anchor. (*see* weigh anchor)

blue pigeon USN (19th c.) a lead used to take soundings in waters where depths were unknown or fluctuating. (ANE)

Blues *See* Federals

blues USA/USMC (20th c.) the dress blue uniform. (SAM)

blueshirt USN (1960s–70s) one who worked on and manhandled aircraft on an aircraft carrier.

blue suiter USAF (1980s) an officer of high rank, one whose duty required him to wear his class A Air Force uniform on a daily basis. (*see* class A uniform)

blue ticket USA (ca. 1900–1960s) a military

discharge granted for a medical problem or mental instability, one step above dishonorable. It was printed on blue paper. (ATK)

blue tuxedos USA (ca.1900–WWII) blue dungarees worn for especially dirty work. (GWD)

blue unction BrA (WWI) foul-smelling ointment used to combat the body lice ever present in trenches.

blue water sailor MM (18th c.–present) a sailor who earns his daily bread on the world's oceans and seas and is looked down upon by those who ply their trade in bays, coastal waters, lakes, or rivers. (AST)

bluff MM (17th–20th c.) a vessel with a blunt, rounded bow; a buxom female. CSA/USA (1860s) a cheater, possibly from an early version of poker called bluff. (LRY) American colonies (1867) a high, steep riverbank. (IHA TON)

blunderbluss MM (17th–19th c.) [Dutch *donderbus*, thunder gun>English *blunderbus*, blunder, possibly to describe such a gun's notably short effective or accurate range] a gun with a wide, funnel-shaped muzzle designed to fire lead, nails, gravel, glass, or other material packed into it in a wide burst. An ideal antiboarding weapon for wooden ships of the era. (DWO TON)

BMGC BrA (WWI) brigade machine gun company. (AGE)

B19 USAAF (WWII) a mythical bomber; a big female, a comparison to something larger than a B17, the largest bomber of the time.

Board you! USN (19th c.) an order for the next drink to be poured, the implication being that a fight would follow if the drink were not forthcoming. This arose from the practice of placing a ship alongside an enemy vessel and sending boarders onto its decks. (ANE)

boat MM (13th c.–present) [Anglo-Saxon *boat*, small vessel or ship] to sailors of old, a craft that could be rowed or was small enough to be hoisted up and placed on the deck of a ship. (OST)

boat chocks BrN (1750s) wooden cradles on the spar deck upon which the ship's boats rested. (*see* spar deck)

boat station USN (20th c.) the assigned place of an individual when a boat is being lowered. (MAN)

boatswain MM>USN/USMM (15th c.–present) [Anglo-Saxon *boatswain*, boat commander] a petty officer who directs work done by the watch stationed on the deck of a ship; aka bosun. In the merchant fleet, boatswains were more commonly called mates. (SLA)

BOB (bob) USAF (1950s) Bureau of the Budget. (AFS)

bobber USA (WWII) a carrier of tales, rumor monger. (GWD SID)

bobbery USN (19th c.) a loud squabble or disturbance, pidgin English from the East Indies. (ANE)

bob-down man BrA (WWI) an air raid sentry. When he sounded the alarm, those in his unit dropped (bobbed) down.

bobstay MM (16th–20th c.) a heavy line used to hold the bowsprit of a ship in its proper place; aka penis. (DVT OST)

bobtail BrA (18th c.) a loose woman, one who flaunts her backside; a eunuch or impotent man. USA (ca. 1900–WWII) a dishonorable discharge written on yellow paper with the lower portion cut off (bobbed). (AFR DVT EMP) (*see also* dishonorable discharge)

boche (bosh) FrA (WWI) [French *boche*, hard-headed ones] a German soldier. (AGE WWW) (*see also* Heine, hun, Jerry, Katzenjammer Kid, kraut, moffer, Ted)

boco (bo•KO) BrA (WWI) [French *beaucoup*, a lot] good, very good, all is well; also spelled boko, bokoo (bo•KOO). (*see also* beaucoup)

boko *See* boco

bokoo *See* boco

body lice *See* louse

body snatcher MM (18th c.) a civilian who served as deputy to the sheriff and whose duty it was to arrest debtors. USN (18th c.) member of a vessel's police force. Ashore: one who disinterred bodies for illegal medical research. (DVT) (*see* Jimmy Legs, master-at-arms) AusA/BrA>USA (WWI) a German sniper. (WWII) a stretcher bearer, who snatched wounded from the battlefield; a member of a raiding party sent out to make prisoners of enemy soldiers. (AGE)

Boer D/BrA (19th c.) a Dutch settler of South Africa.

bogey USAAF>USAF (WWII–present) an aircraft of unknown origin; also spelled bogie. (AFR)

bogie wheel USA (WWII) one of the small wheels inside the track of a tank serving to keep the treads in line. (GWD MD MMD)

boglander BrA (18th c.) an Irishman, for all the bogs on the Emerald Isle; aka bog-trotter. (DVT)

bog pocket USAAF (WWII) one who was tightfisted with his cash, as if "his pockets were as bottomless as a bog." (AFR)

bog-trotter See boglander

BOHICA (bow•HEE•kah) USN/USMC (1960s–present) bend over, here it comes again. A friendly warning that something unpleasant is about to happen.

boiling up USN (19th c.–1960s) approaching at a high rate of speed. A vessel under full steam and moving at a fast pace was said to come boiling up. (WEA)

boite FrA (WWI) [French *boite*, box or case] a jail. (WWW)

bokra BrA (20th c.) [Arabic *bokra*, tomorrow] tomorrow.

Bolo BrA (1918) short for Bolshevik, a member of the Russian Social Democrat Party, which seized power in Russia by the Revolution of November 1917.

bolo USA (1898–1970s) a long, curved knife used with deadly effect by some natives of the Philippine Islands; a soldier who failed to qualify on the rifle range and who would have been better off had he been armed with a bolo. Groups of such men were called bolo squads. (MCT)

bologna USA (WWII) a generic term for cold cuts and cold meats, not necessarily the large smoked sausage from which it took its name.

bolo squad See bolo

bolt¹ BrN>USN (14th–20th c.) to run away from danger in a panic; to gulp down food. (17th–18th c.) to swallow a portion of meat without chewing. (ANE DVT)

bolt² BrA (14th–19th c.) the arrow shot from a crossbow. (*see also* quarrel)

bolt out of the blue BrA (11th c.–present) a surprise attack; an arrow fired from a crossbow at a high trajectory, which appeared to its targets to have fallen out of the sky. (19th c.) a total surprise. (*see* bolt², crossbow)

bolt upright BrA (14th c.) straight up and down, as a crossbow arrow stuck in the ground. (DVT) (*see* bolt², crossbow)

bomb USA (18th c.–present) [Greek *bombos*, buzzing or booming sound>Latin *bombus*, loud sound>Italian *bomba*, explosion> French *bombe*>English *bombard*, bomb thrower] an explosive device, such as a shell (hollow cannonball filled with gunpowder), hand grenade, or aerial bomb. (DWO) BrN> USN (1750s–mid-1800s) a man-of-war that carried shell-firing mortars used to bombard shore positions; aka blazer, bomb ketch, mortar vessel. (19th c.) a specially designed craft used to bombard shore positions. (TWW)

bomb-a-deer USAAF (WWII) bomber personnel, a play on the word bombardier. (GWD) (*see* bombardier)

bombard See bumboat

bombardier BrA (1768) one employed in the loading and firing of a mortar, who filled shells and set fuses. In the language of the day, he was "third rank of a private man in a company of artillery," most likely sergeant of artillery. (MDB)

bomb dodger BrA (WWI) a civilian who moved his family outside of London in the hope of escaping dreaded zeppelin and bomber raids.

bomber BrA>USA (WWI) one assigned to carry a sack of hand grenades when the unit went on a trench raid. (*see* suicide squad) BrAF> USAAF>USAF (WWI–present) an aircraft designed to carry a heavy load of bombs to be dropped on enemy targets from the air.

bomb heaver USA (WWII) pretty girl; very well-endowed young woman. (GWD)

bomb ketch BrN>USN (18th–mid-19th c.) a sailing vessel used to assault shore fortifications and positions, armed with mortars that could fire exploding shells (bombs); aka blazer, bomb, mortar vessel. The mortars fired in a high arc (forty-five degrees or more) to bring fire plunging down upon the enemy. Conventional shipboard guns of the time had very limited elevation, most often no more than five degrees. (*see* bomb)

bombo USN (19th c.) a drink low in alcoholic content and therefore considered to be of poor quality. (ANE)

bomb-proof BrA>CSA/USA (1760s–WWII) an earthen shelter reinforced with heavy timbers and built partially or totally underground. The roof consisted of several feet of packed earth over heavy logs and was intended to absorb the impact of bombs and thereby protect those in the shelter.

bomb-proofer BrA (WWI) one who constantly schemed to get a bomb-proof job. (*see* bomb-proof job)

bomb-proof job BrA (WWI) a soft, cushy job in a safe place, usually far behind the front lines.

bone USA (18th–20th c.) to steal or cheat.

boned BrA (WWI) arrested by military police. USA (WWI) arrested. (DVT)

bone orchard BrA (19th c.) a cemetery or graveyard.

bones See sawbones

bone up USN (19th c.) to review or restudy. USA/USAAF (20th c.) to cultivate, as a friendship; to strive for goal. (AFR ANE MMD)

bonfire BrA (WWI) a cigarette.

bongo-boosh BrA (WWI) a tasty morsel.

booby See booby trap

booby hatch MM (18th–20th c.) originally, a small, square hatch that opened to the deck below. It was usually on the spar deck aft of the wheel, where the officers stood their post. Booby may be a corruption of the word "body," and a booby hatch may have been an opening large enough to allow a body to pass through. USN (1930s) mental hospital.

(SLA)

booby hutch BrA (WWI) a small indentation scooped from the side of a trench. Those who sought safety there, who were about as safe as a rabbit in its hutch, were called boobs (fools).

booby trap BrA>USA/USMC (WWI–pres-

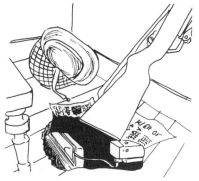

Booby trap: lifting the rifle activates the release igniter, which detonates the charge.

ent) [Spanish *bodo*, stupid>English *boob* (1600), dull or stupid] an explosive device left behind by the Germans and set to go off when triggered by a fool (boob). At first the Allied Forces considered these devices to be cowardly, but by WWII all sides were using them freely. (*see* Allied Forces)

boodle West Point/USA (19th c.–present) candy or other sweets. (ASC) (*see* pogey bait)

boogie woogie boy USA (WWII) a new draftee who wanted to jitterbug more than anything else—the smart-ass punk of his day. (SID)

book it USA (WWII) to foul up anything and everything. (MMD)

boom USAF (1950s) the sound made by a jet aircraft as it exceeds the speed of sound. (ASC)

boom-boom[1] USA (WWII–1970s) a handheld firearm, such as a pistol or rifle; sex. During the 1960s and '70s, the term was used by Vietnamese prostitutes to advertise their trade. (GWD)

boom-boom[2] USA (WWII–1970s) to have sex. (GWD)

boom-boom girl USA/USMC (1960s–70s) a Vietnamese prostitute.

boom-boom house USA/USMC (1960s–70s) a house of prostitution.

boomer USN (1960s–present) a sailor assigned to duty aboard a nuclear-powered vessel; a submarine armed with nuclear warheads.

Boomtown USNA (WWII) the wooden barracks built by the WPA and occupied by the Naval Aviation Cadet Regiment; aka Splinterville. (AFR)

boondockers USMC (1898–present) heavy combat boots worn by Marines when stomping through the boondocks. (PAT SAM)

boondocks USA/USMC/USN (1898–present) [Philippine *Bondoc*, small, isolated village across the bay from Manila] remote site; a foreign station; aka boonies. (SAM)

boonie rat USMC (1960s–70s) an infantryman, especially one in combat; one who has been in the bush for a long time, possibly too long. (*see* bush*)*

boonies *See* boondocks

boot USMC/USN (1900–present) a short canvas legging that gives the appearance of a boot; a raw recruit. (1960s) someone fresh from basic training; new, untested material or equipment. (SAM)

boot camp USMC/USN (1900–present) the basic training camp for United States Navy and United States Marine Corps recruits, most likely named for the uniform leggings (boots) worn from 1900 through the Korean War. (SAM)

bootleg *See* coffee

bootlegger MM (18th–20th c.) a smuggler who carried contraband in the tops of his thigh-high boots. US (1920s–30s) a gangster who smuggled illegal liquor. (TON) (*see* demon)

bootlicker USN (19th c.–present) sailor who goes out of his way to curry favor with the ship's officers; also spelled boot-licker. (ANE)

bootneck BrN (1980s–present) a Royal Marine; aka Jolly. (*see also* Jolly)

boots BrA (18th c.) the youngest officer in a regimental mess, whose duty it was to ring the mess bell, tend the fire, and put out the candles. (DVT)

boots and saddles USA (1860s) [French *boute selle*, put on the saddle>American English *boots and saddles*, a mispronunciation of the French] a cavalry command for troopers to mount their horses. (MCT)

boot top MM (18th c.) a band painted around the outer hull of a ship just above the waterline to mark the ship's normal sailing depth in water. (OST)

boot topper MM (18th c.) a coating of sulphur and tallow, or a mixture of resin and lime, applied to the bottom of a ship after it had been scraped and cleaned in dry dock. (AST OST)

booty BrA>USA (15th–18th c.) [Old German *bute*, to distribute, share>Old French *butin*>Saxon *bote*>English *butin*>English *booty* (18th c.)] military goods and stores seized legally in time of war. (DWO)

booze[1] MM (13th c.–present) [Middle Dutch *busen*, to drink much alcohol>Middle English *bouse*, to drink heavily>*bouse* (16th c.) or *bouze*>*booze* (1714)] to drink to excess, until drunk. (DWO SLA)

booze[2] MM (13th c.–present) strong spirits or other alcoholic drink. (1834) a drinking contest. (*see* demon)

boozed *See* boozy

boozer BrN>USN (1611–present) one who drinks heavily and often. (IHA) (*see also* bottle baby)

boozy BrA>USA (17th c.–present) drunk; aka boozed, bouzy, bowsy, or dowsie. (DVT IHA)

BOQ USA/USAF (1900s–present) bachelor officers' quarters. (AFS) (*see* bachelor's mess)

born under the gun and educated on the bowsprit USN (18th–19th c.) said with pride of a career enlisted man in the age of sail, especially one who had been in much trouble. Troublemakers were often laid over a gun's barrel to be flogged and given the job of cleaning the heads (toilets) located under the bowsprit as punishment for misdeeds. (*see* head)

boss[1] American colonies (1649) [Dutch *baas*,

chief, master>colonial American English *boss*] slave owner or field overseer. (1700s) a factory foreman, a title adopted by free whites, who disliked the word "master." USA (1920s) the top sergeant of a company, battery, or troop. (GWD IHA) (*see also* Big Dad, pop, top)

boss² USA>USMC (mid-19th c.–present) to give directions, have control.

bosun *See* boatswain

bosun's call BrN>USN (17th–19th c.) a silver or brass whistle carried by the boatswain and used to convey orders aboard ship; aka bosun's pipe. Its shrill sound could be heard above most shipboard noises. (pre-17th c.) a pipe worn as a symbol of authority by maritime officials. (*see* boatswain)

bosun's pipe *See* bosun's call

botfly BrA (ca. 1900) a two-winged fly, the larvae of which are parasitic in mammals, especially horses; a bothersome, annoying person.

bottle baby USMC (WWII–1970s) a heavy drinker, alcoholic; aka boozer. (SID)

bottle cap colonel USA/USAF (1950s–70s) a lieutenant colonel, likening the oak leaves symbolic of the rank to the cap of a soda bottle. (AFS)

bottomless pit Br>USA (18th c.) a woman's private parts. USA (19th c.–present) one who seems able to eat without becoming full. (DVT)

boudoir USA (1930s–40s) a mocking reference to a tent that housed a squad of eight men. (GWD)

bought another flag USA (WWI–WWII) said of one required to pay a large fine imposed by a military court, supposedly sufficient to buy an expensive flag for the army. (EMP) (*see* bought another star)

bought another star USA (WWI–WWII) said of one required to pay a small fine imposed by a military court, supposedly sufficient to buy a star for an expensive flag. (EMP) (*see* bought another flag)

bought his girl a chubby *See* chubby

bought the farm USA/USMC/USAF/USN (WWII–1970s) died in the service, possibly a reference to the ten-thousand-dollar life insurance policy payable to a military man's family in the event of his death. (AFS)

bouncer BrN (18th c.) a hefty person; a habitual liar. USN (19th–20th c.) a ship's gun with a violent, mean recoil. (ANE DVT)

bouncing Betty USA/USMC (WWII–present) an antipersonnel mine designed by the Germans and copied by the Allied Forces during WWII. The mine consisted of a cannister filled with ball bearings. When stepped upon, the can was propelled about three feet into the air before it exploded, scattering ball bearings in a 360-degree radius.

bounty BrN (18th c.) bonus money paid to a sailor to persuade him to enlist; a sum of money paid as compensation to a sailor's widow for the loss of her husband. (TWW) USA (1833–1860s) a monetary inducement to reenlist. On March 2, 1833, Congress passed an act authorizing payment of two months' extra wages to soldiers who reenlisted two months before or one month after their date of discharge. Also, depending on the length of enlistment and whim of Congress, one might receive 40 to 160 acres of land. Later both state and federal governments offered payments ranging from one hundred to three hundred dollars. In 1865, the United States government offered a bounty of a thousand dollars for the enlistment of an able-bodied sailor. (ASL MD)

bounty jumper USA (1860s) one who enlisted to receive a bounty payment and then deserted to enlist in another unit in order to receive an additional bounty. If caught, such a man could face a firing squad. (LRY)

bouzy *See* boozy

bow chaser *See* long Tom

bowlegs USA (19th–20th c.) an infantryman's nickname for a cavalryman.

bows on MM (18th c.–present) said of a vessel sailing a straight and determined course; face to face. (SLA) (*see also* end on)

bowsprit MM (13th c.–present) [Old Saxon *sprit*, to sprout, or Dutch *boespriet*, place] the place at the bow of a sailing ship where the figurehead is secured; a spar at the bow of a ship from which lines run to the masts to secure and stabilize them; a human nose. (OST TON)

bows under MM (18th–20th c.) said of a ship laboring under heavy seas, its decks frequently awash; said of a person overwhelmed with work. (SLA)

box the compass MM (18th c.–present) to recite the points of a compass from memory; to answer questions concerning the compass. (DVT)

box the Jesuit MM>BrN>USN (18th c.) to masturbate. (DVT) (*see also* frigging, jack-off flare, wanking pit)

boy's cat MM (17th c.–1880s) cat-o'-nine-tails made of lighter cord than a regular "man's" cat. USN (1770s–1850s) tails had whipped rather than knotted ends. Under US regulations a hand fourteen years old or younger could receive no more than twelve strokes and was permitted a dry flogging. (RAS) (*see also* black Monday, blue Monday, dry flogging, earn your stripes, flog, gunner's daughter, man's cat, thieves' cat)

bozo *See* recruit

BP USAF (1950s) base pay for an airman. USA (1970s–present) battle position. (AFS)

BPO USAF (1950s) base post office. (AFS)

brace[1] USA/USAAF (WWII) to assume a military stance, posture, or position.

brace[2] USA/USAAF (WWII–1950s) an exaggerated stance of attention. (ASC AFR) (*see* bruss)

brag rag USA (WWII) a military medal or decoration.

brain bucket USAF (1950s) a crash helmet. (AFS)

brain cramp *See* brain fart

brain fade *See* brain fart

brain fart USN (1980s–present) a brief loss of intelligent thought; a sudden recovery of a memory; an idea. Aka brain cramp, brain fade.

brass USA (1898–present) senior line and staff officers, from the brass buttons on their uniforms. CSA/USA (1860s) foolishness; courage, steady nerves. (WWI–1970s)

empty shell cases. (IHA) (*see also* brightwork)

brassards BrA>USA/USMC/USN (WWI–present) armbands worn by military personnel to denote specific duties.

brassed off BrA>USA (WWI) totally bored, fed up, and disgusted with life; aka browned off. (MMD)

brasserie FrA>BrA>USA (WWI) [French *brasserie*, brewery, beer hall] a restaurant and beer hall. (WWW)

brass hat BrA>USA/ USMC/USAF (19th c. –WWI) a senior line or staff officer, who wore brass fittings and gold leaves on his hat; the hat itself. (AFS SAM) (*see* red hat, scrambled eggs)

brass hat

brass monkey BrN (18th–19th c.) a brass cylinder in which shot was kept. (*see* cold enough to freeze the balls off a brass monkey)

brat BrA (16th c.) [Old Irish *Bratt*, mantle, covering>Old English *bratt*, cloak>English *brat* (16th c.), worn, ragged, makeshift clothing] a child, possibly from the fact that many children wore ragged clothing. (DVT DWO) (*see also* army brat)

brave Fr>Br>USA (15th c.–present) [French *brave*, uncivilized, wild, savage>English *brave* (15th c.), courageous] a Native American warrior. (DWO IHA)

bread and meat USA (WWI) nickname for a commissary (mess) officer. (MMD)

bread and water USMC (WWI–WWII) reduced rations served in the brig, literally bread and water; aka cake and wine, piss and punk, p & p. (SAM) (*see* brig, punk)

bread basket CSA/USA (1860s) a person's stomach. (LRY)

break[1] USA (19th c.–present) a short rest or respite from regular army routine. (ASC MMD)

break[2] USA (19th c.–present) to destroy one's spirit; to reduce in rank. (ASC MMD)

breaker BrN>USN/MM (15th–20th c.) [Anglo-Saxon *breken*, wave that bursts upon shore, and Spanish *bareca* (18th c.), barrel] a wave that breaks over shoals or rocks. (18th c.) a small water cask kept in a lifeboat for emergency use; a wave that breaks upon shore. (MAN OST SLA)

break out USMC (19th c.–present) to take out of storage and prepare for use. (SAM)

bream BrN (17th–19th c.) USN (18th–19th c.) to burn off the weeds that amassed on the bottom of a ship—dry dock work. (OST TWW)

breechcloth *See* breechclout

breechclout BrA>USA (18th c.–present) loincloth worn by Native Americans; aka breechcloth. (IHA)

breezy BrA (WWI) very nervous or afraid.

brevet Br>CSA/USA (16th–19th c.) [French *brevet*, commission or title of rank] an official written notice giving one the temporary rank of officer. USA (1861) honorary title of rank in effect only for the duration of a war or other conflict. Many obtained such rank through political connections rather than ability. (IHA) (*see* brevet baby)

brevet baby USA (post-1865) an illegitimate child; aka brevet child. (IHA)

brevet child *See* brevet baby

brew USA/USMC/USN (1960s–present) beer; sometimes, coffee. (SAM)

brew up BrA (WWII) to make tea; to blow up with explosives. (WID)

bricklayer's clerk USN (19th c.) a contemptuous name for one who claimed he had been forced to become a sailor by hard times on shore. Until the Civil War, all USN sailors were volunteers; some did join for economic reasons. (ANE)

bridgehead CSA/USA (1861) a field fortification built at the near end of a bridge to protect friendly forces during retreat. (WWII–present) a fortification erected at the far end of a bridge or ford to protect the advancing army. (MD MMD) (*see also* tête du pont)

brief USA (WWII) an all-too-short weekend leave. (GWD SID)

brig MM (1760s) [English *brigantine* or *brigand,* pirate] a pirate ship of the Mediterranean; in Europe, a two-masted, square-rigged vessel; a ship's jail, the place where pirates (brigands) were confined. (OST TON) USN/USMC (1790s–present) jail aboard ship or on a land base. (PAT SAM) (*see also* brigand, jail)

brigade BrA>USA (18th c.–present) BrA (18th c.) four battalions plus eight artillery pieces. USA (18th c.–WWII) headquarters and two regiments. (1950s–present) a unit commanded by a brigadier general and consisting of a headquarters and two or more groups that are equivalent to WWII regiments. (MDB MMD)

brigand BrA>USA (16th c.–1860s) a bandit, outlaw, or pirate. (MCT) BrA (16th c.) a lightly armored mercenary foot soldier, some of whom turned to banditry when wars ended and wages stopped.

brightwork BrN>USN/USMC (18th c.–present) a metal surface that requires polish, including doorknobs, buttons, belt buckles, bells, and other ship's fittings; aka brass. In the early days, most metal to be shined was brass or bronze. (AST SAM)

brig rat USN/USMC (WWII–present) a sailor confined to the ship's brig; a prisoner. (SAM) (*see* brig)

brig's po' juggler AusA (WWI) the brigadier's orderly, who had to manage his senior officer's daily schedule.

bringers-up BrA (1768) those positioned at either end of a line and charged with keeping the line straight and its men from running. (MDB) (*see also* line closers)

bring scummion in USA/USMC (1960s–70s) to bring the maximum firepower available to bear on a target; aka bring smoke, bring the max. (*see* bring smoke)

bring smoke USA/USMC (1960s–70s) to come prepared to shoot someone; to bring the maximum firepower available to bear on a target; to release outgoing artillery fire; to punish or attack. (*see also* bring scummion in)

brisque FrA (WWI) an enlisted man's rank chevron; battle wound. (WWW) (*see* blessure, chevron, dogleg)

British treasury note ANZAC (WWI) an army-issue blanket, said by the soldiers to be as thin as a treasury note.

BRO *See* Big Red One

broadside BrN>USN (17th c.–present) the side of a ship; the complete battery of a ship's guns (from all decks) on one side of the ship; a volley in which all of the guns on one side of a ship are fired at once. (OST TWW)

broken down USA (1960s–70s) inoperable, broken or dismantled.

brolly BrAF>USAAF (WWII) a parachute. Use of this term was very limited among Americans. (GWD) (*see also* life insurance)

brothel creepers BrA (WWII, North Africa) desert boots with thick rubber soles that enabled wearers to move very quietly across rough ground and were worn by some British units in North Africa. Most combatants wore hob-nailed boots, which were quite noisy. (ADW)

broth of a boy USN (19th c.) an excellent yet very high-spirited young sailor. (ANE)

brought up to the mast *See* masted

brow BrN>USN (17th–20th c.) [Old English *bryeg*, bridge] a light plank that bridges the distance from a ship's side to the shore. (1960s) a heavy gangplank with handrails on the top and rollers on the underside that ran from the ship's side to the wharf dock. (MAN OST)

brown bagger USN (WWII) a married man posted to shore duty who carried lunch from home to his station in a brown paper bag. (TON)

brown bar USA (1960s–present) a second lieutenant, from the single gold (brown) bar worn as insignia of rank; aka butter bar.

Brown Bess BrA (1708–1830s) a flintlock musket with the barrel painted brown to match the color of its wooden stock; aka Black Bess. Originally called a brown musquet. (DVT)

brown bomber USA (WWII–1960s) army-issue laxative; aka CC pill. (GWD)

brown boot(er) USAF (1956–1970s) one who had been in the service prior to September 1, 1956, when the uniform switched from brown to black shoes; aka brown shoe. (*see also* brown shoe army)

browned off *See* brassed off

brown George BrN (1693) an exceptionally hard, coarse ship's biscuit named in dubious honor of King George II. (1780) called a brown wig after George III. (17th–20th c.) aka munition bread or jug. (DVT) (*see* biscuit)

brownie BrA/BrN (WWI) a volunteer in the Women's Land Army, which worked the fields to free men for military duty, for the color of her uniform.

Browning automatic rifle USA/USMC/USN (1918–1960s) an automatic rifle weighing 15 lbs. with a twenty-round magazine; aka BAR. Adopted by USA in 1918 as an infantry assault weapon, this .30-caliber firearm remained in service until the early 1960s. It can still be found in the arsenals of many nations. (MMD)

brown musquet *See* Brown Bess

brown shoe army USA (1950s–60s) the army prior to September 1, 1956, the date by which all brown shoes had to be dyed or replaced with black shoes. (*see also* brown boot(er), garrison shoes)

brundook *See* barndook

brunets *See* buffalo soldiers

bruss USAAF (WWII) an extremely exaggerated version of the brace. (AFR) (*see* brace²)

BS USA (WWI) the base section of a military unit; bullshit, used as an expletive. (WWW)

BSA USA (1970s–present) brigade support area.

BSM BrA (WWI) battalion sergeant major, the senior NCO of a battalion. (AGE)

BSR FrA (WWI) [French *Bureau de Service de Renseignement*, bureau of intelligence] French Military Intelligence. (WWW)

BTE BrA (1940, North Africa) headquarters for British Troops, Egypt. (TOC)

bub BrA/BrN (17th c.) [Latin *bibere*, to drink] very strong beer. USN (19th c.) an alcoholic drink. USA (1940) a young soldier. US (1940) a form of address used to hail a male stranger. (DVT)

bubble and squeak USA (WWI) a flat-tasting English pudding. (WWW)

bubble chaser USA (WWII) a dishwasher or anyone assigned to kitchen duty; aka bubble dancer, pearl diver. USAF (1980s) a specialist in hydraulics. (SID)

bubblehead USN (1980s–present) a surface sailor's name for a submariner.

buccaneer MM (17th–19th c.) [Caribe *mukem*>French *boucan*, a mispronunciation of the Caribe word, dryer of meat or woodsman] a pirate of the West Indies. In early days these men were meat dryers who worked as pirates on the side to make ends meet. (DWO OST SLA TON)

buck¹ BrA (18th c.) a brave or daring person, a comparison to a male deer.

buck² USA/USMC (1890s–present) to strive for advancement, not necessarily by the rules, as in *buck for sergeant*; to oppose the established system, as in *buck city hall*. (DVT OST) USA/USAAF (WWII) to oppose, to work against a person, situation, or order. (AFR) (*see* buck for orderly)

buck³ USA (ca. 1900) of the lowest grade within a rank, such as buck general. The lowest-ranking person in the entire army was a buck private, who was not entitled to wear a stripe on his sleeve.

bucket USN (WWI–WWII) a slow-moving vessel, especially a destroyer of WWI vintage. Depending on the speaker's tone of voice, the word could be used affectionately or despairingly.

bucket brigade USA/USMC/USN (WWII) a group of civilian yachtsmen who volunteered to help the navy patrol the eastern seaboard of the United States in search of German U-boats. USN (WWII–1960s) a less-than-polite term for the United States Coast Guard; aka baby navy, freshwater navy, hooligan navy, muddy water sailors.

bucket carriers USA (WWI) the men who carried hot rations to those in frontline trenches. (MMD)

bucket head USA (WWI–WWII) a seldom-used term for a German soldier, from the shape of his steel helmet.

bucket of bolts USAF (1950s) an aircraft and/or its engine. (AFS)

bucket of boost USAAF (WWII) a practical joke played on new and gullible air cadets by pilots. The recruit was sent to the flight officer for a bucket of boost to help the pilot get his plane off the ground. (GWD)

buck for orderly USA (ca. 1900) to maintain an excessively neat appearance in an effort to impress the company commander and be appointed the captain's orderly for the following twenty-four hours. The orderly's job was considered to be very soft and cushy. (EMP)

buck general USA (WWII) a lieutenant general, the lowest-ranking general. (*see* buck³)

buckle¹ BrA (14th c.–present) [Latin *buccula*, helmet's cheek strap, or *boss*, a raised nog in center of shield>French *boucla*>English *buckle* or *buckler*] a strap fastener. (DWO)

buckle² USA (1960s) to be involved in a fight. (DWO)

buckler BrA (14th–20th c.) [Latin *buccula*, helmet's cheek strap, or *boss*, a raised nog in center of shield>French *boucla*>English *buckle* or *buckler*] a small round shield. (DWO) BrN (1750s) a wooden plug used to block the hawse holes when a ship was at sea. (*see* hawse hole)

bucko *See* recruit

buck private *See* buck³

buck sergeant USA (ca. 1900–present) a line sergeant who commands troops in the field; the lowest grade of sergeant, for which the insignia is three stripes on the sleeve. (*see* buck³)

buckshee *See* bakshee

bucksish *See* bakshee

buck up USA (ca. 1900) to polish one's brass items in preparation for inspection; to take heart, to cheer up.

buddy USA/USMC (WWI–WWII) a close friend. (1914) a new recruit; a form of address used when one did not know the name of a person. (*see also* mac)

BUFF USAF (1960s) big, ugly, fat fellow or fucker; the B52 Superfortress.

buff FrA>BrA>USA (16th–20th c.) [French *buffe*, buffalo, buffalo hides, or leather>

English *buff*, yellow-brown color of leather> (17th c.) hide or skin in buff, naked] (16th–17th c.) a yellow-brown buffalo or ox hide used to make leather equipment for the military; the yellow-brown color itself. (19th c.) a soft leather pad used for polishing. (1820) a volunteer or one with an avid interest in a specific topic. USA (1960s–70s) a water buffalo, the traditional beast of burden in the Far East; aka water boo, water bull. (DWO IHA)

buffalo soldiers USA (1873–WWI) members of the Ninth and Tenth Colored Cavalry who served in the American West during post–Civil War years; aka brunets. They were named by the Native Americans for their curly black hair and beards, which resembled a buffalo's mane. (IHA)

bug[1] USAAF (WWII) a recording instrument that was part of Link trainer equipment. (AFR) (*see* Link trainer) USN (19th c.) a naval vessel noted more for its size than for its efficiency. USA/USMC/USN (1920s) a defect of undefined nature found in a machine or vehicle. (WWII–present) an unidentified lump in one's soup, food, or drink; a germ; a hidden microphone. (ANE DWO MMD)

bug[2] (WWII–present) to annoy or bother someone.

bugger[1] MM/BrA>USA (16th–20th c.) [Old French *bougre*>Middle Dutch *bugger*, heretic or bigot>English *bugger*, to ruin> (18th c.) ruin by sodomy] originally, a Bulgarian member of the Eastern Orthodox Church, considered by many Roman Catholics to be a heretic. Calling someone a bugger could be either an insult or a compliment, depending on the tone of voice. (DWO SLA) USA (1860s) a general, disrespectful term for an officer; aka greenhorn, skunk. (LRY)

bugger[2] MM/BrA (18th c.) to ruin or sodomize; to confuse or perplex.

bugle GrA>FrA>BrA>USA (14th c.–present) [Latin *buculus*, small ox> French *bugle*, buffalo or bull>English *bugle horn* (14th c.), bull's horn used as hunting or drinking ves-

sel] a valveless brass instrument resembling a trumpet and used especially for military calls. During the Seven Years' War, Frederick the Great and his corps of hunters, or Jaegers, used horns to relay military orders.

bugle call BrA>USA (1793 c.–present) a tune written especially for a bugle. The Austrian composer Haydn wrote the first bugle calls for the British army. United States bugle calls were a mixture of French and British army calls. (CWO DWO MCT)

bug out CSA/USA>USMC (1860s–present) to retreat in total panic and disorder; to abandon responsibility.

build MM (19th c.) form, such as the external shape of a ship; most commonly, a woman's figure. (SLA)

build a wooden horse USAAF (WWII) to crash a plane. Many early warplanes had wooden frames, and the debris from a crash might provide enough wood to build a wooden (Trojan) horse. (MMD)

built-in head wind USAAF (WWII) said of a plane that was slow and sluggish to handle. (AFR)

bulkhead[1] MM (15th c.–present) the upright wall or partition used to form a cabin on a ship's deck. USN>USMC (WWI–present) a wall within a building or ship. (SAM WEA)

bulkhead[2] USN (1980s–present) to criticize, as an officer, a fellow officer in a loud, vocal manner.

Bull USA (ca. 1900–WWII) Bull Durham brand cigarette tobacco, from the days when most cigarettes were hand-rolled; often capitalized. BrA>USA/USN/USMC (WWI–present) utter nonsense; aka bullshit. USA (WWII) a target. (GWD) (*see also* on the bull)

bulldog BrA (1699) a pistol, from its loud bark and vicious bite. USN (19th–20th c.) a heavy gun on a ship's main gun deck. (DVT)

bulldoze USA (19th c.) to coerce, physically force, or pistol whip. (ANE)

bullet BrA>USA/USN/USMC/USAF (16th–present) [French *boulette*, little ball>English *bullet*, little ball] a projectile fired by small arms or artillery. (DWO) (*see* bullets)

bullet bait USA (WWII–Korean War) one

new to combat and inexperienced in survival techniques.

bullets USN (ca.1900–1920s) beans. (1920) peas, especially hard, dry ones.

bullpen USA (18th c.–present) a guardhouse or other place of confinement; a well-defined, fenced area in which a soldier must walk alone, carrying his rifle. USA (1770s) the fenced area in which prisoners of war were confined.

bull ring USN (19th c.) the area of the spar deck where the captain held his mast, or court. USA (18th c.–present) a fenced area for breaking and training horses. BrA (WWI) an area behind the lines where men were trained for special attacks. (*see* captain's mast)

bullshit *See* bull

bully[1] BrA>USA (16th c.–present) one's sweetheart. (17th c.) someone with a big mouth. (18th–19th c.) a pimp. (18th c.–WWII) canned corn beef or salt beef; aka bully beef, desert chicken.

bully[2] CSA/USA (1860s) great, fantastic; aka hunky-dory. BrA/USA (19th c.) praiseworthy, as in *my bully fellows*. (19th c.–present) excellent, extraordinary. (DWO LRY)

bully beef MM>BrA (18th c.–WWII) salt beef. (WWI–WWII) canned corned beef. (WWII, North Africa) aka bully, desert chicken. (WID)

bully boys MM (18th–19th c.) ordinary sailors, who ate bully beef. (TON) (*see* bully beef)

bully splog BrA (WWI) soldiers' hash made by frying crushed biscuit, water, and bacon grease (if available) with tinned beef. (*see also* biscuit)

bum CSA/USA (1860s) a spree of wine, women, and song.

bumboat MM (17th–20th c.) [possibly from *boomboat*, a trading boat that moored itself near the boom (after section) of the vessel with which it was doing business] a small boat that came out to a larger vessel to sell goods to sailors and passengers. A boat that carried beer to ships at anchor was known as a bombard. (DVT OST)

bumbrusher AusA (1915–18) an orderly; aka batman, dingbat.

bum dope USMC (WWII) unreliable or incorrect information. (SAM) (*see* dope)

bumf *See* bumfodder

bumfodder BrA (17th c.–WWII) toilet paper. Originally, any material with which to wipe one's backside (bum); aka bumf. (17th c.) any type of paper that could be used as toilet paper. (WWI) a derogatory term for an official written order, instruction, or memo that expressed a soldier's opinion of such paperwork. (DVT)

bum-freezer BrN>USN (1750s–1860s) the short-waisted wool coat favored by sailors. It was ideal for mild weather but totally useless in winter, as it left the backside exposed to the elements. (*see* monkey jacket)

Bumfuck, Egypt USA/USN/USMC/USAF (1960s–present) a distant, foreign, or hole-in-the-wall post or base; aka East Overshoe.

bummer USA (1850) [German *bummler*, idler, loafer] a deserter. (1860s) a looter, freebooter, or plunderer; a soldier detailed to find provisions for Gen. William T. Sherman's army as it marched through Georgia. Sherman's bummers were noted for their hostility toward civilians. USA/USAF/USMC/USN (1960s–70s) a bad event or situation; a great disappointment. (IHA MD)

bum-out USA (ca. 1950) an assignment to an easy post or soft duty.

bump off BrA>USA/USMC (WWI) to kill.

bun MM (18th c.) a woman's private parts. It was common for sailors going off to sea to touch bun before they sailed. (DVT)

bundook *See* barndook

bun doop *See* barndook

bung up and bilge free MM (18th–20th c.) all right. The wooden barrels in which food was kept in a ship's hold were all right if the bung hole (the place in which to insert a tap) was at the top of the barrel, above the bilge water. (SLA) (*see* bilge)

bunion breeder *See* infantry

bunion buster *See* infantry

bunk BrA>USA (18th c.–present) a sleeping platform or a bed in the barracks. (18th c.) a double-tiered wooden platform padded with loose straw in lieu of a mattress that slept five men on the bottom and five on top.

bunker MM (19th c.) originally, the storage compartment for the coal that fueled steam vessels. (20th c.) the storage area for fuel aboard a ship. (MAN OST)

bunker buster USA (1950s–present) a satchel charge of C4 explosives fixed with a short fuse and used to destroy fortified enemy positions. (*see* C4, satchel charge)

bunk fatigue USA (19th c.–present) rest or sleep in one's bunk at a nonregulation time. A play on words since fatigue is a military term for work. (SID)

bunk fly USAAF (WWII) to talk about flying while at rest in barracks. (AFR)

bunkie USA/USMC (ca. 1900–60) a close friend in the same barracks. (WWI–WWII) a person with whom one shared a pup tent. In the 1960s, Marines used the term only during basic training. (*see also* bunk in with)

bunk in with CA (WWI) to share a tent or shell hole with another person. (*see also* bunkie)

buntukk *See* barndook

buoy MM (13th c.–present) [Old French *boie*, chain>English *boye*, a float>*buoy*, floating channel marker] a floating channel marker or a float used to mark obstructions in the water or as a mooring for a boat. (DWO OST TON)

BUPERS (BOO•pers) USN (1950s–60s) Bureau of Naval Personnel. (WEA)

Burglar BrA (WWI) a British soldier's comical name for a Bulgarian.

burgoo BrN>USN (18th–20th c.) [Arabic *burgbul*, dried wheat dish boiled to make it edible; Urdu/Hindustani *burgoo,* porridge] BrN: a thick, coarse oatmeal porridge. USN: a mixture of crushed hardtack and molasses; infrequently, any type of stew. (OST TBS) (*see* hardtack)

burka BrA (ca. 1900–WWI) [Egyptian *Shariael Burka*, street of brothels in Cairo] a brothel.

burnout USMC (1980s) a drill instructor who let the stress and strain of training

recruits wear him down.

burn the shitters USMC (1960s) to clean the latrines by moving the half-barrel receptacles to an open field and setting their contents afire.

burnt offering BrN (19th c.) plain roast beef or mutton that has been either undercooked or burnt to a crisp.

Burp USA (1960s–70s) a soldier's nickname for a Marine.

burp gun USA (WWII) a German submachine gun, from the sound it made when fired. (Korean War) a particular machine gun used by the Chinese.

bury the hatchet BrA>USA (17th c.–present) to end a feud, to make peace; aka bury the ax, bury the tomahawk. From the 1660 Native American practice of burying a war club or hand ax prior to a truce as a sign of good faith and peace. (IHA)

bus *See* airplane

bush Br (1700s) [Dutch *bosch*, woods or forest>English *bush*, a mispronunication of the Dutch] wilderness. USA/USMC (1960s) an untamed and/or uninhabited area. USA (1960s–70s) an abbreviation of ambush; backcountry. (IHA) (*see also* ambush, bushranger, bushwhacker)

bush a gun CSA/USA (1860s) to drill out the worn-out vent of an artillery piece and replace it with a circular copper bushing, a metal plug that has been drilled out as a vent. (MD)

bush artillery AusA (WWII, North Africa) the infantrymen of the Australian forces, who manned the captured Italian artillery in defense of Tobruk.

bush country USA (1855) the American frontier. (IHA)

bush hump *See* hump

bushranger BrA/colonial America (1756) a Native American fighter, tracker, and/or frontiersman. (IHA)

bushwhacker USA (1813–present) one who fights from the cover of bushes and woods, an irregular soldier. (1861) a Confederate sympathizer in Kentucky. (post-1865) one who attacks from ambush to make an easy kill. (IHA)

bust[1] BrA/USA/USMC/USN (19th c.–present) to reduce in rank; demote, as in *he was busted*. USAF (1950s) to err or fail. (AFS ASC)

bust[2] BrA/USA/USMC/USN (19th c.) a celebration, such as a beer bust, in which alcohol is the main item on the menu.

bust caps USA (1960s–70s) to fire one's weapon rapidly, as a child would fire paper caps in his toy gun.

Busy Bertha *See* Big Bertha

Butch USA (WWII) an uncommon name for a unit's commanding officer. (DVT) (*see* CO, KO, Old Man, Skipper)

butcher BrA>USA (18th–19th c.) a surgeon who employed bleeding as a treatment; aka butch. USA (WWI–WWII) an army barber.

butcher's bill USN (19th–20th c.) the official list of killed and wounded as prepared by the ship's surgeon and his assistants. (ANE)

butt BrA>USA/USMC/USN (12th–20th c.) [Anglo-Norman *butt*, to strike with the head>*but* (14th c.), barrel>thick end (15th c.)] a barrel in which foodstuffs were stored. (15th c.) the human backside. (18th c.) the target of a joke. (WWI) the time remaining in one's enlistment. (WWII) an unburnt remnant of a cigarette or cigar; the cigarette itself. (DWO GWD OST SLA)

butter bar *See* brown bar

butter-box USN (19th c.) a Dutchman, for his supposed love of butter. (ANE DVT)

butterflies USA (WWII) a serious case of uncontrollable burps. (GWD)

butternut CSA/USA (1861) a Southern sympathizer from Missouri; a Confederate soldier, from the color of his uniform. By 1863, due to a lack of regulation cloth, butternuts were used to dye the uniforms a light yellowish brown. (IHA)

butt fuck USA/USMC (1960s–70s) to attack from the rear; to give a raw deal; to take advantage of in a very serious manner.

buttinski USA (WWI–WWII) someone who interrupts or butts into a conversation.

button chopper USA (WWI–WWII) the

base laundry, where uniform buttons disappeared by the thousands.

button it up USA (WWII) an order to close the hatch on a vehicle or to be silent; aka button your lip.

button up BrA (WWI) to achieve a state of readiness. USA (WWI–1960s) to close all hatches on an armored vehicle. USAF (1950s) to ready, to finish. (AFS)

butts USA/USMC (ca. 1900–present) the far end of a rifle range, where the targets are located; the pit below the targets, to which rangemen lower the targets to mark hits and from which fresh ones are raised. (AGE SAM)

butts up USA (WWII) an order to pick up cigarette butts and other trash lying on the ground.

buy the farm *See* bought the farm

buzz[1] Br>American colonies (1737) a drinking spree. (WWII) a widespread rumor that, like a bee, buzzes from place to place. (IHA)

buzz[2] BrA (WWI) to kill, from the sound of a bullet in flight.

buzzard BrA (16th c.) a dim-witted person or coward. Br (18th c.) someone who is afraid of the dark. BrA>USA/USMC (1850s) the eagle insignia of a full colonel. (1920s) government-issue turkey or chicken. (DVT)

buzzard busters USA (WWII) a soldier's unusual name for the Army Air Force, possibly from the large number of colonels in that branch of the service. A full colonel wears eagles (buzzards) on his collars. (SID)

buzzer USA (ca. 1900–WWI) a member of the Signal Corps, from the sound of the telegraph keys. (*see also* iddy-umpty, Signal Corps)

buzz the town USAAF (WWII) to fly at a low altitude and high speed over a population center. (AFR)

buzzy cot USA (WWI) a makeshift cookstove made from iron bars or metal grates placed over a bed of hot coals. (EMP)

BX USAF (1950s) base exchange, the air force's version of a PX. (AFS) (*see* PX)

by the boards *See* go by the boards

by the numbers USN/USMC (19th c.–present) a step-by-step method of drilling in which each movement is numbered. When a number is called, the trainee knows exactly what he is expected to do. (SAM)

BZO USMC (1980s) battle sights zero, no elevation changes needed; point blank range, when a target is between zero and three hundred yards away.

C

CA USA (1960s–70s) civil affairs; combat assault; combined assault.

cabbage BrA (WWI–WWII) an arial bomb. USA/USMC (WWI–WWII) paper money, for its green color; aka lettuce. (MMD SSD) (*see also* hard cash, toot)

cabin BrN>MM (14th c.–present) [Old French *cabane,* hut] a hut, especially one made of logs. BrN (15th–16th c.) a wooden-framed hammock hung in the captain's quarters for his use. MM (18th c.–present) an officer's quarters. (SEA SLA)

cable tier USN (18th–20th c.) an area on the orlop deck of a wooden man-of-war where the ship's anchor hawsers were stowed. (*see* orlop deck, hawser, man-of-war)

caboose MM (18th–20th c.) [Dutch *kaban buis,* deck cabin] a small cabin on the spar deck of a ship that served as the ship's galley. Br>USN (18th–19th c.) ship's galley located on one of the lower gun decks of a man-of-war. (SLA TON) (*see* galley, man-of-war, spar deck)

cackle jelly USA (WWII) chicken eggs. (GWD)

cacolet (kaa•koh•LAY) CSA/USA (1860s) a litter placed astride a mule and used to transport wounded men, typically one on either side of the mule. Despite the good intentions

of its inventor, transport in a cacolet caused great discomfort to the wounded, who felt every step the mule took. (MD)

cadet BrA>USA (1768) [vulgar Latin *capitellus,* little head>Gascony French *capdet,* chief>French *cadet,* little head> English *cadet,* younger son] a young gentleman who entered service as an enlisted man, rather than an officer, and served, except in the royal artillery, without pay; aka volunteer. (1800–present) an officer candidate who attends a military academy with the intention of becoming an officer and a gentleman. (MDB MMD)

cadet widow USA (1920s–WWII) a popular young (or not-so-young) lady who was well known to several classes of cadets over a period of time. Cadet widows were not prostitutes, but more usually ladies who dated cadets in an effort to remain youthful, at least in their own minds. (GWD)

cadre USA/USMC (WWI–present) [French *cadre,* frame] a core group of officers and NCOs around which a new military unit is formed; an official list of the officers and NCOs of a newly formed unit. (MCT MMD) (*see* NCO)

caisson FrA>BrA>USA (18th c.–WWII) [French *caisson,* large chest or covered wagon] an ammunition chest mounted on a two-wheeled limber and used for transporting shot, shell, and powder; sometimes, the combination of the ammunition chest and the limber. USA (WWI–WWII) a motorized truck that carried artillery ammunition. (MD MMD)

caisson rider USA (19th c.–WWI) an infantryman's term for an artilleryman. Until the artillery became motorized, members of gun crews rode into position on the battery's caissons. (*see* caisson, red leg) (ATK)

cake and arse NZN (1980s–present) a derisive description of an officer's cocktail party.

cake and wine See bread and water

cakewalk BrA (WWI) an easy raid or attack, comparable to "a piece of cake," the civilian phrase denoting an easy task. (SSD)

calculated risk USAAF (WWII) the projected loss of bombers and personnel in an attack on an enemy position; to take a calculated risk was to attempt to match one's projected losses against those of the enemy. Eventually, taking a calculated risk came to mean embarking on a course of action that is hazardous but worth the gamble.

caliber BrA>USA/USMC/USN (18th–19th c.) [an Arabic word meaning a mold for casting metal>Italian *calibro*>French *caliber,* cannon, bore, or template>English *caliber*, diameter of bullet or cannonball] the number of lead shot to a pound; the weight of an artillery shot. (1890s–present) the diameter of the bore of an artillery piece or small arm. (DWO MCT MD MMD)

call USA/USMC/USN/USAF (19th c.–present) a short, formal visit between officers and/or their wives. (AFS)

call a halt GrA>BrA>USA (16th c.–present) [German *Halt machen!*, to make a halt, to stop] to stop and rest troops. (DOC)

called on the carpet BrN>USN (18th–20th c.) faced the captain in his quarters on a disciplinary matter; aka called on the mat. On royal navy ships, there was carpeting or matting in the captain's cabin, the only place aboard the vessel where this luxury was found. A sailor who was "called on the carpet" was in trouble serious enough to be addressed by the captain in his quarters. BrA/USA (WWI) in trouble with a commanding officer. (AGE EMP)

camel MM (15th c.) a floating dock used to raise a ship over a shallow body of water; a floating barrier of wood or logs between a ship and the dock to which it was moored. (SEA SLA) BrA/ANZAC (WWI) a British Sopwith scout plane, sometimes called a Sopwith camel; a Turkish or Egyptian cigarette. The cigarette was said to smell and taste like a dead camel; in the Australian army it was also referred to as camel dung.

Camel Corps BrA (WWI) the infantry's name for itself. Like camels, infantrymen were expected to carry heavy loads—often in excess of seventy pounds—and travel long distances without anything to drink, especially not a rum ration. (AGE)

camel dung *See* camel

camelier (cam•meh•LEER) AusA (WWI) a member of the Camel Corps, which operated in the Middle East against the Turks and their Arab allies 1916–18.

Camel to Consumer BrA (WWII) a nickname for *Cape to Cairo* brand cigarettes, a favorite of British soldiers in North Africa. (ADW)

camel wallah BrA (ca. 1900) [Hindustani *wallah*, person] a native Indian camel driver; one who works with camels.

cammies USA (1960s–70s) government-issue camouflage uniforms.

camouflage FrA/ItA>BrA>USA (WWI) [Italian *camuffare*, to hide or disguise>French *camoufler*, to disguise] to conceal something or someone from the enemy. (pre-WWI) in Parisian street slang, to blow cigarette smoke into someone's eyes to distract him. (CWO DWO)

camouflet (cam•ou•FLAY but: pronounced cam•ou•FLET by United States soldiers) CSA/USA (1860s–WWII) a ten-pound charge of explosives that could destroy an enemy tunnel without causing a cave-in of the ground above it. (WWII) a land mine that did not create a crater when it exploded; aka antipersonnel mine. (MD MMD)

camp It>Fr>Br>USA (16th c.–pre-WWII) [Latin *campus*, open field>Italian *campo*>French *camp*, place where soldiers are quartered] an area occupied by troops during an overnight pause in a march; a temporary living area in which soldiers were quartered in tents and sometimes buildings. (DWO MCT MD MMD)

campaign ItA>FrA>BrA (1768) [Italian *campagna*, to spend winter months in camp>French *campagne*, military operations] seasonal military operations. USA (1861) period during which the army stayed in the field on operations against the enemy, usually through the spring and summer. USA (20th c.) an interconnected set of military operations. (DWO MD MDB MMD)

campaigner USA (WWI–WWII) an old soldier, especially one who had seen combat in various places over many years. (MMD)

campaign hat USA/ USMC (1910–present) a tall-crowned, broad- brimmed felt hat with three indentations in its peak; aka service hat. This design was adopted in 1910 by the USA and USMC for service in the field, was dropped from use in the late 1930s, and is now worn only by USA, USMC, and USAF drill instructors. (1920s) aka cowboy hat (because of its popularity with Western moviemakers) and Montana peak. (GWD) (*see also* overseas cap)

campaign hat

camp candlestick BrA (18th c.) an empty bottle or bayonet pressed into service as a candle holder. (DVT)

camp colours BrA (1768) a flag measuring about eighteen inches square displaying the regimental color and trimmed in the color of the regimental uniform's facing. (MDB)

camp follower BrA>USA (ca. 1810–WWI) [may have been coined by the Duke of Wellington] (ca. 1810–1880s) a prostitute who followed an army and provided laundry and nursing services as well as plying her trade. (1880s–WWI) a wife, sweetheart, or mother who fulfilled the roles of laundress and nurse; a civilian who hoped to sell wares to soldiers. (*see* sutler)

camp happy USA (WWII) off in the head, crazy. (GWD)

can[1] USA/USMC (1900–present) human backside; infrequently, jail. (*see also* jail) USA (1900–present) toilet. USN (WWII–present) a destroyer, more commonly called a tin can.

can[2] USN (WWII–present) to dismiss from a job or military school.

'Canal USN>USA (WWII) Guadalcanal Island. (BCD PAT)

canary BrA>USA (WWI–WWII) an instructor in a bull ring, who wore a yellow armband as a symbol of his position. USA (WWII) a large mosquito of the deep South;

a government-issue gas mask, probably from the use of yellow paint to mark artillery shells containing poison gas. (GWD) (*see* bull ring, canary bird)

canary bird BrA (18th–20th c.) a caged prisoner. (WWI) gas warfare instructors, from their yellow armbands. (DVT) (*see also* canary)

C and E rations *See* MRE

can do MM (ca. 1800) in pidgin English, "I can do it." (SLA) (*see also* no can do)

C and S USN (19th c.) clean and sober, an entry made on the roster beside the name of a sailor returning from liberty in good condition. He had to be able to salute the officer of the deck and the national colors, get to the gun deck without passing out or becoming sick, and be free of contraband. (ANE RAS) (*see also* D and D)

candy-ass Marine USMC (Korean War) a Marine who had served garrison duty stateside or in another noncombat role. (PAT SAM)

canister BrA>USA/USMC (ca. 1799) a metal can filled with iron shot; aka case. Like a shotgun blast, the shot scattered outward in a wide pattern when fired. Canisters are often mistakenly called grapes, which were strictly naval charges. (MMD) (*see also* case, grapeshot)

canister

canker mechanic USA (1960s–70s) an army medic who treated the body sores common to those serving in Vietnam. (*see also* chancre mechanic, corpsman, MC, medic, medi-co, pill pusher, pill roller)

canned cow USA/USMC/USN (WWI–WWII) canned condensed milk. (AFR MMD PAT SAM) (*see also* city cow, galvanized Guernsey)

canned horse USA/USMC/USN (ca. 1898–WWII) canned corned beef. (MMD PAT) (*see also* canned Willie, embalmed meat)

canned up BrA (WWI) dead drunk. (SSD)

canned Willie USA/USMC (WWI–early WWII) canned corned beef, so named in "honor" of Kaiser Wilhelm II of Germany; aka corn Willie. (MMD PAT) (*see also* canned horse, embalmed meat)

cannibalize USA/USAAF/USMC/USN (WWII–present) to remove working parts from a broken-down vehicle or other equipment so as to be able to repair a similar piece of equipment with the recovered parts.

cannon ItA>FrA>BrA>USA (16th c.–present) [Italian *cannone*, large tube>French *canon*, large tube] a large gun; an artillery piece. (DWO)

cannon ball USA (WWII) a grapefruit, so named for its shape and size. (GWD)

cannon cocker USA (1960s) an artilleryman.

cannon fodder BrA (ca. 1900–WWI) infantrymen, especially green, inexperienced troops sent into battle with little or no chance of success. (WWI) all soldiers, infantry in particular, below the rank of major. (DVT)

cannon quickstep USA (1860s) to do the cannon quickstep was to run away in battle, a play on a regular marching cadence. (LRY) (*see also* quick-time)

canoe GrN (WWII) German submariner's nickname for a U-boat. (TOC)

can of worms USA/USMC/USN/USAF (WWII–1978) military-issue canned spaghetti distributed as part of C rations. (PAT) (*see* C rations)

can opener BrAF (1940s, North Africa) a Hurricane fighter plane armed with two 40-mm guns and two Browning machine guns. (WID)

canteen BrA>USA/USMC (1768–present) [French *cantine*, small shop; Spanish *cantina*, small country store, restaurant, or bar; colloquial French *cantina*, flask or bottle] a metal, wooden, or, in modern times, plastic bottle for carrying liquids. BrA/USA (19th c.–present) a store at which soldiers purchase small items of necessity. (MDB) (*see also* post exchange, PX, sutler)

canteen check USA (1880–WWI) metal tokens or, more commonly, scrip (in one-, two-, three-, and five-dollar denominations) issued to soldiers for use in post exchange. A soldier could request canteen checks for up to twenty percent of his pay from the company CO, who had to sign scrip before it could be used. (EMP) (*see* CO, post exchange, scrip)

canteen egg BrA (WWI) a poison gas bomb, a comparison of the odor of poison gas to that of a supposedly rotten egg purchased at the army canteen. (DVT) (*see* canteen)

canteen medal BrA/USA (ca. 1890–WWII) a beer stain on a uniform. During Prohibition United States soldiers, like the general population, could not buy beer legally. When Prohibition ended, they could purchase limited amounts at the post canteen. The term is also a sarcastic reference to an honestly earned Good Conduct Medal, implying that it was not earned but purchased in the post canteen. (AFR SSD) (*see* canteen)

canteen soldier USA (WWII) one who wore a uniform or insignia that was not government issue. Approved copies of government-issue items could be purchased at post exchanges, and canteen soldiers did something comparable to buying generic rather than brand-name items. (AFR) (*see* post exchange)

canteen stinker BrA (WWI) a foul-smelling type of cigarette available at the canteen. (*see* canteen)

cantonment (can•ton•ment) BrA/USA (1777–WWI) an army post not fully fortified. (1906–07) grounds and buildings rented by the government for national guard and regular army troops on joint maneuvers. (1917) a large, temporary army camp. (ATK)

canvasback MM (mid-19th c.) a steamship sailor's term of contempt for a sailing ship sailor. (AST) (*see also* mechanic)

cap¹ BrA>USA/USN/USMC/USAF (1790s–present) any military head covering except a helmet.

cap² USA (1960s–70s) to shoot. (*see also* bust caps)

Cape Cod turkey MM (19th c.) salted cod, a specialty of the Cape Cod region. (TON)

Cape Horn fever MM>BrN>USN (19th c.) a

mysterious and probably mythical illness that befell sailors who wished to avoid hard work and/or foul weather. When the British navy withheld the grog ration from those on the binnacle list in an effort to "cure" this disease, the men reported for duty even when they were truly sick. (RAS TON) (*see* binnacle list, grog)

Cape Horn snorter MM (19th c.) a severe, long-lasting storm, such as those encountered in the turbulent area around Cape Horn. (SLA)

Cape Stiff MM (19th c.) one of many names given to Cape Horn, at the southern tip of South America. The moniker came from the many corpses (stiffs) produced by storms and wrecks in the area. (AST)

Cape to Cairo BrA (WWII) a brand of cigarettes favored by British soldiers in North Africa; aka Camel to Consumer. (ADW)

capsize MM (13th c.–present) [Spanish *capuzan*, to sink] to turn over in the water; to go in reverse; to fall over as a result of drinking alcohol. (DVT OST)

capstan MM (17th c.) a barrel-type structure used to raise anchors or move yards. Poles (aka handspikes) were placed in pigeonholes

capstan

in the barrel's head and used to rotate it in a clockwise direction. (SLA) (*see* yard^3)

captain FrN>BrN>USA/USN/USMC/USAF (14th–17th c.) [Late Latin *caput*, head> Anglo-Saxon *caput*, thane (head lord)> French *capitaine*] the leader of a military force or even an entire army. (18th c.–present) the commander of an infantry company, cavalry troop, or artillery battery. The commander of a ship is given the title and addressed as captain even if his actual rank is lower. (DWO MCT MD MMD OST) (*see also* captain-general)

Captain Copperthorne's crew BrA (1770s) army officers; a unit in which everyone tried to act as an officer. (DVT)

captain-general BrA/SpA (14th–18th c.) title often given to the commander of an entire army or of combined allied armies. (MCT MD MMD OST) (*see also* captain)

captain-lieutenant BrA (18th c.) meat from an older calf that is neither beef nor veal; an officer with the duties of a captain but the rank of lieutenant. (1768) one with field command of a colonel's company or troop. (DVT MDB)

captain of the head USMC/USN (WWII) one in charge of cleaning the toilets of a ship or Marine barracks. Said to be the only man in the company who knew what was going on. (SAM) (*see also* head)

captain's mast USN (18th c.–present) a shipboard judicial hearing at which the captain alone settles minor infractions of military law. In the age of sail, the captain would hear the case at a table just forward of the main mast, hence the name. Since the creation of the Uniform Code of Military Justice on May 5, 1950, the accused sailor has had the right to bring a representative (not necessarily a lawyer) to the hearing. Prior to the hearing the sailor would have met with a naval lawyer and been informed of his rights, one of which is to have a formal court-martial. If the accused does not agree with the punishment, he may appeal. Punishments assigned by the captain's mast do not carry the weight of judicial punishments, so a record of a criminal offense will not be placed in the permanent file of the accused. (RAS) (*see also* captain's table)

captain's table BrN (1800s–present) a shipboard judicial hearing at which the captain is both judge and jury. (*see also* captain's mast)

caput Gr>BrA>USA/USMC (WWI–1960s) [German *kaput*, to be finished or dead] done for, finished, dead. (SSD)

caraburger USA (1900–WWII Philipines) [Tagalog *carabao*, water buffalo] government hamburgers or meatloaf, which supposedly contained carabao meat instead of beef. (MMD)

carcass BrA (1768) a fire bomb, fired from a mortar and designed to set buildings afire; a fused, oval-shaped, iron cage–framed projectile filled with a mixture of mealpowder, saltpeter, sulphur, glass, horn shavings, pitch, tallow, and linseed oil and covered with pitched cloth. (MDB) (*see* mortar)

cards CSA (1860s) cornbread baked in flat sheets measuring 18 x 10 inches. (LRY)

careen MM>US (1500s–1900s) [Latin *carina*, nutshell>English *careen*, nutshell-shaped boat keel>Genoese *carena*>French *en carene,* to expose ship's keel] to turn a vessel over or on its side in order to clean the hull. US (20th c.) to veer out of control, as a vehicle. (DWO OST)

care package USA/USMC (1960s–70s) a package from home, especially one filled with treats and goodies.

carouse[1] GrA>BrA (16th c.) [German *trinken garaus*, to drink completely>English *drink carouse*, to drink fully, and *carouse*, to drink and party with abandon] to drink a full tankard of alcohol or beer. USA (19th c.) to drink and act wildly. (DWO)

carouse[2] GrA>BrA (1690) a drinking bout. (DWO)

carpet bombing USAAF (WWII) a thorough bombing of an enemy position prior to a planned ground attack. (SAM)

carpet, called on the *See* called on the carpet

carpet slipper BrA (WWI) a highly explosive naval shell that passed overhead on its way to the enemy as silently as one walking in his carpet slippers; aka carpet slipper bugger.

carried away MM (18th–19th c.) torn loose and swept or knocked overboard, as a mast, a piece of equipment, or a man. (MAN OST)

carronade BrN>USN (1768–1830s) a short-barreled deck gun that fired a heavy—twenty-four-pound, thirty-two-pound, or sixty-eight-pound—shot to an effective range of two hundred to three hundred yards; aka smasher. (OST)

carry a heavy load USA (WWII) to be fatigued or melancholy. (SAM)

carry in BrA (WWI) the task of a machine gun crew that had to take its weapons to a frontline trench position. (SSD)

Carry me out and let me die! BrA (WWI) an expression of surprise or disgust. (*see also* Good night, nurse!; That's torn it!)

carry on BrA/BrN>USA/USN/USMC (18th c.–present) an admonition to bear hardship with silent patience; an order to resume a duty or operation. (MAN SAM)

carte blanche USA (18th–19th c.) [French *carte blanche*, literally, white card] total power and authority. An officer granted carte blanche was given a blank piece of paper on which to record his manpower and equipment requirements for the mission at hand. (MD MMD)

cartel Br>USA (1768–1865) an exchange of prisoners of war. (MD MDB MMD)

cartridge Fr>Br>USA/USMC/USN/USAF (16th c.–present) [French *cartouche*, paper cornucopia used by grocers to package goods] a single charge of gunpowder for a musket wrapped in heavy paper. (17th–early 18th c.) a paper cylinder filled with a charge of powder and lead shot. (1860s) a brass cylinder filled with powder and shot. (CWO DWO)

CAS USA (1970s) close air support. (LRY)

case BrA (1790s–1815) a canister. USA (1800–60) an artillery shell filled with lead balls and designed to explode well above ground level, scattering its deadly contents on the heads of those below. (MD MMD) (*see* canister, shell, shrapnel)

Casey Jones mission USAAF (WWII) a bombing raid that targeted Japanese railroad yards and installations. (AFR)

cashiered USA/USMC/USAF/USN (1860s–present) disgracefully discharged from the military as a result of court-martial. (MD MMD)

cast about MM (18th c.) to sail on various courses when the navigator is uncertain of the ship's exact position; to attempt different solutions to a single problem; to grasp at straws; to feel one's way. (SLA)

castaway[1] MM (18th c.–present) discarded, abandoned. (SLA)

castaway[2] MM (18th c.–present) discarded or abandoned material. (SLA)

cast loose MM (18th c.–present) to loosen or release lines that secure an object or a ship. (MAN OST)

castramentation BrA>USA (1768–1860s) the art of designing and laying out encampments. (MD MDB)

casual FrA>USA>USAF (WWI–present) a soldier not assigned to a specific military unit. USAF (1970s) a serviceman awaiting discharge for medical or psychological reasons. (WWW)

casual company USMC (1970s–90s) in boot camp, a company in which some or all of the men awaited discharge or reassignment.

casualty USA/USMC/USN/USAF (19th c.) one discharged from service by virtue of death or desertion. (20th c.) a wounded, sick, or captured combatant, as well as a fatality or deserter. (MD MMD)

casualty assembly center (WWI) a place behind the lines where the wounded were gathered for classification and placement in the proper medical facilities. (*see* Charlie Chaplin's Army Corps)

cat BrA (15th c.) an old prostitute of the lowest kind; a woman with a mean disposition; female genitalia. Br>USN (until late 19th c.) cat-o'-nine-tails. USN (1960s–present) the catapult on an aircraft carrier. (*see also* boy's cat, cat-o'-nine-tails, enough room to swing a cat, let the cat out of the bag, man's cat, thieves' cat)

cat beer USA (WWII) milk. (SAM)

Caterpillar Club USAF (1950s) an informal group of pilots and aircrew who had gained entry to the club by parachuting from their damaged aircraft. (AFS)

catfall BrN>USN (18th c.) a block and tackle. (OST) (*see* cat the anchor)

cathead MM (17th c.) one of two stout beams or spars projecting from the ship's bow that provide support as anchors are raised or lowered. A picture of a cat's head, for good luck, was often embossed on the

ends of these beams, a practice possibly arising with the pre-Christian-era Romans and revived during the classical revival of the sixteenth and seventeenth centuries. (AST OST) (*see* cat the anchor)

cat the anchor BrN>USN (18th c.) to hoist an anchor out of the water to the level of the spar deck. A block and tackle called the cat-fall raised the anchor to a protruding spar called the cathead. Catting the anchor was a very dangerous job. (AST OST SEA SLA TWW) (*see also* cathead)

cat lap BrN>USN (18th–19th c.) tea; silly talk; a thin or weak alcoholic or nonalcoholic drink. (ANE DVT)

cat-o'-nine-tails MM (pre-Christian-era Egypt–present) an instrument of discipline that began with the ancient Egyptians, who made a nine-tailed whip from the hide of a cat, which they considered to be a sacred animal. To be struck with the whip was to be blessed by the cat's goodness. BrN/USN (17th–20th c.) a whip with nine tails, eighteen to twenty-four inches in length, and a wooden or rope handle. Strokes with the cat-o'-nine-tails were the most common punishment inflicted on a sailor. (AST RAS) (*see also* black Monday, blood ships, blue Monday, boy's cat, cat, earn your stripes, enough room to swing a cat, flog, gunner's daughter, let the cat out of the bag, man's cat, marry the gunner's daughter, thieves' cat)

cats-paw BrN (16th c.) a makeshift, imitation tool. (DVT) MM (18th c.) a light air that gently ripples the water's surface in a localized area during a period of calm. (SLA)

cattle boat USA (1950s) a troop transport. (ASC) (*see* transport)

catwalk BrA/MM (19th c.–present) a narrow walkway suspended above an open deck that enables crew to move fore and aft in foul weather. One has to be as surefooted as a cat to move along it. BrA (WWI) a narrow (nine-inch-wide) brick pathway common to the front yards of Belgian houses. (20th c.) a narrow walkway around a ship's smokestack. (OST)

caught in a downdraft USAAF (WWII)

caught in an embarrassing situation. (GWD)

caulk off BrN>USN (17th c.–WWII) to sleep or nap. On old wooden ships, the deck seams were caulked with tar, and when men lay down to catch a few winks, the tar often left its imprint on their backs and clothing. (OST TON)

cav USA (1960s–70s) airborne cavalry.

cavalier FrA>BrA>USA (16th–20th c.) [Latin *caballus*, horse>Italian *cavaliere*> French *cavalier*, horseman>English *cavalier*, a mounted knight or soldier] (16th c.) a gentleman of the court. (1648) a follower of Charles I who was disdainful, having a cavalier manner; a troop of cavalry. BrA (1790s–1820s) an artillery piece or a battery set up on a raised platform within a fortification. BrA/USA (19th–20th c.) a romantic name for a cavalryman of the Confederate States of America; a disdainful man. (DWO)

CAVU (ca•vu) USAF (1950s) ceiling and visibility unlimited. (AFS)

CB Br/USA (ca. 1900–WWII) confined to barracks, a punishment given to soldiers upon return to camp for offenses committed in the field; counter (artillery) battery fire. USA (1970s–present) a chemical/biological military unit. (GWD)

CBU USAF (1970s) cluster bomb unit.

CC USA/USMC/USN/USAF (1960s) company commander.

CC pill USA (WWII) a laxative; aka brown bomber. (GWD)

CC pusher USA (WWII) a member of the Army Medical Corps. According to many veterans, this group was overly concerned with regularity. (GWD) (*see* CC pill)

CCRA BrA (WWII) commander of the Corps of Royal Artillery. (TOC)

CCS BrA (WWI) casualty clearing station, a first aid post immediately behind the front lines. (AGE)

centry box *See* sentry box

ceremonial flag USAF (1950s) a flag used only for official occasions. It was made of very fine materials and trimmed on three sides with silk fringe. (AFS)

CEV USA (1970s–present) combat engineer vehicle.

C4 USA/USN/USMC/USAF (1960s–present) a white plastic explosive that will not explode unless triggered by a detonator. The material burns with an intense heat and can be used for cooking. It is very pliable, so it can be molded to fit the application. (*see also* DuPont lure)

CG USA (WWII–1950s) commanding general. (ASC)

chai BrA (1880s–WWII) [Arabic *chai*, tea] tea. The term was borrowed by British forces serving in the Middle East. (TBS) (*see also* char)

chain of command USA/USN/USMC/ USAF (WWII–present) a series of officers in order of the authority of their ranks. (ASC) (*see also* pipeline)

chain pump BrN (1750s) a pump comprising in part a leather washer fixed to chains. As the chains are drawn up and around by the action of the pump handles, the water rises through the pump and spills out onto the ship's deck. (*see also* pumpdale)

chairborne USA (1960s) a play on the word airborne that described a chair-bound, pencil-pushing government or military bureaucrat.

chalk USA/USMC/USN (WWII) powdered milk, from its color and taste. (PAT SAM)

chalk, walk the *See* walk the chalk

challenge for orderly USA (ca. 1900–WWII) a competition between the adjutant's orderly and those who wish to have his position. The smartness of a candidate's appearance and equipment was judged. (EMP) (*see* buck for orderly)

chamade (cha•MADE) Br>USA (1768–1860s) a drumbeat used to signal a meeting between representatives of opposing armies. (MD MDB)

chancre mechanic (CAN•ker) USMC (1960s) medic; aka corpsman. (*see also* canker mechanic, corpsman, MC, medic, medico, pill pusher, pill roller)

changee for changee MM (18th c.) an even trade or exchange, from Far East pidgin English.

change of station USA (1950s) the reassignment of military personnel from one post to another. (ASC)

change tack USAAF (WWII) from the naval term meaning to change course of movement or thought; to change one's approach to a woman. (SID)

chapel flag USA/USMC/USN/USAF (WWII–present) the flag that marks the location of a unit's chaplain or religious services; aka chaplain's flag. The blue flag has a white symbol representing the chaplain's denomination at its center. (AFS)

chaplain BrA/BrN>USA/USN/USMC/USAF (17th c.–present) [Latin *capellanus*, cape> French *chapele*, cape] a military clergyman. From the legend of St. Martin, who gave a beggar half his cape, the remains of which were preserved by a holy order of knights called *caoellani*. In the 1640s in Great Britain, chaplains were appointed to the army and navy as the guardians of men's souls by Charles I and paid a fee for each man in the unit. In the 1770s, chaplains in the United States Army were appointed by George Washington. Each served for six months and was paid as if a major without the rank. On March 2, 1791, the office of chaplain was officially established by the United States Congress. (NCT) (*see also* GI sky pilot, gospel grinder, Holy Joe, padre, sky pilot, and sky scout)

chaplain's flag *See* chapel flag

chaplain's fund USA (1950s) a fund administered by the post or unit chaplain and used for the maintenance of the troops' piety, morals, and morale. (ASC)

chaplain's shirttail *See* crying towel

char BrA>USA (18th–20th c.) [Hindustani *char*, tea] tea that was charred or burned before it was served, according to United States troops serving with the British in WWI. (TBS) (*see also* chai)

charge of mess USA (ca. 1900) an NCO in charge of a company's affairs—drills, sick call, guard details, cleanliness of the barracks—for a twenty-four-hour period was said to be in charge of the mess. (EMP)

Charley USA (post-1945–present) a stupid or inept soldier.

charlie USA (1910–WWI) an army field pack. (Korean War–present) military parlance for the letter "c". (1960s–70s) a member of the Vietcong.

Charlie Chaplin's Army Corps CA>BrA (WWI) a casualty assembly center for the Canadian forces that served with the British forces in Europe. Later, the Central Casualty Assembly Center at Shornecliff, England. In both cases, an irreverent reference to the way the wounded men were handled/cared for. (*see* casualty assembly center)

Charlie Chaplin's Corps *See* ASC

Charlie Harry BrA (1940, North Africa) the coordinates of the main axis or centerline of a brigade or division's advance, an area where most of the enemy's snipers were located; aka Charlie Iffer, Charlie Love. (DRA)

Charlie Iffer *See* Charlie Harry

Charlie Love *See* Charlie Harry

Charlie Noble BrN>USN (19th c.–1980s) galley stovepipe, so named for British captain Noble, who took great pride in keeping the copper stovepipe of his ship's galley well polished inside and out; also spelled Charley Noble. (MAN TON) (*see also* shoot Charlie Noble)

Charlie USN (19th c.) a civilian officer of the law on the lookout for smugglers. (ANE) (*see also* Victor Charlie)

charlie tango USA (1960s–70s) the letters "c" and "t" in military parlance, a radio call sign for the control tower.

char wallah BrA (WWII, North Africa, India, Middle East) [Hindustani *wallah*, person] a servant who serves tea; literally, a tea servant. (TBS) (*see also* char)

chase BrN>USN (18th c.) a ship that is being pursued; one ship's pursuit of another. (TWW)

chase port BrN (1750s) each of the two forward-most gun ports on a man-of-war, one to port and one to starboard. The bow chasers were placed in these ports. (*see* bow chasers, port, starboard)

chase prisoners USA (WWI–WWII) to guard prisoners detailed to labor outside of a prisoner-of-war camp, usually on public, government, or private farms or on roads in the United States, Canada, or United Kingdom. (EMP GWD MMD)

chatt *See* louse

chatter box USA/USMC (18th c.–WWII) one who talks constantly. (WWI–WWII) a constantly firing antiaircraft gun. (WWII) base public address system. (DVT GWD)

chatty BrA (WWI) [English *chattel,* livestock or cattle] covered with lice; aka chicot (CHEE•ko). (*see* chicot, louse) (SSD)

Chauchat automatic assault rifle USA/ USMC (WWI) a French rifle made of stamped metal parts; aka hot cat, sho-sho, tin lizzie. It fired an 8-mm round and, because of its violent recoil, proved difficult to keep on target. (GWD)

chaw[1] USA/USMC/USN (19th c.–present) to chew something, especially tobacco; to talk or converse. (PAT)

chaw[2] USA/USMC/USN (19th c.–present) a plug or twist of tobacco. (PAT)

ChC USAF (1950s) chaplains' corps. (AFS)

cheap Charlie USA/USMC (1960s–70s) a man who refused to spend much money on bar girls or prostitutes.

check USA (1900) the 11 P.M. bed inspection/head count of all men not on duty or off base with a pass. (EMP)

check out USA/USMC (1960s–70s) to examine closely; to die.

check pass USA (1900) a pass that allowed one to miss the 11 P.M. curfew but not morning reveille. (EMP) (*see* check)

check your six USAF>USNA/USMC (1950s–present) a warning issued by a fighter pilot to a pilot with an enemy plane directly behind him.

Cheerly, men! MM (19th c.) an order to move quickly and with effort; also spelled cherrilymen. (AST)

cheese off BrA/BrAF (pre-WWI–WWII) a Liverpool civilian term meaning "get lost." (1914–18) to be totally fed up or bored, used mainly by troops from Liverpool. In 1935, the term came into general use by members of the British Army. By 1940, it was mainly used in the Royal Air Force. (SSD)

cheese-parer MM (20th c.) a tightwad, a nipcheese, one who nipped (stole) ship's goods intended for the sailors' comfort. (RAS TON) (*see also* cheese paring, nipcheese)

cheese paring MM>USN (18th–19th c.) committing petty theft, from dishonest practice of a captain or ship's purser who cut small slices of cheese from a large wheel and created extra wheels by pressing the scraps into smaller molds, which he then sold as good wares. (*see also* nipcheese) (TON)

cheese toaster BrA (18th c.–WWII) a sword. USA (19th c.–WWII) bayonet. Practical uses included digging holes, opening cans, and toasting bread. (DVT GWD) (*see also* frog sticker, Josephine, paring knife, pig sticker, Rosalie, toadsticker)

cherry USA/USMC/USN/USAF (1960s–70s) virginal, said of a newly arrived replacement or an untouched item in perfect condition.

cherrypicker USN/USAF (WWII–present) a large crane used to move machines, equipment, and other heavy items. (BCD)

cherry picker BrA (1940, North Africa) a member of the Long Range Divisional Reconnaissance. (DRA)

chest hardware USA/USMC (ca. 1900–WWII) awards and decorations worn on the walking out or dress uniform; aka chest gongs. (PAT SAM) (*see* dress uniform, gongs, walking out uniform)

cheval-de-frise (shay•VAL•de•FREES) DA> FrA>BrA>USA (15th c.–WWII) [French *chevaux de frize,* horses of Friesland] originally, a reference to the Dutch Army, which was mostly infantry and faced the Spanish, who had large cavalry units. BrA (1768) USA (1861) large beams with pointed, often iron-tipped ends used to fill gaps or breaches in defense lines.

cheval-de-frise

BrA>USA (WWI–WWII) sawhorse-type frames over which fencing and concertina wire were secured. They could be moved by two to four men. Plural: chevaux-de-frise (shay•VOH•de•FREES) (CWO MD MDB MMD) (*see* concertina wire)

chevrons USA/USMC (WWI–Korean War) stripes worn on the sleeve of the service jacket which, by their color and number, can

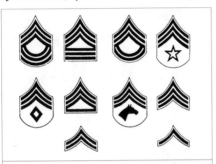

Chevrons, U.S. Army. Top row: regimental sgt. major, regimental supply sgt., battalion and squadron sgt. major, color sgt. Middle row: first sgt., company supply sgt., stable sgt., sergeant. Bottom row: corporal, lance corporal.

indicate rank, length of service, and number of wounds suffered. (SAM)

chew out USMC (WWII) to severely reprimand. (PAT SAM) (*see also* give chocolate)

chew the fat USN/USMC (19th c.–present) literally, to chew the fat that was part of (or most of) one's salt beef or pork ration; to talk idly; to sulk or be resentful. (PAT SAM SLA) (*see also* chew the rag)

chew the rag BrA/BrN (18th–20th c.) to waste time talking, to engage in idle conversation; to sulk or be resentful. (DVT) (*see also* chew the fat)

chick USAF (1950s) an aircraft, especially a fighter plane. Began as a code word but quickly passed into general use. (AFS)

chicken USN/USMC (19th c.) a regular partner of a known homosexual. USA (1850s) an irreverant reference to the newly designed eagle insignia of a full colonel. (1860s) a tentmate, usually a young recruit. USN/USMC (20th c.) a coward. USMC (WWII) a young Marine or recruit. (RAS

SAM) (*see* eagle)

chicken cach (catch) USA (1993, Somalia) chicken cacciatore, an MRE served almost daily. (*see* MRE)

chicken colonel *See* bird colonel

chicken guts USA/USN (1861) an elaborate gold braid worn by Confederate officers on their cuffs to mark rank. (1960s) a gold braid worn on an officer's dress uniform. USN (1950s) a naval aide's gold aiguillette. (WEA) (*see* aiguillette)

chicken hearter BrA (18th c.) a coward. (DVT)

chicken of the sea USN (1970s–present) a surface sailor's derogatory reference to a submariner serving on a ballistic missile submarine or the submarine itself. The job of the Ballistic Submarine Service is to hurt the enemy while avoiding detection by any means possible. The unofficial, tongue-in-cheek motto of the Ballistic Submarine Service is "We hide with pride."

chicken plate USA (1960s) body armor, such as that worn by helicopter pilots.

chicken shit USA/USMC/USN/USAF (WWII–present) rules and regulations regarded as trivial. (PAT SAM)

chicot (chee•ko) FrA>BrA (WWI) loaded with lice; aka chatty. (*see* louse)

chief cook and bottle washer CSA/USA (1860s) one who could and was expected to do anything and everything that needed to be done. (LRY)

chief housemaid BrN (19th c.) a ship's first lieutenant, who was second in command and bore full responsibility for the ship's cleanliness. (TON)

chief of staff USA/USMC/USN/USAF (WWI–present) the senior ranking officer of a branch of the military; a member of the chiefs of staff. (AFS) (*see* chiefs of staff)

chiefs of staff USA/USMC/USN/USAF (1950s–present) the heads of the various branches of the military. (AFS)

chieu hoi (choo HOY) USA (Vietnam) a surrender campaign aimed at the NVA and Vietcong. (BLO) (*see* NVA, Vietcong)

chili bowl USA (WWII) an army-style haircut. The suggestion was that the army barber put a bowl on his victim's head and then cut off all the hair that stuck out. (GWD)

chime in USN (19th c.) to jump into a conversation with or without an invitation from those involved; to speak freely, to express one's opinion. (ANE)

chimes, on the See on the chimes

China Boy Company See Mobile Guerrilla Forces

china clipper USA (WWII) one who washed dishes at a fast pace. (ATK SID) (*see also* bubble chaser, pearl diver)

chinaman USN (1870s–WWII) a sailor assigned to duty in ship's laundry. In the nineteenth-century United States, many Chinese immigrants took up the laundry trade. (ANE)

Chinaman, John USN (19th c.) a generic name for a Chinese man. (ANE)

Chinese attack BrA>USA (WWI) a simulated attack; a noisy attack that does very little damage; a false attack meant to trick the enemy. (MMD)

Chinese fire drill USA/USN/USMC (1930s –present) an energetic yet pointless display of activity. (MMD PAT) (*see also* cluster fuck)

Chinese junk See junk, Chinese

Chinese landing USAAF>USAF (WWII– 1950s) a poor landing caused by dipping one's wing. So named for the mythical Chinese pilot conjured by United States airmen during WWII—Won Hung Low. (AFS)

Chinese Rolls-Royce BrA (WWI) a mocking name for the Ford vehicles used by the Royal Army Medical Corps.

Chinese three-point landing USAAF (1930s–WWII) a crash landing. (GWD)

Chinese tobacco USA (1900–WWII) opium. (PAT SAM)

Chink Br>USA/USMC/USN/USAF (1790s– present) an offensive term for a person of Chinese ancestry. Used in the maritime services of England and the United States from the 1790s, it was in general usage in the United States from the Gold Rush of 1849 onward. (MMD)

chino USA (ca. 1900–WWII) cheap, poor-

quality cloth. (AGE EMP) (*see also* chino khaki)

chino khaki USA (ca. 1900–WWII) high-quality, khaki-colored cloth made in China. In this case, chino refers to the origin of the product rather than its quality. (EMP) (*see also* chino)

chinstrap See come in with a chinstrap on

chip his molars USA (WWII) to talk a great deal but say nothing; aka chip his teeth. (AFR)

Chips USN (18th–20th c.) a ship's carpenter. Until WWI, the term was also used in the British army. (AST)

chip with a rubber hammer MM (19th c.) to work at a useless or meaningless task, from the fear that sailors in hell spent eternity trying to chip lead paint with a rubber mallet. (TON)

chit Br>USA/USMC/USAF (18th c.–1980s) [Hindustani *chitti*, to be marked] a receipt or voucher. (18th c.) a baby; anything small. USAF (1950s) a requisition form or voucher. (1960s) a paper granting approval of one's request. USMC (1980s) a soldier at the bottom of the official ranking system. (ASC DVT SAM TBS TON)

chivey (SHIV•ee) BrN>USN (18th c.–present) a knife, especially a switchblade; aka shiv. (ANE)

chock USAF (1980s) a worthless person.

chocolate chip USA/USMC (1991, Desert Storm) the camouflage uniform worn by American troops in the field. (*see* Gulf War, Desert Storm)

choggie[1] (CHOH•gee) USA/USMC (Korean War) to carry a heavy load, especially uphill: *he can choggie a bigger load than a man twice his size*. (SAM)

choggie[2] (CHOH•gee) USA/USMC (Korean War) a Korean who carried supplies for the United States military. (SAM) (*see also* coolie)

choker See fag

choke the luff USN (19th c.) to jam the sheave of a pulley with the end of a line, jam the block; to cut someone off verbally; to put someone in his or her proper place, verbally or physically. (ANE AST) (*see* block)

choke up USA (WWII) to freeze at a critical time, to lose one's nerve temporarily. (GWD)

chokey BrA/BrN>USN (19th c.) a jail or detention cell; also spelled choky. (*see also* jail) (AGE)

chop BrAF (WWII) to shoot down. To *get the chop* was to be shot down. (*see also* chop girl)

chop-chop MM>USA/USMC (19th c.–present) an order to hurry, be quick. Pidgin English used by American forces serving in the Far East. (1946, Japan, and 1960s–70s, Vietnam) food.

chop dollar USN (19th c.) a badly mauled United States silver dollar, in part from the Chinese custom of stamping a coin every time it went through a bank or money exchange. One Chinese coin was similar in size to the United States silver dollar. (ANE)

chop girl BrAF (WWII) a woman who had successive flier boyfriends shot down. (SID) (*see* chop)

chopper USA/USMC/USN/USAF (WWII) a Thompson .45-caliber submachine gun, which "chopped" its victims down; aka tommy gun. (1950s–present) a helicopter. (*see also* helicopter, tommy gun, whirlybird, windmill)

chopsticks MM (1790s–present) [Chinese *kwai-tsze*, nimble ones, and English *chops*, mouth, jaws, and lips] pidgin English from Far East meaning slender sticks used as eating utensils. (SLA)

chow USA/USMC/USN/USAF (1848–present) [Chinese *chia*, food] food. Used widely during the gold rush of the late 1840s because of the influx of Chinese laborers into the gold fields of California. (AFS ATK SAM)

chowderhead USN (19th c.) a stupid person. (ANE)

chow down USA/USMC/USN/USAF (1848–present) to eat in a hearty manner whatever is set before one. USMC (1980s) an announcement to begin eating. (*see* chow)

chow hound USA/USMC/USN/USAF (1848–present) one who eats with total abandon and at every opportunity, a glutton. USA (WWII) aka meat hound. USN (20th c.) a pelican. (TON) (*see* chow)

chow line USA/USMC/USN/USAF (ca. 1900–present) line of people waiting for food to be dished up. (PAT SAM) (*see* chow)

chow rag USN (19th c.) a pennant flown from the masthead at mealtime; aka bean rag, meal flag. (AST)

Christmas tree order BrA (WWI) an order to march with a full field pack. A full field pack weighed more than sixty pounds and included spare shoes and uniform, two to three days' worth of rations, a rifle, bayonet, shelter half with poles and stakes, full one-liter canteen, at least one wool blanket, wool overcoat, rubberized ground sheet, helmet, 80 to 120 rounds of ammunition, and possibly an entrenching tool. After mid-1915, one or more hand grenades would also have been found attached to the web straps of the pack. (*see* full marching order) (SSD)

chubby USA (WWII) a cheap date, usually spent at a girl's home with her parents at their expense: *He bought his girl a chubby.*

Chuck USA (1960s–70s) a black soldier's derogatory term for a white soldier.

chuck a dummy USA (WWI–WWII) to faint while in formation. (MMD)

chuck-a-luck USA (ca. 1900) a game played with three dice. Players bet that 1) a specific total would be rolled, 2) three identical numbers would show, or 3) a specific number would show on one die. The thrower determined which bets could be called. In the case of multiple winners, the winnings were divided. If there were no winners, the money was anted for the next game. (ANE)

chucks his weight around BrA (WWII) said of an arrogant, self-important person; aka throws his weight around. (AGE)

chum BrA (17th c.) one who shares living quarters. (17th–19th c.) a constant companion. (19th c.) a helpmate. (WWI) a best friend. Less widely used by non-Cockneys, who preferred "mate" or "pal." (DVT EMP) (*see also* long-haired chum)

church key USMC (WWII–Korean War) a

bottle opener. A gentle poke at devout non-drinkers. (PAT SAM)

churchyard watch *See* graveyard shift

CIA US (late 1940s–present) Central Intelligence Agency, heir to the wartime Office of Strategic Services.

CIB USA (1944–present) combat infantry badge, awarded to infantrymen who have served in a combat zone for a specific period of time.

CID USA (Vietnam) Criminal Investigation Division. (BLO)

CID, el *See* el Cid

CIDG *See* Civilian Irregular Defense Groups

cigarette *See* coffin nail, fag, scag, shag, skag

CINC (sink) USAF (1950s) commander in chief, the president of the United States.

cinch[1] Br>USA (WWI–WWII) a sure thing, an easy, guaranteed feat. (AGE EMP GWD)

cinch[2] USA (WWI–WWII) to take the last piece of bread without refilling the basket. (AGE EMP GWD)

CINCPAC (SINK•pak) USA/USMC/USAAF/USN (WWII) commander in chief in the Pacific theater.

Cinderella liberty USN/USMC (1960s) liberty, or free time ashore, that ended at midnight.

cingalis (sin•GAHL•is) FrA (WWI) the caterpillar-tracked, 155-mm long-range field gun. (WWW)

circle jerk USA/USMC (1960s–70s) action without purpose; a contest among a group of men to see who could be the first to achieve erection and climax.

circumvallation CSA/USA (1860s) a field fortification built to protect the rear areas of an army while that army was laying siege to an enemy fort or town. (WWII) fortifications used by a besieging army that encircled an enemy fort or town. (MD MMD)

circus water USA (WWII) an iced drink served at any time, but especially at meals. During the early to mid-1900s, many Americans enjoyed the treat only when the circus was in town. Many United States homes lacked the luxury of a refrigerator

until just prior to WWII. (MMD)

cit BrA (17th c.) a citizen of London. (DVT) USN (19th c.) a civilian. (ANE)

citadel BrA/USA (1740s–1860s) a small but strong fort situated within or near the town or fortification of which it was a part. If the outer fort was breached, the citadel served as the last defensive position. (MD MMD)

citation USA/USAF/USMC/USN (WWI–present) an official acknowledgment of a unit's or an individual's valor; the document in which the act of bravery was described. (ASC)

cits USA/USAF/USMC/USN (WWI–WWII) civilian clothes; aka civvies. (PAT)

city cow USA (WWII) canned condensed milk; aka canned cow, galvanized Guernsey. (GWD)

Civilian Irregular Defense Group USA (1960s) a unit of South Vietnamese civilians trained to defend their villages by the United States Special Forces; aka CIDG (SID•gee).

civil serpent USA (1960s–70s) civil servant, a friendly jab at civilians employed by the military.

civvies USA/USMC/USN/USAF (ca. 1900–present) civilian clothes. During WWI and WWII, enlisted men were not permitted to wear civilian clothing, even when off duty. (ATK MMD PAT SAM SID) (*see also* cits)

civvy BrA (WWI) a civilian; anything related to a civilian. (SSD)

clamp down MM (19th c.) to wash down a ship's deck.

clap BrA>USA/USMC/USAF/USN (16th c.–present) gonorrhea. Until the 1830s, "the clap" was considered the polite term to use in general discussion of the disease. (DVT)

clap a stopper on your tongue MM (18th c.) an order to be silent. Often hissed when too many officers or informants were about. (RAS) (*see also* white mice)

clapchecker USA (1960s) enlisted medic, especially one who checks for venereal disease. (*see also* clap, pecker checker)

clap on MM (19th c.) to add sail; to grasp and haul on, as a line. (ANE)

clap shack USA/USMC/USN/USAAF

(WWII) a clinic that treated venereal disease. (*see* clap)

Clara BrAF>USAAF (WWII) the siren that sounded when an enemy air raid was over and all was clear. (MMD SSD)

clarion FrA (WWI) an army bugle or trumpet. (WWW)

class A offense USA/USN (WWII) a minor infraction of the rules and regulations. (AFR)

class A pass USAAF (WWII) a pass that permitted one to go off base when not on duty, a reward for efficiency and good conduct. (AFR)

class As USA/USMC/USN/USCG (WWII–present) semi-dress or service uniform (as opposed to fatigues); walking out uniform. (PAT) (*see* walking out uniform)

class A uniform USA/USMC/USN/USCG/USAF (WWII–present) the standard dress uniform worn for ceremonies, walking out on the town, and on base between sunrise and sunset; not a uniform worn in the field, in combat, or on a work detail. Aka service dress, walking out uniform.

class B pass USAAF (WWII) a pass that permitted one to be off base overnight, from lights-out until reveille. (AFR) (*see* reveille)

classified matter USA (1950s) material or information that, according to the government, had to be kept from the general public. Classified matter was categorized as top secret, secret, or confidential, depending upon its sensitivity. (ASC)

claymore USA/USMC (1960s–present) an antipersonnel mine that throws tiny steel cubes in a sixty-degree fan pattern to an effective range of fifty yards and a maximum range of a hundred yards. (*see also* animal, monster)

clean bill of health MM (18th c.) an official document given to a ship's captain

claymore

stating that the crew was free of contagious disease, which permitted the vessel to enter port. (OST)

cleansweep MM (18th c.) a wave that breaks over the spar deck and sweeps away unsecured materials and persons. (SLA) (*see also* weather deck)

clean sweep, make a MM (18th c.) to rid oneself of all possessions in order to start over; to capture everyone or everything in a designated area. (SLA)

clear away BrN>USN (18th c.) to remove items; to disengage, unfasten; to unfoul, untangle. (TWW)

clerks and jerks USA/USMC (1960s–70s) rear area personnel who performed the clerical work of the military and were looked down upon by those in the field. (*see also* cluck jerk, company clerk, stooge)

click[1] BrA (18th c.) to grab, snatch, or nab, as in *He clicked the butter*; to give a blow to the body, as in *I clicked him right good;* to hit it off, as in *The gal from the motor pool and I really clicked.* (WWI) to be placed on the duty roster; to perform a drill with smartness; to receive a wound that required a return to England; to be killed. (DVT)

click[2] BrA (18th c.) a blow to the body. USA/USMC (1960s–present) a kilometer, also spelled klick; a piece of good luck, as in *I had a bit of a click.* (DVT) (*see also* clicker)

clicker BrA (WWI) a man skilled at picking up women. (DVT)

client BrA (WWI) one who caught a venereal disease, thus becoming a doctor's client. (SSD)

climb all over USA (WWII) to scold severely. (GWD)

clink BrA (ca. 1880) jail, from the name of a prison in Southwark, London. (DVT) (*see also* jail)

clinker BrA (18th c.) a sly, sneaky person; a distinctive style of hard, yellowish brick used by the Dutch.

clinker built MM/BrA (16th–20th c.) said of a method of shipbuilding in which the upper planks overlap the ones below to form the ship's sides. BrA (1880s–WWII) said of a person who has served time in jail. (OST SLA SSD) (*see also* clink)

clinkers BrA (18th c.) iron cuffs worn by prisoners, so named because of the sound they made. (DVT)

clip[1] USA (1860s) to cheat or steal. (IHA SID)

clip[2] USA/USMC/USN/USCG (WWI–present) a stripper clip or box that holds ammunition for easy loading into an automatic weapon. The clip is inserted into the open receiver of the weapon, the bullets are pressed into the magazine, and the clip is removed. (MMD PAT SAM) (*see* magazine)

clipper MM (19th c.) [Old English *clipper*, to run or fly fast] a square-rigged, graceful, fast sailing ship. The first clipper was built and launched in Baltimore, Maryland, in the 1830s. (OST SLA)

clipper built MM (19th c.) said of a person, especially a female, who was neat and trim in appearance. (SLA)

clobber BrA (WWI) a full field pack. (AGE)

clock BrA (WWI) a human face; aka dial, map. (AGE)

clod[1] BrA (WWI) to shell heavily, from the clods of earth that rained down as the result of an exploding shell: *Our boys are going to clod Jerry good tonight.* (AGE)

clod[2] USA (WWII) a penny. (GWD)

clod-hopper USN (18th c.–present) a farmer, one who works amid mud and rocks; a clumsy, unseaman-like sailor. (ANE DVT)

close aboard MM (18th c.–present) nearby. (MAN)

close order knuckle drill USMC (WWII) a fistfight. (SAM)

close quarters BrN>USN (18th c.) [Old English *close quarters*, closed quarters] a restricted area or room; a small cabin on an open deck that served as the crew's last refuge in the event of attack by pirates; very close range, as hand-to-hand fighting. (SLA TON)

close shave MM (18th–20th c.) literally, a shave by a barber using a straight razor, which could be a life or death matter on the rolling deck of a ship at sea; a close call, a narrow escape from a disaster or accident. (SLA)

clothes stop USN (19th–20th c.) a cloth tie sewn into clothing and used to secure wet clothes to a clothesline; a cotton lanyard

used to secure rolled clothing in a seabag. (MAN OST) (*see* seabag)

cloth in the wind USN (19th c.) one who is half drunk; a vessel that has sailed too close to the wind and is difficult to handle. (NCT RAS) (*see also* half seas over, three sheets to the wind and the fourth a shakin')

clown USMC (1930s–Korean War) a Marine who is totally useless to himself and others; aka dud, feather merchant, knucklehead, shit bird, yahoo, yo-yo. (SAM) (*see also* acey-ducey)

clubmobile USA (1950s) a mobile unit of the American Red Cross that tended to isolated posts and maneuver areas. (ASC)

cluck jerk USA (ca. 1940) the company clerk, from the sounds made by a typewriter. The clerk was often looked down upon by the other men in the unit. (*see also* clerks and jerks, company clerk, stooge) (GWD SID)

clueless BrAF (1940, North Africa) said of someone who had no idea what was going on in relation to the military situation—or anything else, for that matter. (DRA SSD)

cluster belt *See* clutch belt

cluster fuck USA (1960s–70s) a scene of mass confusion; soldiers gathered for no apparent reason. (*see also* Chinese fire drill)

clutch belt USMC (1960s) an ammunition belt issued by the United States Marine Corps; aka cluster belt.

clutching hand BrA (WWI) an army quartermaster, who reputedly grabbed and held onto anything and everything. (AGE)

CMH USA (1950s) the Congressional Medal of Honor. (ASC) (*see* Medal of Honor)

CO USA/USMC (WWI–early WWII) the commanding officer of a unit, especially the commander of a camp or base. (WWII–present) the commanding officer of a unit, usually a company, regiment, or division. Also spelled Kay O, KO. (SAM)

coal box BrA (WWII) German 5.9-inch high explosive shell, from the huge cloud of black smoke it created upon explosion. (AGE)

coal bucket *See* coal scuttle

coal scuttle USA/USMC (WWI) a German

steel helmet; aka coal bucket. (AGE)

Coasties USN (1960s–70s) one of many nicknames for United States Coast Guardsmen. (*see also* bucket brigade)

coast is clear MM (16th c.) the area is safe, no danger is in sight. (DOC)

cockpit BrN>USN>USAAF (18th c.–present) a small area of blood and death. On a man-of-war, the cockpit was a small area on the orlop deck below the waterline where the surgeon and his mates tended to the wounded. (20th c.) the area of a plane from which the pilot controls the craft. (1970s) the area of a boat occupied by the crew. (MAN OST)

cockpit fog USAAF (WWII) instability; confusion, befuddlement. (GWD)

cockpit trouble USAAF (WWII) an aircraft mishap due to pilot error. (AFR)

cocksure BrN>USN (16th–20th c.) absolutely certain, especially of oneself. From the cocking mechanism on a flintlock musket, a more dependable device than the old matchlock. (ANE DVT)

cocktail BrN>USN (ca. 1860) an alcoholic drink made by mixing spirits and crushed bitters. (ANE)

coconut juice USMC (WWII) home-brewed booze commonly made from fruit juice and yeast by sailors or Marines in the Pacific islands. (SAM)

coffee MM>USA (1860s–WWI) government-issue coffee was as strong as bootleg liquor and as thick as blackstrap molasses; aka blackstrap and bootleg, originally New England whalers' terms for the beverage. Other military names for coffee include battery acid, blackout, blackstrap, ink, jamocha, java, joe, lifer juice, and paint remover. See individual entries. (EMP)

coffee boiler CSA/USA (1860s) a loafer, said to be waiting for coffee to brew. (EMP MMD) (*see also* coffee cooler)

coffee cooler CSA/USA (1860s) a loafer, said to be waiting for his coffee to cool before getting to work. (EMP MMD) (*see also* coffee boiler)

coffee grinder USAAF (WWII) an aircraft engine; a portable telephone, which rotated from place to place like the handle of a coffee grinder.

coffin nail BrA (WWI) a cigarette. The red glow of the tip was a good target for a German sniper, and with each puff the smoker put another nail in his coffin. (SSD) (*see also* fag)

cogmen USN (19th c.) maritime tramps, shipwrecked sailors who maintained themselves by begging and stealing. (ANE)

cog the nose USN (19th c.) to get cozy with a mug of hot grog. (ANE) (*see* grog)

cohorn USN (19th c.) a small mortar. (ANE)

cohort BrA (early Middle Ages) [Latin *cohort,* one of ten divisions of the Roman legion, each consisting of three to six hundred men] an army camp. In later use, an enclosed farmyard that served as an army camp. BrA (19th c.–present) a colleague or partner in crime.

coin BrA (1768) a wooden wedge placed under the breech of a gun to increase or decrease its elevation; also spelled quoin (pronounced coin). In 1861, coins were still used by the United States Navy and some fortress artillery units. (MD MDB MMD)

cold biscuit USA (ca. 1800) a physically and emotionally unattractive person; aka cold fish. (LRY)

cold bottle *See* cold fish

cold cock USA (ca. 1800) to knock someone out without warning using bare fists or a weapon. (TON)

cold enough to freeze the balls off a brass monkey BrN (18th–19th c.) very cold. On some men-of-war, shot was kept in brass cylinders called monkeys. In the cold of winter the monkeys contracted, and the shot popped out onto the deck, causing no little nuisance to the crew. (ANE) (*see* monkey)

cold feet USA (ca. 1895–present) fear or doubt that prevents one from taking action. (MMD SSD)

cold fish USA/USN (ca. 1800–present) an unfriendly, cold, dull, withdrawn person; one who shows no real emotions or feelings toward others; aka cold bottle, cold jug.

(LRY) (*see also* cold biscuit)

cold iron BrA>USA/USN (18th c.) an edged weapon used to stab or cut. (DVT) (*see also* cold steel)

cold jug *See* cold fish

cold meat BrA>USA/USN (18th c.) a corpse, a dead body. (DVT)

cold meat cart USA (1820) a hearse. (LRY)

cold meat ticket BrA (WWI) an identification disc or tag used to identify a dead soldier. USA/USMC (WWI) an identifying tag secured with string to the big toe of a soldier's corpse when his dog tags were removed. (SAM SSD) (*see* dog tags)

cold motherfucker USA/USMC (1960s–70s) one who remained cool, calm, and collected while under fire; one who could kill without a show of emotion or strain.

cold steel USA/USMC/USN (19th c.) an edged weapon made of steel, especially a bayonet. (ANE) (*see also* cold iron)

collateral damage USA (1960s–present) damage caused by shells falling outside of a target area and the civilian casualties caused thereby.

collision mat USN (WWII) a heavy piece of canvas fitted with securing lines that is hauled over the side and used as a stopgap measure to plug holes below the waterline of a ship. USN/USMC pancake or waffle; aka shooting pad. (SAM SEA)

colonel BrA>USA/USMC (17th–18th c.) [Italian *colonnela*, commander of company>Old French *coronel*>English *colonel*] the commander of the company that marched at the head of a regiment. (18th–20th c.) the commander of an entire regiment. (DWO MCT) (*see also* lieutenant colonel)

colonel's wife's silk stockings *See* silk stockings, colonel's wife's

color guard USA/USN/USMC/USAF (18th c.–present) those assigned to carry the unit's flags. (19th c.) those who carried flags into battle and acted as a rallying point for the regiment. (AFS) (*see* colors)

colors BrA>USA/USMC/USN/USAF (17th c.–present) flags used for unit identification

on the battlefield; the British spelling is colours. BrA (1768) "Flags of silk carried by ensigns (except by fusiliers) but never carried on detachment." (MDB) USA (1861) unit and regimental flags of silk flown one at a time. In actual service, the regimental flag was usually displayed. USA (1942) any flag carried by a military unit; the ceremonial raising and lowering of such a flag. (MCT MD MDB MMD SAM) (*see* ensign, fusilier)

color salute USA (1950s) the dipping of the standard or colors as an honor. (ASC) (*see* colors, standard)

colors flying BrN>USN (17th c.) a term indicating that flags were flying from every mast: *The victorious fleet returned to its home port with colors flying.* (1692) figuratively, descriptive of a proud celebration. The British spelling is colours. (CWO)

COLT USA (1970s–present) combat observation and laser team.

colt BrN>USN (18th–19th c.) a short piece of stout line with a large knot at the business end; aka starter. Used by petty officers to spur slow sailors to action or to inflict punishment if ordered by an officer to use a touch of the colt. (RAS RSC) (*see also* persuader)

column USA (1960s) an army battalion.

comb USA (1930s) to search or inspect thoroughly, from the use of a fine-toothed comb to rid hair of dirt or vermin. (GWD PAT SID)

combat Br>USA (16th c.–present) [Latin *combattere*, to fight or beat>French *combattre*, to fight>English *combat*] a fight or battle. (DWO)

combat command USA (1950s) a major segment of an armored division that corresponded to a regiment in the infantry: a tactical headquarters with command and staff, communications, and equipment to which battalions and smaller units were attached for military operations. (ASC)

combat fatigue USA/USMC/USN/USAF (WWI–1990s) a condition of total exhaustion sometimes accompanied by shakes, comatose staring, manic-depressive behavior, nightmares, and/or flashbacks to battle conditions; aka battle fatigue. (WWI) aka shell shock. (1970–present) more commonly called post-traumatic stress syndrome or post-traumatic stress disorder; aka PTSD. (PAT SAM) (*see also* battle fatigue, PTSD)

come about MM (16th c.–present) to change course, to turn around. (OST)

come along BrA (WWI) a length of barbed wire fashioned into a noose and used to encourage prisoners to come along quietly and peaceably.

come and get it USA/USMC/USN/USAF (19th c.) cook's call to meals. (EMP)

come boiling up *See* boiling up

come down upon BrN>USN (18th c.) to attack with the wind in one's favor and have the advantage of maneuverability; to verbally rebuke; to lose one's temper. (AST) (*see also* take the wind out of his sails)

come in with a chinstrap on BrA (WWI) to be totally exhausted. The implication was that only the chin strap of one's hat or helmet was keeping one on one's feet. (AGE)

come up MM (18th c.) to slacken a line or rope. (OST SLA)

coming the acid BrA (WWI) boasting; lying. (EMP)

commandant USA/USMC/USN/USAF (WWII–present) the officer in command of a service school. (AFS ASC)

commandeer Boer/BrA>USA/USMC/USAF/ USN (1880s–present) [Afrikaans *commandeer*, to force into military service or seize for military use] to take, as material or items, for military use. (1900) to take goods for one's personal use.

commander BrN (18th c.–present) lesser captain. The term was coined by William III and applied to the captains of brigs and sloops. BrN (1827) a rank directly below that of full captain. USN (1835) captains of third- and fourth-rate ships who, on shore, served as aides to commodores and flag officers. In 1838, the title was changed to master commander, possibly to show that the USN was not merely a copy of the British Royal Navy. USAF (1950s) the commanding officer of an air force unit. (AFS)

commander of the relief USA (1950s) the NCO of the guard, who posted and gave directions to the sentries of the relief force. (ASC) (*see* NCO)

commanding general USA (1950s) the general officer in command of a post, military installation, or unit. (ASC) (*see also* commanding officer)

commanding officer USA (1950s–present) an officer below the rank of brigadier general who commands a post, unit, or military installation. (ASC) (*see also* commanding general)

commando BrA (WWI) [Portuguese *commando*, command>Afrikaans *kommando*, mounted troop of Boers or local unit of militia] an expedition or raid with a specific objective. Br>USA (WWII–present) an elite, specially trained group of military raiders; a highly trained and efficient soldier. (DWO)

command pilot USAF (1950s) the highest possible rank for an airman. (AFS)

command post USA (WWII–present) a headquarters unit with a commanding officer and necessary staff. (ASC)

COMMFU (com•foo) USA/USMC/USAF/ USN (1960s) completely monumental military fuck up.

commissary BrA (1790s–1815) a supply officer. USA>USAF (WWII–present) a government-operated department store found on some military bases. (AFS ASC) (*see also* canteen, sutler)

commissary of horses BrA (1768) an artillery officer responsible for inspecting the unit's horses and acquiring horses as needed or ordered. (MDB)

commissary of provisions BrA (1768) an officer appointed to inspect and maintain the supply of "bread and provisions." (MDB)

commissary of the musters BrA (1768) an officer appointed by the commanding general to enlist men. The commissary of the musters needed to know and maintain the combat strength of each unit. (MDB)

commissary of the stores BrA (1768) an artillery officer directly responsible to the ordnance department and charged with maintaining the artillery's supply of gunpowder and weapons. (MDB)

commission BrA>USA/USMC/USN/USAF (18th c.–present) a written order that formally grants the rank of officer to a person in the military. (AFS)

commission pennant USN (19th–20th c.) the official pennant flown at the main mast of a man-of-war when she was under the command of a commissioned officer of less than flag rank. (SEA)

commo USA (1950s–70s) a communications officer.

commodore DN>BrN (1652–WWII) [Dutch *komandeur*, commander] an honorary title given to a naval officer who had commanded a squadron, coined to avoid the use of admiral. BrN (1680s) a commander. The word was brought to England from Holland by William III in 1680 but not officially adopted by the Royal Navy until 1806. USN (1799–WWII) an honorary title or rank given to a captain who was in command of a squadron. (NCT OST)

commodore's privilege USN (1860s) an unfastened trouser fly. No one would dare bring it to an officer's attention. (NCT)

communicator USMC (WWII) a Marine assigned to communications, a radio or phone operator, or one who laid the wire. (SAM)

companion ways USN/USMC (1970s) ladders or steps between decks. (MAN)

company BrA>USA (18th–19th c.) [Latin *cumpane*, with bread, a group of men who shared their daily bread] a military unit usually consisting of one hundred or more men. (MCT) USA (1800–present) an army unit that is smaller than a battalion but larger than a platoon. In the artillery, the equivalent unit is called a battery; in the cavalry, a troop. In all cases the unit is commanded by a captain. Companies have varied in size from 100 to 250 men. (ASC) (*see* battery, platoon, squad, troop)

company clerk USMC (WWII) one who handled paperwork in the company head-

quarters. (SAM) (*see also* clerks and jerks, cluck jerk, stooge)

company grade officer USA/USMC (20th c.) a commissioned officer, often a second lieutenant, first lieutenant, or captain, who commands a company. (ASC)

company punishment USAAF (WWII) a punishment assigned to the entire company by the company commander. (AFR)

company screwball USA (WWII) company Jonah, who brought bad luck to one and all. (GWD) (*see* Jonah)

company stooge *See* stooge

completely cheesed USA (WWII) totally bored. (MMD)

compo BrN>BrA (WWI) soldier's pay, an abbreviation of compensation. (SSD)

compre (com•PRAY) BrA (WWI) to understand, British soldier's version of French *comprendre*. Sometimes spelled compray. (AGE)

comrade Sp/BrA (13th–18th c.) [Latin *camera*, room>Spanish *camerado*, roommate> English *comrade*] one with whom quarters are shared; a close friend; a fellow soldier from one's unit. BrA (1768) "two men who share one billet and lie together." (MDB) SpA (18th c.) one with whom quarters are shared. It was customary for five men to live in one room. (DVT MCT MDB)

com rats USMC (1970s–90s) commuted rations, an allotment of money for those who did not eat on base, in the mess hall.

COMSEC (COM•sek) USA (1970s) communications security.

con¹ MM (18th c.) a step or platform against a ship's sides, on both sides of the wheel, from which the officer of the deck could look over the side to see anything directly in front of the vessel. This officer gave directions to the helmsman, who steered by compass and could not see obstacles in ship's path. (OST SLA)

con² MM (18th c.) to navigate or steer a ship, especially within sight of land. (OST SLA)

CONAC (CON•ack) USAF (1950s) Continental Air Command. (AFS)

concertina wire BrA/FrA>USA/USMC

(WWI–present) coiled barbed wire (as opposed to traditional fencing wire). It is shipped in compressed rolls that expand when set up, like the musical instrument of the same name. (MMD)

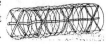
concertina wire

conchie (CON•chee) Br>USA (WWI–WWII) a conscientious objector; aka conchy. The shortened term passed to Americans during WWI and was revived during WWII. (MCT)

condition purple USAAF (WWII) a warning that enemy aircraft are approaching. (AFR)

condition red USAAF (WWII) a warning that the enemy aircraft are in sight and attacking. (MMD)

condom *See* cundum

Confed CSA/USA (1860s) Confederate money; a soldier or civilian of the South. (LRY)

Confederate beef USA (1860s) any Confederate livestock, including horses, pigs, and cows. (IHA)

congee (CON•jee) USN (19th c.) rice gruel. (ANE)

congo (CON•go) BrA (1725) [Chinese *congou*, tea] tea, a mispronunciation of the Chinese word. (DVT)

conk out BrAF>USA/USMC (WWI) to stop working, from the coughing noise made by a failing airplane engine before it stopped working entirely. (WWII–present) to pass out or fall asleep; to stop; to give up.

connex USA (1960s) a large metal box used for shipping and/or storage.

CONOP (CON•op) USA (1970s) continuous operations.

conservatory *See* glasshouse

consigne (kon•SINE) FrA (WWI) [French *consigne*, instructions, orders] forbidden. (WWW)

contraband BrA>USA (16th–19th c.) [Italian *contrabbando*, proclamation ban> French *contrebande*>Old English *contraband*, prohibition] smuggling or other illegal trade, especially in the Spanish colonies during the wars between Spain and England.

(17th c.) goods seized in time of war. USA (1861) slaves or runaways freed or seized by federal forces during the Civil War. (DWO)

convoy[1] BrA (1768) USA (1861) a supply of men and/or goods transported into a town or to an armory; a member of the troops guarding such a supply. USA/USMC/USN/USAF (1942–present) army troops were carried overseas in a convoy of naval ships; on land, a USA/USMC convoy consisted of various military vehicles bound for a specific destination. (MD MDB)

convoy[2] USA/USMC/USN/USAF (1942–present) to escort persons or ships. (MMD)

cook BrN>USN (17th–20th c.) enlisted men's cook aboard a man-of-war; aka cookie. From the 1660s to the late nineteenth century, sailors who were too old or infirm to perform regular duties customarily became cooks, the ability to start a fire and boil water guaranteeing them shelter and work until death. The British ended the practice in the mid-1800s, when the government established homes for aged and infirm servicemen, but the USN kept the custom alive until the early 1900s. (NCT) (*see also* doctor)

cooker BrA (19th c.–WWI) [Nepalese *kukri*, fighting knife>English *cooker*, a mispronunciation of the Nepalese] the time-honored fighting knife of the Gurkhas, which by custom must draw blood before it can be returned to its sheath. (TBS) (*see* Gurkha)

Cooke's Tour BrA (WWI) an official visit by civilians, usually politicians, to a quiet or safe sector of the line. So named for a famous prewar travel agency, Cooke's Tours of Europe, noted for its ability to ensure pleasant views and good room and board.

cookhouse official BrA (WWI) an unfounded rumor.

cookie *See* cook

cookie duster USMC (1930s–Korean War) mustache. (SAM)

cool USA (19th c.) to sit back and take it easy; aka cool one's heels. Also, to knock someone out, as in *cool him*. (MCT)

cooler BrA (18th c.) a cold and unaffectionate woman. USA (1884) a prison. BrA

(WWI) a place of solitary confinement. The term was borrowed from Americans serving in the British Expeditionary Forces (BEF). Br/USA (WWII) a detention cell, especially one intended for solitary confinement. (DVT) (*see* BEF)

coolie Hindu>Port>India>China>MM/BrN> USA/USMC/USN/USAF (17th c.–present) [Hindu *kuli*>Tamil *kuli* to hire] a native laborer hired to do manual labor. Applied mainly to the laborers of the Far East. (DWO)

cooped up BrA>USA/USMC/USN (18th–20th c.) caged, as a bird in a coop; confined to a location due to circumstances rather than choice. (DVT)

cooties *See* louse

copacetic (co•pah•CEH•tik) Rus>USA (1918–19) all right or good. Borrowed by United States soldiers serving in Archangel and Siberia during a brief, undeclared war with the Red Army in 1918–19. (MCT)

copain (co•PAN) FrA>BrA>USA/USN/USMC/USAAF (WWI) a comrade. Mispronounced co•PANE by the British and US soldiers. (WWW)

cop a Sunday USA (WWII) to hit someone without warning. (GWD)

copper USN (19th c.) a large cast-iron pot lined with copper sheeting in which sailors' food was boiled. (RAS)

copperhead USA (1775–present) a poisonous snake. (1809) one who is hostile, mean, or vindictive. (1838) a white man who sided and fought with the Native Americans; a Native American. (1862) a Northerner who sided with the Southern cause. (IHA)

corking mat USN (WWII) a sleeping mat or air mattress. (PAT)

cork off USN (WWII) to take a nap.

corned Sc>BrA (19th c.) [Scottish *corned*, to be drunk] drunk. (DVT)

corned dog USA/USMC/USN (1898) canned corned beef. (GWD)

corner pocket USA (WWII) a guardhouse. A prisoner in the guardhouse was like a ball in the pocket of a pool table—both were out of circulation. (ATK)

cornet BrA (1768) the youngest cavalry officer of a troop, who was given the honor of carrying the unit's standard and expected to defend it to the death. (1790s–1815) a second lieutenant in the cavalry. (MDB) (*see also* ensign, standard)

corn squeezings USA (WWII) home-brewed whiskey. (GWD)

corn Willie *See* canned Willie

corporal ItA>FrA>BrA>USA/USMC (16th–20th c.) [Italian *capo de squadra*, head of squad>French *corporal*>English *corporal*] a squad leader in British, and later in U.S., land forces. (DWO MCT)

corporal's guard Br>USA (18th–19th c.) a squad of men led by a corporal; a small group of people working for the same cause or on the same project. (DOC)

corps USA (WWII–present) a tactical unit larger than a division and smaller than an army; a branch of the army, such as the Army Corps of Engineers or the Quartermaster's Corps. (ASC)

Corps, the USMC (19th c.–present) the United States Marine Corps. (PAT) (*see* United States Marine Corps)

corps commander *See* louse

Corpse USN/USA/USMC (19th c.–WWII) a sailor's reference to the USMC. USA (WWII) a common reference to the army corps. (ANE GWD)

corpse ticket BrA (WWI) a body tag, a paper tied to the big toe of a body that listed the name, rank, and unit of the deceased; aka cold meat ticket. (*see also* cold meat)

corpsman USMC/USN (WWII–present) a sailor assigned to a Marine unit as the first-aid man in the field; aka bed pan commando, Doc. By custom, the corpsman carried no weapons. (SAM) (*see also* chancre mechanic, pill pusher, pill roller, shanker mechanic)

corpuscle USA (1940s) corporal, a play on the word. (GWD)

Cosmoline gang USA (1898–WWII) impolite reference to both the coast artillery and the United States Coast Guard, which used great quantities of Cosmoline to keep their guns from rusting; aka Cosmoline, Cosmoline slingers. It was said that the coast artillery had to keep its guns especially well oiled since it never had a chance to fire them. (ATK GWD MMD) (*see* Cosmoline soldiers)

Cosmoline soldiers USA (WWI) men of the heavy artillery. (AGE) (*see* Cosmoline gang)

Coughing Clara BrA>USA (WWII) an anti-aircraft gun that had a rasping, harsh bark, as compared to the boom of larger artillery pieces. (MMD)

countermarch BrA (1768) USA (1861) a maneuver in which an entire army reverses the direction of its advance in an effort to counteract an enemy assault. USA (1942–present) a maneuver on a parade ground in which a military band or special parade unit reverses its direction of march without coming to a halt. (MD MDB MMD)

coup de grâce (Fr: coo de GRAH; Br/US: coop dee GRACE) FrA>BrA>USA (1700–present) [French *coup de grâce*, blow of mercy] a fatal cut or jab in a duel or fight; a final blow or finishing touch.

cousin USA (WWII) a close friend; aka country cousin, kissing cousin. (AFR)

covered wagon USN (WWII) rarely used nickname for an aircraft carrier. (*see also* flattop)

cover your ass *See* CYA

cow AusA (1915–18) something or someone considered to be useless, helpless, and/or hopeless. USA (WWI–WWII) milk. (EMP) West Point (WWII–1950s) canned milk; a second classman, or junior. (ASC)

cowboy USA (1775–1960s) a farmer who preferred to raise cattle instead of crops. (1775) a loyalist, a Tory who ambushed farmers and stole cattle. (1830s, Texas) an American who stole Mexican cattle. (1920s–30s) an expert in a mechanized corps. (1960s) an untrustworthy person, a gangster. (IHA)

cowboy hat *See* campaign hat

cow-gun BrN (WWII) a heavy naval gun.

cowhorn USN (19th c.) sailor's mispronunciation of cohorn, a small mortar. (ANE) (*see also* cohorn)

cow juice BrA>USA (18th c.–WWII) fresh milk. (AFR DVT)

cow's tail USN (WWII) the frayed end of a line or rope. (SEA) (*see also* Irish pennant)

coxswain BrN>USN (18th c.–present) [Old English *cockswain*, commander of a small boat] a petty officer who commands the crew of the ship's small boat when no commissioned officer is present; also spelled cockswain, coxsun. Often, the coxswain mans the boat's tiller or wheel. (NCT)

CP *See* command post

CPO USN (20th c.) chief petty officer. (MAN)

CQ USA (WWII) the man in charge of quarters. The CQ followed the bugler with his whistle at the ready to rouse the men from sleep. (GWD)

CR USA (WWI) a crossroad. (WWW)

CRA BrA (WWII) a battery commander in the Royal Artillery. (WID)

crab[1] BrA>USA (18th c.–present) a type of body louse that lays eggs at the roots of hair, so named for its resemblance to the sea animal. (DVT) USA/USAAF (WWII) a chronic complainer. (AFR) BrN (1980s–present) a sailor's name for a member of the Royal Air Force, whose uniform is the same color as the crab fat used to lubricate naval gun breeches. (*see* crab fat, louse)

crab[2] USA (WWII) to complain or find fault. (AFR)

crab fat BrA (WWI) whale oil, used to prevent frostbite and combat body lice in humans and to lubricate naval gun breeches. (*see also* antifrostbite)

crabs BrA>USA (18th c.–present) an infestation of crab lice. (*see* louse, crab[1])

crack BrA>USA/USN/USMC (18th c.–present) said approvingly of the elite: *a crack unit, a crack shot, a crack crew.* (DVT OST SLA)

crack-brained USN (19th c.) mentally defective. (ANE)

crack-hemp USN (19th c.) someone destined to be hanged by a noose made of hemp rope, from the sound of a neck snapping; aka crack-rope. (ANE)

crack up USMC (WWII) to experience combat fatigue. (SAM) (*see* combat fatigue)

craft MM (17th c.) a ship, boat, or person. (OST SLA)

cranky USN (19th c.–present) touchy, tempermental, easily upset or irritated. (ANE)

crapaud BrA/BrN>USN (1790s–20th c.) [French *Jean Crapaud*, John Toad, disparaging name for common sailor] disparaging nickname for a French soldier or sailor; aka Johnny Crapaud, Johnny Crappo. (ANE AST)

Crapaud, Johnny *See* crapaud

crapper GrN (WWII) a U-boat, from the combined smells of people, food, and machinery; aka hearse. USA/USAF (WWII–1960s) a toilet. (*see also* iron coffin, latrine)

Crappo, Johnny *See* crapaud

crash USAAF (WWII) an omelette made from scrambled (crashed) eggs. (GWD)

crash and burn USAF (1980s) to go to bed in a state of exhaustion at the end of a hard day.

crash and dash USAF (1980s) a landing and almost immediate takeoff by an aircraft, a perilous business for its pilot.

crash tag USAAF (WWII) an identification bracelet used as a backup to dog tags. (GWD) (*see* dog tags)

crate *See* airplane

C ration USA/USMC/USN/USAF (WWII–1978) literally, canned ration: preserved, precooked, canned food carried by armed forces in the field, including stew, tuna, and spaghetti and noted for its high content of preservatives. C rations could be heated if the situation allowed or eaten cold (as opposed to K rations, which consisted of dry foods, such as crackers and cheese, which were meant to be eaten cold); aka Cs, C rats, can of worms. (*see also* MRE)

C rats *See* C rations

crawfish NZ>USA (WWII) to beat a hasty retreat by crawling backward.

crawl all over USA/USMC/USN/USCG (WWI–Korean War) to bawl out or admonish: *the old man crawled all over Joe.* (AFR MCT)

crawl in with one's eyebrows on BrA (WWI) to be totally exhausted.

crazy with the heat USA (1898–WWII) a state of delirium often marked by the victim's speaking gibberish. Coined by soldiers and Marines in the Philippines, where the heat sometimes caused men to become delirious or incoherent. (EMP)

creased BrA (1940s, North Africa) to have been wounded, not fatally. (DRA) (*see also* kaput, topple off one's perch)

creep and crawl *See* snoop and poop

creeper BrA (18th c.) a gentleman's term for a louse. USA (1860s) a soldier's wrought-iron frying pan, carried in a haversack over the right hip and near the small of the back. The pan had a habit of riding (creeping) up during a march, causing no little discomfort to the back and kidneys. (DVT) (*see* louse)

creeping crud *See* jungle rot

crew[1] MM (17th–19th c.) [French *creue*, reinforcements] all the sailors aboard a ship, a ship's complement and any additional men. (OST TON)

crew[2] MM (pre-19th c.) [French *creue*, reinforcements] to reinforce sailors' numbers on a ship. Most ships sailed with the fewest men safety would permit; when required, a ship's complement was augmented by legal or semi-legal means. (OST TON)

crew chief USN (WWII–present) a petty officer in charge of a detail of men, such as a painting crew or aircraft maintenance crew.

crew chief magnet USNA (1980s) an aircraft's fire bottle/extinguisher, a favorite leaning post for the crew chief prior to the plane's launching.

crew dogs USAF (1980s) the flight crew.

cricket ball BrA (WWI) a spherical hand grenade. (AGE)

crimp MM (18th–19th c.) a job broker for sailors who usually took their three months' advanced wages. He guaranteed a sailor's presence on board ship at a prescribed time. (BMO)

crispy critters USA/USMC/USAF (Vietnam) those unfortunates who had been burnt to a crisp by flaming napalm, from the popular children's cereal by that name.

critique USA (1950s) a written review of a military operation or exercise. (ASC)

crooked shoes USA (1860s) shoes cut in the modern style, with distinct right and left patterns (as opposed to the standard shoe of the day, which was cut straight and worn on either foot). (IHA)

croot *See* recruit

crossbar hotel USA (WWII) a guardhouse or jail. (GWD) (*see also* jail)

crossbow ItA>BrA (13th–16th c.) a short, sturdy bow secured horizontally to the end of a stock, which was held against the shoulder when fired. Its missile was a short, stout arrow called a bolt, capable of penetrating most types of mail and armor at ranges of a hundred yards.

cross-country flight USAF (1950s) a flight from coast to coast. (AFS)

Crotch USMC (1960s–present) a derogatory name for the Marine Corps.

crotch rot *See* jungle rot

crow[1] USA (WWI–WWII) government-issue chicken, which was as tough as an old crow. USN (WWI–present) the eagle in the insignia of naval petty officers; aka buzzard. (DVT GWD) (*see also* eagle, get a crow)

crow[2] BrA (18th c.) to boast; to keep an opponent in a state of subjection: *He'll have to crow the bugger if he hopes to win the fight.* Possibly a mispronunciation of cow. (DVT GWD)

crowd[1] BrA (WWI) a military unit; aka mob.

crowd[2] MM (18th c.) to put up as much sail as the mast and yards can stand in an effort to gain more speed. (OST SLA)

crow hooks USA (1860s) the chevrons of an NCO; aka crow tracks. (ATK) (*see* chevrons, NCO)

crow's feet BrA>USA (1768–1860s) four-pronged, iron stars used to obstruct the path of oncoming infantry and cavalry. When thrown on the ground, one spike was in an upright position. (MD MDB)

crow's nest MM (19th c.) a ship's highest yards or mastheads, on which

crow's feet

lookouts—said to be *in the crow's nest*—were posted. The term arises from the era of the Vikings, who carried ravens in cages atop ships' masts. When released, the birds found the most direct course to land. (TON)

crow tracks *See* crow hooks

CRP USA/USMC (1960s–1980s) Soviet combat reconnaissance patrol.

crud USMC (WWII) a Marine who was untidy in personal appearance or uniform; aka crum. (SAM) (*see also* crummy)

cruise[1] MM (17th c.–present) [Dutch *kruizer*, to cross or wander] to put to sea without a predetermined course or destination; to wander about town during liberty; for a ship, to go to war at sea, to patrol an enemy coast constantly.

cruise[2] USMC/USN (1860s–present) a full four-year enlistment; a duty assignment aboard a ship. (OST SAM)

cruise missile USAF/USN/USA (1977–present) a jet-powered, winged, unmanned missile that is stable in flight and very accurate against sea or land-based targets. The Harpoon and Tomahawk missiles are currently in use. (*see* Harpoon missile, Tomahawk missile)

cruiser BrN>USN (18th c.–present) a ship designed for patrol duty off an enemy coast. (18th c.) a highwayman who prowled a particular length of road in search of victims; a fast, light commerce raider from the Mediterranean; a warship, usually of frigate class or smaller, sent on detached service alone or with two other ships. (DVT MCT TWW) (*see* detached service, frigate)

cruiser, Confederate CSA/USA (1860s) a Confederate warship built in England or France. (IHA)

crum *See* crud

crumb bosun' (BOW•sun) USN (19th c.) a ship's cook's helper. (ANE)

crumb hunt USA (WWII) a thorough kitchen inspection. (AFR)

crummy BrA>USA/USN/USMC (18th c.–WWI) fat, very fleshy. Br>USA/USMC (WWI) loaded with lice; aka chatty, chicot. (DVT) USMC (WWII) said of a Marine who

68

was untidy in personal appearance or uniform. (SAM) (*see also* chatty, crud)

crump BrA (WWI) a German high explosive shell that made a "crump" sound upon impact. (AGE)

crump hole BrA>USA (WWI–WWII) the hole made by the German high explosive shell known as a crump. (WWII) a hole made by a shell. (GWD) (*see* crump)

crunchies USA (1960s) infantry, so named for the sound of marching feet.

crusher BrN (1980s–present) a member of the naval shore patrol.

crying towel USA/USMC (WWII) a towel hanging in the chaplain's office and used to dry tears; aka chaplain's shirttail. (GWD SAM)

CS USAF (1950s) chief of staff; certificate of service, a paper that details one's duties and length of military service. USA (1970s–present) combat support. (AFS)

Cs *See* C rations

CSM BrA (19th–20th c.) company sergeant major. (AGE WID)

C2 USA (1970s) command and control group. USN (1970s) a navy transport plane, the Grummand Greyhound.

cuckoo USAAF (WWII) a dive bomber. (GWD MMD) (*see also* hornet)

cuddy MM (19th c.) a small cabin on a ship (usually a merchant ship) reserved for the ship's carpenter. (OST)

cuff leggings USA (1860s–Korean War) short canvas leggings that extended from just above the ankle to the foot and kept trouser legs from being snagged and torn. (EMP)

cumshaw MM (18th c.–present) [Chinese word for alms or gifts] pidgin English for a gift or item given gratis, most commonly a graft or bribe. Used by British and American troops with service in China. USN (1960s) any item obtained by bribery or other illegal means. (MMD SLA TON)

cundums BrA (18th c.) condoms, which were invented by a Colonel Cundum. He made the first such item in 1776 from dried sheep intestines. (DVT)

cunt cap *See* overseas cap

Cuntsville USA (1960s–70s) the United States—home.

cup and wad BrA (WWI) a cup of tea and a hymn at the Church of England, an army hut, or the YMCA.

curio AusA (1915–18) a souvenir taken from the enemy; aka souvy.

curtailed watch *See* dog watch

cushy BrA>USA (19th–20th c.) soft, easy, comfortable. Borrowed from the British by Americans during WWI. (AGE GWD)

cut and come again USN (19th–20th c.) beans and bread left out for the crew to nibble on during the course of the day. The phrase arose from the naval battle tactic of firing broadside and then maneuvering to strike again. (AST NCT)

cut and run BrN>USA/USN (18th–20th c.) to cut the anchor cable to effect a hasty withdrawal. USA/USN (18th c.–present) to make a swift attack on a position, then withdraw before the enemy can strike back effectively. (OST SLA)

cutlash USN (19th c.) cutlass, sailors' mispronunciation. (ANE) (*see* cutlass)

cutlass BrN>USN (16th–20th c.) [Old French *cutelas*, large knife] a heavy bladed sword used by sailors fighting in close quarters. (DWO)

cut of one's jib MM>BrN>USN (18th–20th c.) the general appearance of a person or ship. In the eighteenth century, it was possible to identify the size and nationality of a ship by the style and number of jib sails the vessel carried. (AST MCT OST)

cut the painter MM (18th–20th c.) to die. When a ship's painter, the line by which it is moored, is cut, the ship drifts out to sea. When a person cuts his painter, his soul drifts aloft to Fiddler's Green—or below to Davy Jones's locker. (AST) (*see* Davy Jones's locker, Fiddler's Green)

cutty MM (18th–20th c.) [Scottish *cutty*, short chemise] a short-stemmed pipe; a loose woman, as such ladies often wore short-waisted chemises. (ANE)

CYA USA/USMC/USN/USAF/USCG (1960s) cover your ass, watch out for yourself.

cyclo USA (Vietnam) a three-wheeled, motor-powered vehicle. (BLO)

cylindrical sirloin *See* horse cock

D

Dad USA (WWII) the oldest enlisted man in the unit. (MMD)

daddy mammy beat BrA (18th c.) the first beats of a drumroll. (DVT)

DAF (daf) USAF (1950s) Department of the Air Force. (AFS)

dago BrA (17th–20th c.) [Spanish *Diego*, James] a Spaniard; aka diego. USA (1840s) term of insult for an Italian. (NCT TON)

daily bulletin USAAF (WWII) orders issued by the commanding officer of a regiment. (AFR)

daily detail USAAF (WWII) one of possibly several groups of men assigned to carry out the work orders of the first sergeant. (AFR)

daily eyewash BrA (WWI) the official, daily news release concerning the war. It presented the facts in the best possible light. (*see also* eyewash)

daisy cutter BrA (18th c.) a horse that did not lift its legs high enough while running and thus stumbled frequently. BrA (19th c.) a cricket ball that skipped along the ground. BrA (WWI) a shell that exploded very close to the ground. USA (1960s) a bomb capable of clearing a large area instantly. (DVT)

daisy pusher BrA (WWI) a fatal wound.

damage the pepper box USN (18th–19th c.) to drop a shot (cannonball) through an open hatch onto the head of the ship's master-at-arms, who was considered fair game unless the one inflicting damage was turned in by one of the ship's white mice; to cause or receive head damage. (RAS) (*see* white mice)

damn-my-eyes tar MM (19th c.) a greenhorn who puts on the airs of an experienced sailor and is all talk and little substance. (RAS) (*see* greenhorn)

dance at the gratings USN (18th–19th c.) to be flogged with cat-o'-nine-tails. (RAS) (*see* cat-o'-nine-tails, flog)

D and D USN (18th–19th c.) drunk and dirty. The notation was made beside a sailor's name if he returned from liberty drunk and/or in poor physical condition. Those who received such a notation drew punishment. (RAS) (*see also* C and S)

dandy funk MM (18th–20th c.) pudding made from ground ship's biscuit, slush, and molasses. The ingredients were mixed together, then boiled or baked; aka duff. (TON) (*see* duff, slush)

dank USN (19th c.) moist or damp. (ANE)

darbies BrN>USN (17th–20th c.) wrist or leg irons. (DVT RAS) (*see* double darbies, irons)

dark greens USMC (1980s–90s) African-American Marines.

Davy Jones *See* Jones, Davy

Davy Jones's locker MM (17th c.–present) the bottom of the sea. (*see also* Jones, Davy)

dawn patrol USAAF (WWII) activity that takes place before reveille. (ATK)

day of absence USA (1950s) a day when a member of a specific unit was away from that unit, usually with permission. (ASC) (*see also* AWL, AWOL, French leave)

day room USA (WWII–Korean War) enlisted men's recreation room. (AFR ASC)

day's duty USN/USMC (1960s) the twenty-four-hour shipboard routine. (MAN)

DB *See* deadbeat

DD BrN (1750s) entry made by the purser in his muster roll beside the name of a man who had died at sea. (*see* purser) USAF (1950s) Department of Defense; dishonorable discharge. (AFS MOW)

dead MM (17th c.) absolute, exact. Often used to emphasize an object's position in relation to the vessel that sights it: *dead ahead*. (BJM)

dead angle CSA/USA (1860s) area that cannot be seen by defenders of a position, barricade, or fortification and therefore is not covered; aka dead ground. (MD MMD) (*see also* dead space)

deadbeat CSA/USA (19th c.–present) a lazy or worthless person; aka DB. (GWD) (*see also* beat)

dead dog USA (WWII) an empty liquor or beer bottle. (MMD)

dead ground *See* dead angle

deadhead MM (20th c.) a partially submerged piece of wood that can hinder navigation. (BJM)

dead horse MM>BrN>USN (17th c.–early 20th c.) advance pay. Usually received when a sailor signed aboard a merchant or navy ship and used to refit him for the new cruise. Sailors served for one to three months without pay to work off advanced wages, and during this period one was said to be *paying off his dead horse*. (TON) (*see also* work for a dead horse)

deadline[1] USA/CSA (1860s) low rail fence set inside the perimeter of the Confederate prisoner-of-war camp at Andersonville, Ga., where many thousands of federal soldiers were held. A prisoner who crossed the barrier was shot without warning by the guards. USA (WWII) barbed wire barrier within the wire fencing that defined the outer boundaries of a prisoner-of-war camp; the date on which a project was due to be completed.

deadline[2] USA/USMC/USN/USAF (WWII–1960s) to place a military vehicle in the camp's maintenance area for repairs. (AFR MCT MMD)

dead marine BrN>USN (18th c.–present) an empty bottle; aka dead soldier. At a dinner, William IV, Lord of the Admiralty, ordered that the dead marines (empty bottles) be removed from the table. A Marine major who was present was offended by the comment, but William soothed him by saying that the Marines "are good fellows who have done their duty and are ready to do it again." Empty spirit or beer bottles have been known as dead marines ever since. (OST TON)

(*see also* Marine officers)

dead months USN (19th c.) winter, which was characterized by a lack of activity, especially among vessels under sail. (ANE)

dead reckoning MM (17th c.–present) plot of a ship's position on a chart based on the estimated distance covered. The term is a corruption of deduced reckoning or positioning; there wasn't room in a ship's log to write the word deduced, so ded or dead was noted. (OST NCT)

deadrun USA/CSA (1860s) open ground between stockade and deadline. (*see* deadline) (MMD)

dead soldier *See* dead marine

dead space USA/USAAF>USAF (WWII–present) area that cannot be covered by fire from a friendly position due to obstacles that block the line of sight. USAAF>USAF the area around an aircraft that cannot be covered by the defensive weapons of that plane. (MMD) (*see also* dead angle)

dead stick landing USAAF (WWI–WWII) a landing made after engine failure. The joystick, the sole steering mechanism of WWI–era airplanes, was useless without power. (AFR) (*see also* joystick)

dean o' the latrine USA (WWII) one in charge of cleaning the latrine. (SID) (*see* latrine)

Dear John USA/USMC/USCG/USN/USAF (WWII–present) letter from military man's wife or sweetheart telling him that their relationship is over.

death gratuity USA (1950s) a lump sum payment of six months' basic pay (eight hundred dollars minimum, three thousand dollars maximum) to the beneficiaries of a serviceman who died on active duty or within 120 days of discharge from the service. The death gratuity was forfeited if the serviceman died as a result of misconduct. (ASC)

debark BrA (1768) to go ashore from a ship or boat. (MDB) (*see also* embark)

debus BrA (WWI) to exit a military transport or bus; also spelled debuss.

decamp BrA (1768) to break camp. Used only when the entire army, not a unit thereof, broke camp. (MDB)

deck MM (15th–16th c.) [Middle Dutch *dec*, covering, roof, cloak>English *deck*, tarpaulin or canvas boat covering, sometimes layered] something stacked atop another; ship's flooring. USN/USMC (18th–20th c.) the floor of a building or the ground. USN/USMC (WWII) aircraft landing strip. (AFR DWO SAM)

deck ape USMC (WWII–present) Marine's derogatory term for a sailor; aka seaweed, squid, swab jockey. (TON) USN (1960s) sailor assigned to gun and/or deck duty. (*see also* anchor clanker, flatfoot, knuckle dragger, Popeye)

decode USAAF (WWII) to explain or clarify. (AFR)

decon (DEE•con) USA (1970s–present) decontaminate.(VET)

deeps BrN (1980s–present) a surface sailor's name for a submariner; aka bubblehead, chicken of the sea.

deep six[1] MM (18th c.–present) six fathoms (thirty-six feet); the bottom of the ocean. (DOC OST)

deep six[2] MM (18th c.–present) to dispose of or throw away, perhaps in deep water; to bury a body at sea in at least six fathoms (thirty-six feet) of water; to drown. USN/USMC (1960s) to discard, throw away, or kill. (DOC OST PAT SAM TON)

deep six turkey USA (WWII) canned salmon. Probably from the suspicion that the meat had been spoiled and condemned (deep sixed) before it was canned and issued to the army. (SID) (*see* deep six)

défaitisme (day•fa•TEEZ•muh) FrA (WWI) [French *défaite*, defeat or evasion] a defeatist, a quitter. (WWW)

defaulter USA (1860s) an army finance officer who misused government funds, either by putting them in his own pocket or by using them for projects other than those for which they were earmarked. Usually also meant that the officer had failed to have his books ready for required inspection. BrA (19th c.) a soldier given extra pack drill for a minor infraction of army regulations. (AGE

MD)

defile CSA/USA (1860s) [French *défiler*, to march in column, or *défilé*, narrow pass] a narrow passage, such as a ford, pass, or bridge, through which soldiers must pass in single column or file. (DWO MCT MD MMD)

defrost USA (WWII) to drink alcohol in an effort to keep warm. (SID)

dekho *See* dekko

dekko BrA (WWI) a glance or glimpse; also spelled dekho. (AGE)

Demon Rum USNA (WWII) strong rum, especially aged or bootleg rum; aka bootleg, bootleg whiskey, booze. Likely stemmed from old-time preachers' fire-and-brimstone sermons on the "Demon Rum." (AFR)

dentist USA (WWI–WWII) one detailed to fill various types of military balloons with gas, a comparison to a dentist and his laughing gas. (SID)

departure USA (WWI) the firing of an outbound artillery shell. (WWW)

dependents USA/USMC/USN/USAF/USCG (WWII–present) individuals recognized by the federal government as having legal claim to support by a member of the military. (AFS)

deplane USAF (1950s) to exit an aircraft. (AFS)

depot BrA>USA (18th c.–present) [French *dépôt*, place where an item is left or deposited] a site designated as a gathering place for soldiers; an area where supply reserves are temporarily stored for use by frontline troops. (DWO MD MMD)

derelict MM (17th–20th c.) [Latin *derelictus*, to be forsaken] a vessel that is afloat but abandoned; a person without roots, a bum, wanderer. (OST SLA)

DEROS USA (1960s) date of expected return from overseas; date eligible to return from overseas; sometimes rendered deros.

derrick MM (late 16th c.) hoisting apparatus designed by royal hangman Thomas Derrick. (16th c.–present) a boom and swivel system used to hoist and load cargo. (DWO NCT TON)

der uffs BrA (WWI) [French *deux œufs*, two

eggs] two eggs. British soldier's mispronunciation of the French. (AGE)

desecrated USN (19th c.) sailor's term for dehydrated, a deliberate mispronunciation of desiccated. At sea, men were fed eight to sixteen ounces of desiccated vegetables (boiled to revive the greens) daily. Sailors felt that desecrated was a more accurate description of the state of the vegetables. (RAS)

desert chicken *See* bully beef

deserter USMC (1930s–60s) one who was AWOL for more than thirty days. (PAT SAM) (*see* AWOL, over the hill)

desert rose BrA (WWII, North Africa) a latrine; a striking natural rock formation; a soldier's urinal, consisting of a tin can punctured as a sieve and inserted into sand, aka desert lily. Once used, the can was pulled up and the hole filled in to prevent wet patches of sand or depressions in sand, which might be detected by an enemy. A term peculiar to the British Eighth Army. (ADW WID)

Desert Shield USA/USMC/USAF (1991) the official name for the military protection of Saudi Arabia and the buildup of allied troops and supplies in preparation for Desert Storm. (*see* Desert Storm, Gulf War)

Desert Storm USA/USMC/USAF (1991) the official name for the combat phase of the Gulf War. (*see* Gulf War)

desertworthy BrA (WWII, North Africa) fit for use in the desert, said of both men and machinery. Peculiar to the British Eighth Army. (ADW)

desk pilot USAF (1950s) a qualified pilot assigned to office rather than flight duty. (AFS)

destroyer USN (19th c.–present) a light, fast warship that began in the late 1800s as a torpedo boat. The first United States destroyer of the modern style was built in 1898. (OST) (*see also* tin can)

detached bastion CSA/USA (1860s) a fortified structure separated from the main defenses by a trench. (MD)

detached duty USA/USMC (WWI–present) duty performed while a soldier is temporarily assigned to a post away from his unit's home base. During the Civil War, aka detached service. (EMP MMD)

detached service *See* detached duty, DS

detached works CSA/USA (1860s) a fortification that is beyond rifle range of the main work. USA (WWII) a site out of range of main works' support fire, artillery included; totally isolated post. (MD MMD)

detail USA (19th c.–present) a small group of men assigned to a specific task for a specific period of time or until completion of the task. (ASC)

deuce and a half USA/USMC (WWII–1960s) a medium-size, two-and-a-half-ton military truck.

devil dodger Br/GrA (WWI–WWII) a military chaplain; a Bible scholar, not necessarily a chaplain, who constantly quoted chapter and verse.

Devil Dogs *See* Teufelhund

devil's bonnet USA (WWII) a steel helmet. (SID)

Devil's Brigade GrA>CA/USA (WWII) a nickname given to the First Special Forces Brigade, which consisted of American and Canadian rangers, by the Germans.

devil seam MM (17th c.) the longest side seam on a ship, always nearest the waterline and therefore most difficult to repair, especially when the ship was under sail. (NCT OST)

devil's piano USA (early WWII) a machine gun. (GWD)

devil's smile USN (19th c.) a ray of sun piercing an overcast sky; a glint of a smile on the old man's (captain's) face. (ANE) (*see* old man)

devil to pay and no hot pitch MM (17th c.–present) [French *poix*, pitch, which the English sailor pronounced pay] said of a no-win situation, from the practice of applying pitch to the devil seam on a ship. (NCT OST) (*see* devil)

D4D *See* K-9 Corps

dhobi (DOH•bee) BrA (WWII) [Arabic *dhobi* or *dhoby*, to wash] to wash, a term peculiar to the British Eighth Army; also spelled

dhoby. A dhobi wallah is a laundryman. (WID) (*see* wallah)

dhobie itch (DOH•bee itch) USA/USMC/ USN (1898–WWII) a nasty skin disease affecting mainly the genital area, often contracted in the Philippine Islands. (EMP)

DI USMC (WWI–present) drill instructor at boot camp. (1980s) aka the hat. (PAT SAM)

dial BrA (WWI) a human face; aka clock, map. (AGE)

diary USA (1950s) a detailed, daily account of a military unit's actions. (ASC)

dibbs USN (19th c.) cash (as opposed to vouchers); small pool of water. (ANE)

dich (DIK) USA/USMC (1960s) [Vietnamese *dichdick*, dead] a dead casualty, especially an enemy. (SAL)

dichdick (dik•dik) USA/USMC (1960s) [Vietnamese *dichdick*, dead] dead. (SAL)

dick the dog USN (1980s–present) to goof off, be unproductive.

dicky leave BrA (WWI) absence without leave, the implication being that the soldier in question is AWOL because he has sexual needs to fulfill; also spelled dickey leave. (*see also* AWOL)

diddy bop USA/USMC (1960s) to walk in a carefree, careless, or bold manner. Used chiefly among black soldiers.

diddy pin (DIE•dee pin) USA (WWII) the single gold bar of rank worn by a second lieutenant. Soldiers compared the gold bar to diaper (ditty or diddy) pins, reflecting the age-old contempt enlisted men have for new lieutenants. (GWD)

di di (dee dee) Viet>USA/USMC (1960s) [Vietnamese *di di*, to move quickly, to hurry] to run or move quickly.

diehard BrA>USA (1811) one who stands his ground regardless of the odds. Supposedly coined by Sir John Inglis, who commanded the Fourth Battalion, Fifty-Seventh Regiment of Foot in the war against France. At the battle of Albuera, Spain, the severely wounded colonel told his men to "never surrender" and "die hard"; three quarters of his unit reportedly suffered casualties and became known as the Diehards.

Dieu et mon droit (d'you eh moan dwa) FrA>BrA (WWI) [French *Dieu et mon droit*, God help me] misunderstood by British Tommies, this phrase came to mean "Fuck you, mate! I'm all right!" (*see* Tommy)

differential pay USAF (1950s) extra compensation for doing a job not in the direct line of duty, especially special or hazardous duty. (AFS)

different ships, different long splices USN (19th c.) a sailor's expression meaning that there is more than one way to do a job— depending upon who is in command. (TON)

digger AusA (19th c.) a guardhouse; a miner, especially a gold digger, who had legal claim to land (as opposed to a farmer or illegal squatter); a fellow Australian soldier, friend, or sometimes stranger. The Australians and New Zealanders at Gallipoli called each other diggers because they had to dig trenches for protection and shelter.

digger, jigger up the *See* jigger up the digger

dig in BrA>USA/USMC (WWI) literally, to dig into the ground for protection; to stand one's ground, braced for an approaching storm.

Dilbert USNA (WWII–1970s) a dumb person. (AFR)

Dilbert dunker USNA (1960s) a simulator used to teach air personnel how to escape a plane downed in water.

dilly bag *See* ditty bag

dilly-wreck USN (19th c.) a sailor's mispronunciation of derelict. (ANE) (*see* derelict)

dingbat AusA>USA (WWI) [Australian *dingo* (short form *ding*), mad or wild dog, and *batman* (short form *bat*), officer's servant] officer's servant. AusN (WWI) deck mop. (1914) one who is sightly mad or eccentric. USA (WWII) headquarters clerk, in employ of commanding officer. (MCT) (*see also* batman)

ding how USN/USA/USMC (19th–20th c.) [Chinese *ding ho*, very good] everything's all right. Until the Korean War, the phrase was used only by those who had seen service in China or the Far East prior to WWII. (AFR ATK)

dinghy MM (18th c.–present) [Hindi *dinga, dinhi,* or *dengia,* small round-bottomed boat] small, nimble boat carried on the deck of a larger vessel. (OST TON)

dingle-dangle parade AusA (WWI–present) medical inspection for sexually transmitted disease. (*see also* short arm inspection)

dingo AusA (19th c.) wild dog of Australia; person who is slightly insane or crazy. (SSD)

dining hall USAF (1950s) chow or mess hall. Air force terminology was more formal than that of the other branches of service. (AFS)

dining room orderly USA (1900) a soldier detailed to wait on tables, set tables, and cut bread in the mess hall. (EMP)

dink USA/USMC/USAF/USN (1960s) derogatory term for an Oriental.

dinkums AusA (WWI) men of the First Australian Division, which served at Gallipoli in 1915. (SSD)

dinner's up BrA (WWI) the meal is ready. (AGE) (*see also* come and get it)

dipper USMC/USN (19th c.) a tin cup used to dip water from a barrel.

dirt bag USA (WWII) one assigned to garbage detail. (GWD)

dirt sailor USN (1980s–present) a Seabee, a member of a naval construction team. (*see also* Seabees)

dirty officer USA (1960s) nickname for a duty officer. (*see* duty officer)

disasters *See* ackers

discharge without honor USA (1900) a discharge for disability and/or ineptness in the line of duty that did not entail a loss of citizenship. (EMP)

disco belt USAF (1980s) a belt with reflectors worn at night to prevent its wearer from becoming roadkill.

Dish USA/USMC (1990s) Mogadishu, capital of Somalia.

dish USN (1850s–WWII) a class A flat-style sailor's hat that served as the service hat until the introduction of the dixie cup. (BMO) (*see* campaign hat, dixie cup)

dishonorable discharge USA (20th c.) a discharge that includes loss of citizenship.

(EMP) (*see also* bobtail)

dish out BrA (WWI) to disper food or medals. (SSD)

dislocation allowance USA (19 tary allowance provided to a who was transferred from one b er. (ASC)

dispensary USAF (1950s) the medicine and dental care wer (AFS) (*see also* sick bay)

disrate BrN (18th c.) to reduc rank. (TWW)

dit-dat artist USA (WWII) a operator, from the sound made ing key. (AFR GWD)

ditty bag MM/BrN>USN/USMC c.) [possibly from Anglo-Saxo and tidy, or *ditto,* duplicate, or *d* tobacco, or a Hindu word for a t from which ditty bags were ma canvas bag in which a sailor's personal items, such as socks, valuables, were kept. BrA/ANZ WWII–present) a small cloth b storage of such toiletry items as and towel. USMC (1980s) zi issued for athletic gear; aka dill OST) (*see also* ditty box, ferman b

ditty box MM (19th c.) a sma served the same purpose as a dit merchant ships and whalers, the was used primarily for personal it the ditty bag was reserved for to in the navy were permitted only because they were easily stored. (*see* ditty bag)

dive-bomb USAAF (WWII) to police or clean up an area, to div trash like a dive-bomber attacks (SID) (*see* police)

division BrA>USA>USMC (18th ent) BrA (18th–19th c.) a unit that of four brigades, each with eigh pieces, and four battalions. U$ c.–WWI) a square division of f ments of four battalions each. US (WWII) triangular division of th ments of three to four battalions ea

ivisional comic cuts BrA (WWI) daily communiqués from division headquarters that contained very little truth. Named for a prewar periodical intended for children and gullible adults.

ivy BrA (WWI) division; also spelled divvy.

ixie CSA/USA (early 1800s–present) the Southern states of the Union; aka Dixieland. In the early 1800s, the Citizens Bank of Louisiana issued bilingual English/French bank notes, some of which displayed the word *dix*, French for ten. From this, New Orleans and then the entire South came to be called Dixieland. In 1859, the term was popularized in the song "Dixie Land." (IHA)

ixie BrA (19th c.) [Hindu *degschai*, cooking pot] a large, oval, metal pot used for stews, soups, rice, and tea, while the lid was used for puddings and biscuits; cooking pot for a group of men. (WWII) a soldier's mess kit. (*see* mess kit)

ixie cup USN (1880s–present) white cloth fatigue or work hat introduced by Adm. Robert "Fighting Bob" Evans, who began his naval career during the Civil War and ended it in 1908; aka gob hat. The hat was intended to permit the "dish" to be reserved for formal occasions, but by the end of WWII the dixie cup had been adopted for wear on all occasions. The name probably came about

dixie cup

in the 1920s, from a comparison between the shape of the hat and the paper cups made by the Dixie Paper Cup Company. (PAT) (*see* dish)

dizzies USA (WWI) mounds of earth at the intersections of communication trenches with the main trench. (MMD)

dizzy pilot USAAF (WWII) a pilot who took too many dangerous chances while in flight. (MMD)

DO USA/USAAF>USAF (WWII–Korean War) duty officer. (AFS) (*see* duty officer)

DOA USA (1970s–present) direction of attack.

do a mike BrA (WWI) to break camp; to avoid duty.

do an alley BrA (WWI) [French *aller*, to go] to depart, especially in a hurry.

do a rug dance US (1950s) to take a long and passionate farewell from a loved one. (AFS)

Doc *See* corpsman

dock¹ BrN (16th c.) to deflower, ravish a woman. BrN (18th c.) to lie with a woman. USA (WWII) to deduct a certain amount of one's pay as a result of court-martial. (DVT MMD)

dock² USA (WWII) an army hospital. (MMD)

docked watch *See* dog watch

dock fever *See* yellow fever

doctor MM (18th c.) a ship's cook, who on merchantmen whalers and small naval vessels often filled the role of ship's surgeon or doctor. (SLA) (*see also* cook)

doctor's discharge MM (1880s) a false discharge. An ordinary seaman paid the ship's cook (doctor) to write up phony discharge papers stating that he was an able-bodied seaman (a higher rating than he deserved), thereby entitling the sailor to a greater sum of discharge pay when he presented his papers to pay clerk. (TON) (*see also* doctor)

dodger BrA (WWI) a sandwich. The meat often slipped out from between the slices of bread, thus dodging the would-be consumer.

dodge the column BrA>USA (WWI–WWII) to avoid dirty, hard, or hazardous work. Phrase began with British mobile forces serving in South Africa and India and was probably picked up by American troops serving alongside the British during WWI. (GWD) (*see also* ghost, goldbrick, gold brick, lead-swinger)

dodo USAAF (WWII) an aviation cadet who had not soloed; ground school pilot. Both named after flightless and extinct dodo bird. (AFR AFS ATK GWD MMD)

doff MM/BrN>USN (14th c.–present) [Middle English *doff*, to remove] to remove an article of clothing. (DWO)

dog BrN>USN (15th c.–present) a piece of metal shaped into a latch or handle and used to secure hatches, scuttles, and watertight

doors. USA (1910–present) foot, although usually used in the plural: *My dogs are killing me!* USA (WWII) infantryman's term for cavalryman's horse. USMC (1980s) another man's girlfriend. (MAN OST PAT SAM SID)

dog and bystander USA (WWII) life-size figures, both prone and standing, used as targets on practice range. (MMD)

dog-barking navigator MM (19th c.) a seagoing sailor's term of insult for a coastal navigator, who was never out of sight of land and supposedly navigated by the sounds of dogs barking on shore. (AST)

dogface NatAm (1840s) Native American pejorative for a white, western soldier, many of whom went unshaven. USMC/ USN (WWI–Korean War) a soldier in the army (as opposed to a Marine, sailor, or airman). USA (WWI–Korean War) an infantryman (as opposed to an artilleryman or cavalryman); a raw recruit (the implication being that he was dirty, unshaven, and not real military material). (ASC IHA MMD PAT SAM) (*see also* doggie, recruit)

dog fat USA (WWII) government-issue butter. (GWD)

dogfight Br>USA/USMC/USN/USAF (WWI–present) an aerial combat between fighter planes, which circle each other like dogs preparing to fight. (*see also* air combat maneuver)

dogged up USA (WWII) dressed in one's best uniform or civilian street clothes. (GWD)

doggie USMC (1960s) army infantryman.

doghouse MM>USA (18th–20th c.) a small deckhouse that served as officers' quarters on slave brigs. Like doghouses, they were small and cramped. To be *in the doghouse* came to mean being in a very difficult situation or in trouble for making a mistake. USA (WWII) guardhouse. (GWD OST TON) (*see also* jail)

dogleg USA (WWII) a chevron that denotes rank and resembles the raised hind leg of a dog about to urinate; aka dog's leg. (MMD)

dog robber CSA/USA/USAAF>USAF (1860s–1960s) officer's orderly or servant, who supposedly stole scraps left by the officer (dog) he served. (AFR AFS ATK MCT) (*see* striker)

dogsbody MM (18th–20th c.) a pudding made of peas boiled in a cloth sack; a junior officer. (SLA)

dog show USA (WWI–Korean War) a foot inspection conducted by a medical officer. Because infantry travels on its feet, dog shows were a regular ritual. (GWD) (*see* dog)

dog tags USA/USMC/USN/USAF/USCG (WWI–present) identification discs that resemble old-style dog licenses. (WWI) a tag with "U.S.A." stamped on one side and name and serial number on the other. (WWII–present) two tags, each bearing a serviceman's name, serial number, and blood type. Some versions include religion, next of kin, and home address. One tag remains with the corpse, wedged between the front teeth, while the other goes to the records office. USA (1960s) an identification bracelet, tags, or jewelry. (AFS ATK GWD MCT) (*see also* crash tag)

dog tent USA (1860s–WWII) a small two-man tent, possibly so named because it was occupied by two dogfaces (soldiers). In the 1860s, dog tents were made of drill and sometimes rubberized to make them waterproof. From WWI to WWII, they were made of canvas. (EMP IHA) (*see* dogface, pup tent)

dog vane BrN>USN (17th c.–WWII) a strip of cloth or a line hung from a vertical pole and used to show the direction from which the wind was blowing. In days of sail, it was set in a place where it could be seen by the officer of the deck and the helmsman. (BJM OST) (*see* OOD)

dog watch BrN>USN (16th–20th c.) a rotating system of watches instituted to prevent men from standing the same watch day after day, originally called curtailed watch or docked watch. The first and second watches alternated days and times. Two dog watches existed in the old navy—the first from 4 to 6 P.M. and the second from 6 to 8 P.M. (BJM NCT OST) (*see* old navy)

doherty wagon USA (1860s–WWI) a small covered wagon used to transport soldiers or, more often, officers' wives and children from post to post. (EMP)

doings BrA (WWI) jail. To be *in the doings* was to be in the guardhouse. (*see also* jail)

do it again USA (WWI–WWII) to reenlist. Often spoken in a sad tone of voice. (EMP)

dolly dancer USA (WWII) a soldier assigned to office duty who catered to the needs and whims of officers. (GWD)

dolphins USN (WWII–present) the insignia of the submarine service; aka pukin' fish, tin tunas.

domani (doh•MAH•nee) It/ItA>BrA (WWII, North Africa) [Italian *domani,* tomorrow] tomorrow. The implication was that tomorrow would never come, much as Americans use the Spanish *mañana.* (ADW)

Don BrN>USN (15th–19th c.) [Spanish *don,* duke or lord] a Spaniard. (ANE)

don BrN>USN (15th–19th c.) to put on an article of clothing. (ANE DWO)

donk BrAF (WWII) an aircraft engine, possibly from the sound made when it stopped suddenly and without warning.

donkey breakfast MM (19th c.) a sailor's mattress, which was stuffed with straw. (SLA TON)

donkey engine MM (19th c.–present) a small engine on the deck of a ship used to hoist gear and other supplies aboard using a block and tackle. Originally, the job was done by a donkey. (TON)

don't break the shovel USA (WWII) a sarcastic comment made to one who obviously was not working hard. (SID)

don't give me a bad time USA (WWII) don't bother me! (SID)

donut dollies See biscuit bitches

doodle bug USA (WWII) a light armored car used for reconnaissance duty. (AFR GWD)

doo-flicker CA (WWI) a tool, instrument, or gadget.

doo-hicky BrAF (WWI) a generic name for any small, detachable airplane fitting.

dooly BrA (WWI) [French *du lait,* milk] milk, a mispronunciation of the French term; aka doolay.

doo-mommie USA/USMC (1960s) [Viet-

namese *du ma,* (roughly) fuck your mother] fuck your mother, an expression commonly directed at the enemy. (ITF)

door knocker GrA (WWII, North Africa) an American, 37-mm antitank gun. The name arose from the sound of its shells hitting and bouncing off the sides of heavy German tanks. (FOD)

doowhistle USAAF (WWII) a new aviation cadet; anyone or anything whose name was not known or didn't come instantly to mind; aka doo-whistle, doo-willie, ducrot, dumb-flicker, dumbguard. (AFR)

doo-willie See doowhistle

dope BrA (WWI) a fool or bungler. USMC/USA/USN (1980s) a change in settings for distance and windage on a rifle. (AFS IHA PAT SAM) USA/USMC/USN (WWII–present) informative rumors. USA (ca. 1901–1906) reliable inside information. One who had such information was said to *have the dope.* (IHA) (*see also* bum dope, griff)

dope off¹ USMC (WWII) to loiter; to avoid work with forethought; aka goof off. USNA/USAAF (WWII) to act dumb or stupid. (AFR SAM)

dope off² USNA (WWII) a fat, lazy, or stupid person. (AFR)

dope out USA (1906) to figure out. (IHA)

dopey crate USAAF (WWII) an airplane that was poorly constructed and/or difficult to fly. (GWD)

DORA (DOH•ra) BrA (WWI) Defense of the Realm Act, wartime regulations that attempted to control every aspect of life in the British Empire, especially in Great Britain.

do them in BrA (WWI) to kill German soldiers. (AGE)

double darbies BrN/USN (17th–20th c.) shackles that bound hands and feet together. (RAS) (*see also* darbies)

double dead USA/USMC (1960s, Vietnam) indisputably dead; aka very dead. (SAL)

double Dutch MM (18th c.) unintelligible speech, nonsense. (IHA SLA)

double private USA (WWII) a corporal, from the two stripes on his sleeves. (SID)

double the grog tub USN (19th c.) to

attempt to get back in line for grog issue. Sailors doubling the grog tub were usually stopped by the master-at-arms and/or an armed Marine sentry posted for that purpose. (RAS) (*see* grog, master-at-arms)

double time USA (18th c.–present) a marching cadence of 180 36-inch steps per minute.

double-time USMC (WWII) to move at double time specifically or quickly in general. (SAM) (*see* double time, on the double)

double veteran USA (1960s) a man who had raped and killed a Vietnamese woman.

doughboys BrN>USN (early 19th c.) hard dumplings boiled in saltwater before being eaten; aka doughballs. USA (1840s) soldiers who served in the Mexican War. They were caked with white dust and looked as if they were made of dough. USA (1860s) a seldom-used name for uniform buttons that resembled doughnuts. USA (WWI) United States servicemen in France, who preferred the name doughboys to Yanks and Sammies. USA (1930s–40s) infantrymen. (ATK IHA MMD) (*see also* Sammies, Yanks)

dough-puncher USA (WWI–WWII) baker. (MMD)

douse MM (17th–20th c.) [German/Dutch *dossen*, to take down] to take down or to put out; also spelled dowse. (BJM OST SLA)

dout (dowt) USN (1880s) to put out, as a light. (ANE)

doves *See* war hawks

DOW USA/USMC/USN/USCG/USAF (1960s) died of wounds, an entry made beside the names of mortal casualties on official lists.

downcheck USNA (WWII) a poor preflight check. (AFR)

downdraft *See* caught in a downdraft

downhill USA (WWII) the last half of one's enlistment period. (MMD)

downrange USA/USMC/USN (1900–90s) the distance between a rifleman or artillery and a target on the target range; the distance from the firing line.

downtown USA/USMC/USN/USAF (1993) any part of Mogadishu, Somalia, except for the American embassy, university, airport, and stadium.

downtown K-Mart USA/USMC/USAF/USN (1993) heavily congested market area of Mogadishu, Somalia.

downwind[1] USA (WWII) one who constantly preened before a mirror to ensure that his hair was neat and not windblown. (SID)

downwind[2] MM (18th c.) leeward (being in or facing toward the direction in which the wind was blowing); aka down the wind. (AST)

dowsie or **dowsy** *See* boozy

DP USA (1945) displaced person.

draft dodger USA/USMC/USN/USCG/USAAF (WWII–1970s) one who avoided, or attempted to avoid, being conscripted into the military. (PAT SAM)

draftee *See* recruit

drag[1] USA (WWII) lady friend, date. (MMD)

drag[2] USA (WWII) to attempt to influence a superior. (MMD)

draped USA/USMC/USN/USAAF (WWII) intoxicated, dead drunk. Possibly from the fact that intoxicated people tend to drape themselves over other people and things. (AFR MMD)

draw crabs BrA (WWI) to draw enemy fire intentionally.

draw midnight small stores USMC (WWII) to steal government food or property from other military units for the good of one's own unit; aka make a midnight requisition, moonlight. (SAM)

draw the longbow Br>USA (1300–20th c.) to be long-winded; to tell a tall tale in which such figures as distance, casualties, and other details are simply too exaggerated to be believed. From tales of Robin Hood, the famous archer who could draw the string of a longbow back farther than any other man and achieve accuracy at any range. (CWO MMD)

dreadnaught BrN>USN (16th c.–WWI) [Anglo-Saxon *dreadnaudgt*, one who fears nothing] a heavily armed ship considered almost invincible. The term was little used until 1906, when Britain launched the 17,900-ton HMS *Dreadnaught*, the first of the modern battleships. By WWI, all battleships were called dreadnaughts.

dream sheet USA (1960s) official form upon which members of the army indicated their choice of next assignment and station. Only dreamers, it was said, believed that they would get what they wanted.

dress blues and tennis shoes USMC (Korean War) dress uniform with all medals on display. (PAT SAM)

dress parade USA (1950s) a ceremony in which soldiers were in their dress uniforms and under arms. (ASC) (*see* dress uniform)

dress uniform USA (1950s) the authorized uniform for social, official, and ceremonial affairs. (ASC)

drift MM (19th c.–present) understanding, gist. (SLA) (*see* get the drift)

drifter USA (WWII) draftee (as opposed to a volunteer); aka yearling. (GWD)

drill[1] BrA>USA/USMC/USN/USAF (17th c.–present) [Dutch *drillen*, to turn] to practice a military exercise until it is habit. (MCT MD MMD)

drill[2] BrA>USA/USMC/USN/USAF (17th c.–present) [Dutch *drillen*, to turn] (17th c.–WWI) an exercise of maneuvers and tactics by troops. (WWII–present) a practice of set acts that become habitual and aid in the establishment of discipline and control; routine, as in *you know the drill*. (MCT MD MMD)

drill a hole BrA (WWI) to shoot someone with a small arm, such as a pistol, rifle, or machine gun.

drill order in USA (WWI) the order to assemble with full packs, rifle, canteen, ammunition belt, and gas mask. (AGE)

drink USN/USMC/USAAF>USAF (WWII–present) ocean, sea, any body of water. (AFS)

drink a toast MM (18th c.) to offer words that honor a dinner guest. Originally, it was the custom to place a piece of toasted bread into a hot toddy or a glass of hot mulled wine. (TON)

drive it to the hangar USAAF (WWII) to shut up or change the topic. (GWD)

drive the train USAAF (WWII) to lead two or more squadrons of planes in flight. (MMD)

drive up USAAF (WWII) to arrive. (AFR)

dropshort BrA (WWI) an artillery round that did not reach the intended target but instead fell on friendly troops; aka fallshort. (*see also* fallshort)

drub BrN>USN (17th–18th c.) to beat or thrash. (ANE DVT)

drubbing BrN>USN (17th–18th c.) a pummeling. (ANE DVT)

drum up BrA (WWI) to collect or gather together, an allusion to civilian peddlers, who sometimes used a drum to attract crowds. (SSD)

dry canteen USA (WWII) a state in which no alcohol was sold. (GWD)

dry-duck USN (19th c.) a punishment in which the convict was suspended in a painful manner above the water so that his body barely touched it. (ANE)

dry fire *See* snap in

dry flogging USN (18th–19th c.) a flogging during which the victim was permitted to wear his shirt. (ANE) (*see* flog)

dry run USA/USMC/USN/USAF/USCG (WWII–present) a practice on a rifle range without live rounds; a practice of a maneuver or drill; a rehearsal; aka dummy run. (AFR AFS ASC MCT MMD SAM)

dry seaman USN (1860s) a sailor after September 1, 1862, when Congress rescinded the sailors' beer and grog ration but not the officers' booze. (ANE)

DS USA/USMC/USN/USAF/USCG (WWI–present) detached service, temporary duty away from one's regular unit. USA (1970s) direct support. (AFR EMP)

DSC USA (WWII) Distinguished Service Cross, which is awarded for valor and is second in esteem only to the Congressional Medal of Honor. (ASC) (*see* Medal of Honor)

DSM USA (WWII) Distinguished Service Medal, awarded for outstanding merit in a position of high responsibility in time of war. (ASC)

DSO BrA (WWI) Distinguished Service Order. (1915) dick shot off, after method by which enlisted man supposedly could win the medal; aka dugout service order, because officer could win the medal by staying safely in a dugout. (EMP)

DT USA (WWII) double time march step, faster than normal movement. (AFR)

dual USAAF (WWII) to fly with an instructor in the cockpit; to go on a date with a chaperone in tow. (AFR)

dubbin USA (WWI) waterproof grease for use on boots and other leather items. (AGE)

duck USA/USAAF>USAF (WWI–Vietnam War) a draftee or inductee; a small sum of money deducted from one's pay by order of a military court. USAAF (WWI) an amphibious plane. (1960s) an American POW who cooperated with the enemy. (AFR ATK) (*see* POW)

duckboard glide BrA (WWI) the act of navigating a trench and its duckboards at night with little or no light. (*see* duckboards)

duckboard harrier BrA (WWI) a company messenger or runner who had to find his way through a maze of trenches. (*see* duckboards)

duckboards BrA (WWI–WWII) wooden planks placed in the bottom of muddy trenches to keep passing soldiers' feet dry; aka mats. (1916) ribbon bars. (AGE EMP) (*see* ribbon bars)

duck fucker BrN (18th c.) a sailor assigned to tend to the live poultry, intended for the consumption of the officers, aboard a man-of-war. (DVT) (*see also* manger)

ducrot *See* doowhistle.

dud USA/USMC/USN/USAF/USCG (18th c.–present) [Dutch *dood*, dead] an unexploded shell; a disappointing experience; one who is dull, boring, or useless. (AFR GWD MCT) (*see also* clown, feather merchant, foul ball)

dude *See* recruit

duff MM (18th c.–WWI) a pudding made from flour or ground biscuit, water, molasses, and slush boiled together in a canvas sack or baked in a shallow pan. (1880s) human backside. USN>USA>USAAF (18th c.–WWII) a pudding made from flour or crushed biscuit mixed with water, slush, and dehydrated raisins or plums. USN (18th–20th c.) any sweet or candy. USA>USAAF (WWI–WWII) any candy, sweet, or pastry. (AFR ANE) (*see also* dandy funk, duffer, slush)

duffel MM (17th c.) [Belgian town of Duffel, noted for its production of heavy, coarse wool that was often used for sailors' clothing] a sailor's clothing and other transportable items; also spelled duffle. (DWO OST) (*see also* duffel bag, seabag)

duffel bag USA (WWI–present) a heavy canvas bag in which a soldier carries all his belongings. (AFR OST) (*see also* duffel)

duffer MM (18th c.) a common sailor (one who eats duff); a common, low-class peddler; a woman who assisted smugglers; one who was stupid or a coward. (ANE)

duff gen (duff jen) BrA (WWII, North Africa) unreliable information. (SSD) (*see* gen)

dugout BrA>USA/USMC (WWI–WWII) a chamber dug into the side of a trench. Dugouts provided protection for soldiers in the trenches and served as living quarters, hospitals, and more. (AGE EMP)

dugout disease BrA (WWI) a mysterious nervous disorder, probably related to shell shock, that caused men to stay deep in the safety of a dugout whenever possible. At the time, it was seen officially as a form of cowardice. (AGE EMP) (*see also* battle fatigue, dugout king, PTSD, shell shock)

dugout king BrA (WWI) an officer or enlisted man who stayed in the dugouts out of fear of dugout disease. (EMP) (*see* dugout disease, PTSD, shell shock)

dugout service order *See* DSO

Dulalley tap USA (WWII) sunstroke. (GWD)

dulay and dupan (doo•LAY and doo•PAN) BrA (WWI) [French *du lait and du pan*, milk and bread] milk and bread. Another attempt by the British soldier to speak French. (AGE)

dumb bomb USA/USMC/USN/USAF (1960s) a bomb not guided by laser or radio technology, a bomb that fell blindly through the air when released from a plane and may or may not have hit its target.

dumbflicker *See* doowhistle

dumbguard *See* doowhistle

dumb insolence BrA (WWI) the act of purposely breaking wind while on parade as an expression of one's opinion of the army; aka silent insolence.

dummy run *See* dry run

dump¹ BrA (WWII) to put a person down in any possible manner.

dump² USA/USMC (1960s) a morgue, a place where human corpses were piled.

dumpster diving USA/USMC/USAF (1960s) destitute Vietnamese's practice of going through American trash dumpsters and salvaging anything that could be used or eaten. USMC (1970s–90s) act of rescuing food discarded from the mess hall.

dungarees Br>USN/USMC (18th c.) [Hindu *dungri*, work clothes] a sailor's work clothes (as opposed to his regular uniform). (TON)

dunnage MM (19th c.) a sailor's clothes and personal gear; originally, lumber used to shore up the cargo in a ship's hull. A sailor's clothes "shored him up" and made him look like a true sailor. (TON)

DuPont lure USA/USMC/USN (1960s) a C-4 explosive or hand grenade detonated under water to stun fish, which floated to the surface and were easily caught. From the DuPont Chemical Company, which manufactured munitions used in the Vietnam War.

dust USN (19th c.) crumbs and broken bits of hardtack. (ANE) (*see* hardtack, midshipman's nuts)

dustbin USAAF (WWII) machine gun turret on the underbelly of a bomber. (GWD)

dust disturbers USA (WWI–WWII) infantry. (EMP)

dust inspector USA (WWII) a very fussy officer who noticed the smallest particles of dust during inspections. (ATK)

dust off USA/USMC (1960s) to evacuate by helicopter.

Dusty *See* Jack o' the Dust

Dutch consolation USN (19th c.) unwelcome or unwanted news or advice; negative advice. (ANE)

Dutch courage BrN>USN (1812) false courage induced by the consumption of alcohol. The Dutch issued their sailors liberal amounts of schnapps immediately before they went into battle. (IHA NCT TON)

Dutch leave USA/USN/USMC (1898) absence without leave or permission. (ANE) (*see also* AOL, AWOL, French leave)

Dutchman USN (1960s) a patch or plate used to cover a defect or crack in metal sheeting or plate. Possibly from the age-old belief that the Dutch will go to extremes to save money and material. The term may be several centuries old.

Dutchman's breeches MM (18th c.) a small patch of blue sky, "enough to make a pair of breeches for a Dutchman," in the midst of the clouds that signaled the beginning of the end of a storm. (NCT)

Dutch reckoning USN (19th c.) a badly done day's work. The phrase mocked immigrants, who were considered a threat to the "American" workforce. (ANE)

duty Br>USA/USMC/USN/USAF/USCG (13th c.–present) [Old French *deu*, owed> Anglo-Norman *duete*, to owe] an obligation, something owed, whether conduct, service, or items. (DWO)

duty officer USA/USAAF>USAF (WWII–present) the officer on call for emergencies for a set period of time, usually from 4 P.M. to 8 A.M.; aka DO. (AFS ASC) (*see also* officer of the day, officer of the deck)

duty roster USAF (1950s) a posted listing of each person's assigned duty. (AFS)

duty station USA>USAAF>USAF (WWII–present) post base station, to which one is sent to serve his tour of duty; one's assigned military post. (AFS)

dynamite pills USA (WWII) very effective laxatives. (SID)

E

EA USA (1970s–present) engagement area.

EAD USA/USAF (1950s) extended active duty; a formerly active member of the service serving time in the Army Reserve. (AFS ASC)

eagle USA (June 11, 1832–present) the insignia worn by full colonels in the army and Marine corps. (ATK) (*see also* buzzard) USAAF (WWII) a flying student; a bomb. (MMD)

eagle

eagle day USA (WWI–WWII) payday. From the eagle on silver dollars used for payment. (GWD) (*see also* eagle farts, ghost walk)

eagle eye USA (1960s) a periodic surveillance patrol that examined groups of Vietnamese civilians, their homes, and their vehicles, in a continuing search for North Vietnamese regulars or members of the Vietcong. (*see* Vietcong)

eagle farts USMC (Korean War) what happens on payday; aka eagle shits. (SAM) USN (WWI–WWII) aka eagle screams. (BJM) (*see also* eagle day)

eagle shits *See* eagle farts

eagle screams *See* eagle farts

eagle walker USA (WWII) an orderly who accompanies a colonel wherever he goes. (GWD) (*see* eagle)

E and E USA/USMC/USAF/USN/USCG (1960s) "Escape and Evasion," a handbook that spells out dos and don'ts for personnel facing capture by the enemy; the act of dodging dangerous work: *If the old man wants volunteers, I'm going on E and E.*

ear banger USA/USMC (WWII) an enlisted man who constantly talked to or attempted to talk to officers and was believed to be currying their favor. (SAM SID)

early out USA/USMC/USN/USAF (1960s) a sudden and unexpected end to one's tour of duty in Vietnam; an honorable, yet less than ideal, discharge "for the good of the service."

earn BrA (WWI) to steal, work for, or win.

earn your stripes USN (19th c.–present) to be flogged so intensely that scars result. USA: to work toward promotion to NCO. (RAS) (*see* NCO)

East Overshoe *See* Bumfuck, Egypt

easy! USN (1960s) an order to be careful.

EAT USAF (1950s) earliest arrival time. (AFS)

E-base USNA (WWII) the elimination base, which was set aside for V-5 air cadets eliminated from the flight program. (AFR) (*see* United States Navy Volunteer Reserve)

e-boat GrN>USN (WWII) a fast German patrol boat. (MMD)

ECCM USA (1970s) electronic counter-counter measures, satellite surveillance.

ED BrA (WWI) extra duty, assigned as punishment. (EMP)

effectiveness report USAF (1950s) an evaluation of an air force officer's command ability, professional growth, and general competence. (AFS)

efficiency expert USA/USMC (1960s) a member of the army special forces. (*see* special forces)

efficiency pay USA (WWI) additional pay granted as a reward for long military service. (EMP)

egg[1] USN>USAAF (19th c.–WWI) [Anglo-Saxon *eggion*, to urge on] to provoke, push to excess: *Don't egg him on, or we'll have a real problem.* (ANE)

egg[2] USAAF (WWII) a bomb dropped from an airplane.

eggbeater USA (WWII) a propeller-driven aircraft. (AFR)

egg in your beer USA (WWII) too much of a good thing. (ATK)

egg sucker USA/USMC (1960s) an enlisted

83

man who brownnoses or kisses up to officers.

eight USA (1960s) one with an E-8 rating, a master sergeant.

eight ball USA (WWII) one who is constantly in trouble. (SID)

82nd Airborne Division USA (WWII–present) aka the All-American, Almost Airborne, Eighty Deuce, and Air-Mattress during WWII. They 82nd was known as the All-African, All-Afro, and eighty niggers and two white men division during the Vietnam war, from a belief that more blacks than whites were present.

elbow grease Br>USA (18th c.) hard labor done with extra effort. (DVT)

el Cid USA (1960s) Central Intelligence Agency; any spy and intelligence organization, but especially the CIA.

electro-optically guided bomb *See* EOGB

elephant dugout BrA (WWI) very large, steel-reinforced dugout. (AGE)

elephant grass USA/USMC/USAF (1960s) high jungle grass with razor-sharp leaves, found in Vietnamese highlands.

elephant gun *See* M79 grenade launcher

elephant intestines USA/USMC (1960s) long canvas tubes used by Vietcong and North Vietnamese to carry rice and other foodstuffs.

elephant trap USA (WWII) a large hole dug for garbage burial. (GWD)

eleven bang-bang USA (1960s) MOS 11-B combat infantryman; aka eleven bravo, eleven bush. (*see* MOS)

eleven bravo *See* eleven bang-bang

eleven bush *See* eleven bang-bang

eleven on a side BrA (WWI) army regulations prescribed that an officer's mustache was to be kept pencil thin and neatly trimmed. Soldiers joked that there were eleven hairs on each side. (*see also* Australian eleven)

elm tree pump BrA (1750s) ship's pumps fashioned from hollow elm trees. These pumps could issue twenty-five gallons a minute. (MOW) (*see also* chain pump, pumpdale)

ELS USMC (1980s) entry level separation, a discharge from the United States Marine Corps while still in basic training.

Elsie USA (WWI) monetary fine imposed by military court: *He got a ten-dollar Elsie for returning late from leave.* (EMP)

EM USA (WWII–present) enlisted man.

embalmed meat USA/USAAF (WWII) canned meat. (AFR) (*see also* canned horse, canned Willie)

embark MM (16th c.) to board a boat. (1830s) to enter into an affair of any nature. (DWO TLL) (*see also* debark)

embrasure CSA/USA (1860s–WWII) an opening in a parapet that enabled artillery pieces to have a protected field of fire without exposing gun or crew to direct enemy fire. (MD MMD)

emergency leave USA (1950s) leave granted because of a personal emergency. It could not exceed the leave earned to date plus thirty days. (ASC)

emma gee Br/USA (WWI) machine gun, especially a German machine gun. "Emma gee" was the verbal expression of the abbreviation MG. Such codes were employed extensively in an attempt to enhance clarity and avoid confusion when using wireless or field telephones. (MMD)

emplane USAF (1950s) to board an aircraft. (AFS)

encamp Br>USA (1768–WWII) to set up camp for an army on the march. USA (1942) to place a person or unit in camp. (MDB MMD)

end on USN (1960s) said of a vessel approaching bows on, an action likely to result in a head-on collision, as in *she's coming end on at full speed!* Also applied to people or vehicles other than ships. (*see* bows on)

E-nothing USA (1960s) an imaginary rank lower than that of a recruit, one who simply does not rate.

enough room to swing a cat USN (18th–19th c.) ample space in which to use a cat-o'-nine-tails without fouling its tails in overhead beams or rigging. The bosun's mate stretched the cat out behind him and took full overhead (180-degree) swings. (*see also* flog, let the cat out of the bag, master-at-arms, rigging) (RSC)

en repos (en ray•POZ) FrA (WWI) [French *en repos*, to be at peace or resting] the status of a unit or men who have been taken out of the front lines for a rest. (WWW)

ensign BrN>BrA>USA/USN/USAF (16th c.–present) [Old Norman *ensigne*, badge] the officer who carried the national flag, or ensign, in a cavalry troop. BrN (16th c.) USN (1862) a passed midshipman, not yet posted to the rank of lieutenant; a large flag flown from the mizzen mast of a ship at sea. BrA (17th c.) the lowest-ranking lieutenant, who traditionally carried the unit's colors. BrA (1790s–1815) a second lieutenant in the infantry. USA (1861) the lowest officer rank in the infantry. During the twentieth century, the rank changed to second lieutenant in United States services except the navy, where it was retained and its bearers addressed as mister or ensign. USN/USAF (1940s) the national flag. (AFS MD MMD NCT OST TON)

Ensign Ralph *See* ralph

entanglement CSA/USA (1860s) barrier against attacking infantry or cavalry formed of trees felled in such a way that their branches became intermeshed. (MD)

EOGB USA/USMC/USN/USAF (1972–present) electro-optically guided bomb, which is guided to the target by the aircraft that drops it.

epaulette Fr>Br>USA/USMC/USN (mid-18th c.–1940s) a bundle of ribbons secured to shoulder straps, a symbol of an officer. BrN/USN (mid-18th c.–1940s) aka swabs, because of resemblance to mops, or swabs. (late 18th c.) gold or silver knotted cording or fringe attached to quality fabric or metal shoulder boards. (NCT) (*see* swabs)

EPD USMC (WWII) extra police (cleanup) duty. (SAM) (*see* police)

EPW USA (1970s–present) enemy prisoner of war.

erk BrN>USAAF (WWII) a British sailor's term for an airman; in American parlance, an airplane mechanic. (GWD)

errand boy USAF (1950s–60s) a pilot whose daily flights carried military correspondence; aka Pony Express.

ersatz valentia (air•SATZ va•LEN•tee•ya) GrA (1942, Russia) jury-rigged snow boots, made of straw with wooden soles. Five pairs were issued to each company. (TOC)

escort of honor USA (WWI–1950s) group of men assigned to escort VIPs. It was meant as an honor to the VIPs, but it was also an honor to be chosen as an escort. (ASC)

escort of the colors USA (WWI–1950s) the ceremony of retrieving and receiving the colors. (WWI–WWII) the escorting of the national colors or unit standards by a color guard. (ASC MMD) (*see* color guard, colors, standard)

E-7 *See* gunnery sergeant

esplanade CSA/USA (1860s) area within a fortification where troops could be drilled. (MD)

esprit de corps CSA/USA (1860s) [French *esprit de corps*, spirit of the body] pride and brotherhood felt among and exercised by the members of a military unit. (MD)

estaminet BrA (WWI) small French tavern where one could get French beer at a penny per glass. (EMP) (*see also* muddy water)

ETA USAF/USN/USMC (1950s) estimated time of arrival. (AFS WEA) (*see also* ATA, ATD)

état major FrA (1790s–WWI) a staff officer. (WWW)

ETC USAF (1950s) estimated time of completion of a task. (AFS)

ETD USAF (1950s) estimated time of departure. (AFS)

ETE USAF (1950s) estimated time en route. (AFS)

e-tool USA (1960s) entrenching tool.

ETR USAF (1950s) estimated time of return. (AFS)

EUCOM (ee•U•comm) USA (1950s) European Command. (ASC)

evak'd (EE•vact) USA (1960s) evacuated from the battlefield.

evening dress uniform USAF (1950s) special uniform worn by officers for diplomatic and state functions. (AFS)

evening gun USA (19th c.–present) the gun that is fired to signal the lowering of the national colors at the evening retreat. (ASC MMD) (*see* retreat)

even keel *See* on an even keel

every bullet has its billet BrA (WWI) a British soldier's expression that arose after the brutal battle of the Somme in 1916, a recognition that everyone has to die sometime.

everything is jake USA (WWII) everything is all right. (GWD)

EW USA (1970s) electronic warfare.

excess leave USA (1950s) leave, without pay, above and beyond all accrued or advance leave. (ASC) (*see also* advance leave, AWL, AWOL)

exec USN>USAF (1881–present) executive officer (second in command) of a man-of-war, military unit, or aircraft; aka first luff. (SEA) (*see also* first lieutenant)

exercise the landing gear USAAF (WWII) to walk, use one's legs; aka exercise the running gear. (GWD)

expectant USA (1960s) a wounded man who is expected to die.

expense magazine CSA/USA (1860s) a small powder magazine placed in each bastion of a fortress for immediate use by those in that position. (MD)

expert USA (1775–late 1800s) an excellent marksman, one who is better than just a good shot. (20th c.) anyone who scores very high on the shooting range. (ATK) (*see also* sharpshooter)

WWII expert marksman's badge

extend USA/USMC/USN/USAF (1960s) to volunteer for an extra tour of duty in Vietnam.

extra duty[1] USA/USMC/USN (1860s–1920s) special duty performed by enlisted personnel; a detail for which extra money is paid. USA/USMC (WWI–1960s) special or extra work for which a soldier received additional pay. (WWII–present) additional work assigned as punishment for a class A offense. In USMC, extra duty means walking or running with a rifle in the company of an NCO for a prescribed amount of time. (AFR ASC MMD) (*see also* class A offense, extra duty pay, NCO)

extra duty[2] USA/USMC (1960s) to be extracted from the battlefield by helicopter.

extra duty pay USA/USN/USMC/USAF (19th–20th c.) additional pay for special assignments above and beyond pay based on one's specialist rating. (AFR MMD)

extra time USNA (WWII) extra flight instruction or training. (AFR AFS)

eye relief USMC (1980s) distance on a rifle between the eye of the rifleman and the rear sight of his weapon.

eyeties BrA (WWII) Italians, both civilian and military. (ADW)

eyewash Br>USA/USMC/USN/USAF (WWI–Korean War) lies in official bulletins; superficial additions intended to make things look good on the surface but not necessarily better or more effective—for example, the beautification of the post/base in preparation for an inspection. (ASC GWD MMD)

F

FA USA (1950s) field artillery. USMC (1980s) first aid.

FAAD (fad) USMC (1980s) forward antiair defense.

FAC USA (1970s) forward air controller.

face the music USA>CSA (pre-1830s–60s) to be dismissed from the regiment in a protracted ceremony. With the entire regiment watching, disgraced soldiers had the insignia and buttons removed from their uniforms and then faced the regimental band, which played the "Rogue's March." Those being punished then followed the regimental fife and drums as they marched through the line of assembled troops. (1851) to face a difficult situation or the owing of a debt. (CWO)

faded USA (WWI) said of something that was stale, flat, or unprofitable. (WWW)

FADR USA (WWI) Field Artillery Drill Regulations. (WWW)

fag¹ BrA/BrN>USA/USN/USMC/USAF (18th c.–present) a servant to an officer. Br>USA (WWI–WWII) cigarette, possibly from a comparison of the smell of a burning bundle of wood, or faggot, and the smell of a cigarette; aka choker. (AGE ANE DVT MMD) USNA (1980s–present) acronym for fighter attack guy, a rude reference to a fighter pilot. (AGE MMD) (*see also* faggot, gasper)

fag² BrN>USN (18th c.) to beat. USN (19th c.) to untwist or fray the end of a line. (ANE DVT)

faggot Fr>Br>USA/USN/USMC/USAF (18th c.–present) [Old French *faggot*, bundle of sticks] a bundle of sticks for a campfire. BrA (1700) one who gave up pay to avoid service with his regiment, considered something less than a man because he did not perform the duties of a soldier. (1768) a bundle of wood stuffed into a military coat with a hat on top that represented an absent soldier at roll call. This way, when a nose count was taken, he was counted as present. USN (1888) one hired by a recruit to serve in his place, a paid substitute. US (20th c.) a homosexual, possibly from the British definition of 1700. (ANE DVT)

fag issue BrA (WWI) the regular Sunday issue of government cigarettes. (AGE)

faint wagon USA (WWII) army ambulance. (SID)

fair-weather friend USN (1885) someone who can be counted on only when times are good; aka fair weather sailor. (ANE)

fairy light BrA (WWI) a flare, a pun on Very light, named for the man who invented that type of flare. (*see* Very light)

fall in USA/USMC (WWI–present) to assemble in formation prior to an inspection, parade, or drill. (PAT SAM)

fall out USA/USN/USMC/USAF (19th c.–present) to leave formation; to leave ranks but be ready to return to the proper formation. (ASC PAT SAM)

fallshort BrA (WWI, especially 1915–16) an artillery round that fell among friendly troops due to worn gun barrels and faulty ammunition; aka dropshort.

false colors See sail under false colors

false muster USN (19th c.) incorrect report of the number of men in a ship's company; aka Quaker muster. (ANE) (*see also* Quaker guns)

fancy man USN (1860s) a regular informer for the master-at-arms. (RAS) (*see* master-at-arms, white mice)

fancywork USN (19th c.–present) macramé, knotted designs that decorate the interiors of ships; aka lace. (ANE MAN)

FANG USNA (1970s–present) acronym for the fictitious Florida Air National Guard or, more commonly, Fucking Air National Guard, used by regular naval fliers to insult Air National Guardsmen.

fang bosun USN (1980s–present) the ship's dentist.

fanny USAAF (WWII) the tail section of an aircraft. (GWD)

Fanny See FANY

Fanny Adams BrA (WWI) nonsense, fuck it all.

fantassin FrA (WWI) [French *fantassin*, infantryman] infantryman. (WWW)

fan-tod USN (19th c.) a nervous or fidgety officer. (ANE)

FANY BrA (WWI) First Aid Nursing Yeomanry, a women's unit organized prior to the war that served with British and French units at the front; also spelled Fanny. During the war the unit traded horse-drawn ambulances for motorized ones.

farangs (fah•RANGZ) USA/USMC (1960s) foreigners.

farmer USA (1860s) aka hay shaker, hen wrangler. (LRY)

fart sack USA/USMC/USN (WWII–present) a bed or sleeping bag. (SAM)

fascine (fa•SHEEN) CSA/USA (1860s–WWII) a cylindrical bundle of wood used in the building of fortifications. (MD MMD)

fast mover USA (1960s) a jet fighter plane.

fat USA (1960s) personnel in a unit in excess of its regulation strength.

fat cat USA (WWII) one who received special treatment and favors. (PAT)

fat dog GrAF (WWII) a large formation of Allied Forces bombers and fighters. (TOC) (*see* Allied Forces)

fat friend USA (WWII) a military observation balloon; aka flying elephant. (GWD)

fat head BrN (1750s) the sensation of having one's mouth or head feel as if it had been filled with copper coins. A fat head often resulted from sleeping in a crowded, stuffy berth.

fathom[1] MM (12th c.–present) [Anglo-Saxon *faehom*, distance between fingertips of one's outstretched arms>English *fathom* (16th c.)] a nautical unit of measurement equal to six feet of water depth. (BJM SEA SLA)

fathom[2] MM (18th c.–present) to determine the depth of a body of water. (20th c.) to comprehend or understand. (NCT TON) (*see also* sound)

fatigue duty USA (19th c.) work detail that does not involve drilling or training of a military nature; aka fatigue. USA/USN/USMC/USAF (1800–present) manual labor (as opposed to regular duty). Fatigue duty included, but was not limited to, building fortifications and surveying roads. As of March 2, 1819, enlisted men east of the Rocky Mountains who were assigned to fatigue duty for ten days or more were paid an extra twenty-five cents a day and mechanics and teamsters forty cents per day. After August 4, 1854, the additional pay was thirty-five cents for fatigue duty of ten days or more and fifty cents for mechanics and teamsters for men stationed west of the Rocky Mountains. As of March 2, 1829, soldiers on fatigue duty were also issued an extra gill (two ounces) of whiskey per day. USA/USMC (1830s–present) any duty that requires the men to wear a working, or fatigue, uniform. (ASC ATK MD MMD) (*see* fatigues)

fatigues USA/USN/USMC/USAF (WWI–1950s) work uniform; combat uniform; aka fatigue clothes. From WWII through the 1950s, fatigues were generally made from denim, heavy cotton, or a similar material. (AFR) (*see also* fatikees, utility clothing)

fatikees (FAT•ee•kayz) USA (1960s) standard jungle fatigues or combat uniform, a purposeful mispronunciation. (*see also* fatty-gewa)

fat squad See MRP

fatty-gewa (fat•ee-JEE•wah) USA (1960s) fatigues, a mocking mispronunciation. (*see also* fatikees)

FEAF (feef) USAF (1950s) Far East Air Forces, air forces stationed in Asia. (AFS)

feathered USAF (1950s) stopped cold, especially after having been chewed out by a commanding officer or any officer of superior rank. (SLA) (*see* chew out)

feather merchant USA/USMC/USN (WWII–Korean War) a civilian employee of the government, particularly a lazy one; a naval reserve officer commissioned upon going on active duty; a sailor with a soft or easy job; a physically small Marine; a useless Marine. (GWD PAT SAM) (*see also* clown)

feather the prop USAAF>USAF (WWII–1950s) to stop the propeller from turning in the event of engine malfunction by turning the plane into the wind so as to reduce the drag. (AFS)

FEB (feb) USAF (1950s) Flying Evaluation Board. (AFS)

Federal CSA (1860s) a member of the Union army; aka Fed, Blue, blueback, and, most commonly, bluebelly. (IHA)

Federals CSA (1860s) the Union army. (*see*

Federal)

fed up Br>USA/USMC (WWI) totally bored and disgusted. As the British soldiers often put it, "Fed up, fucked up, and far from home." (EMP)

feel the way MM (19th c.) to proceed with caution. (BJM)

feint Br>USA (17th c.–present) a false attack or diversion. (DVT)

Feldazaret (felt•ah•zah•ret) GrA (WWI) field hospital. (WWW)

feloos BrA (1940, North Africa) money; aka akkers, disasters. (DRA) (*see also* ackers)

fencible BrA>USA (1790s–1815) a member of a local militia organized for home defense. In 1814, some of the defenders of Fort McHenry were Sea Fencibles, sailors assigned to man shore batteries.

fender belly USN (1960s) an overweight sailor.

ferman bag USN (19th c.) a small canvas bag in which tobacco was stored. (ANE) (*see also* ditty bag)

FFI FrA (WWII) Forces Français de L'Intérieur, the original resistance forces. (TOC)

fid BrN>USN (18th c.) a twisted fuse inserted into a gun's vent and used to set off the powder charge. (DVT)

Fiddler's Green MM (18th c.) heaven, the place to which a sailor's soul rose when he died. His body went below, to Davy Jones's locker. (SLA) (*see also* Jones, Davy)

fid of tobacco BrN>USN (18th c.) a quid, plug, or twist of tobacco, from its resemblance to the gunner's fid. (DVT) (*see* fid)

field USA/USMC/USAF (WWII–1960s) combat zone; any location in the combat zone or away from the base of operations. (AFR) (*see also* in the field)

field day Br>USA (1750s) a day spent in military exercises and maneuvers. (1860s) the removal of troops from the combat area to a safer place for practice and drill. USN (1900) a day set aside for the general maintenance of one's clothing and gear. USMC (1900) usually, Friday, a day designated for barracks cleanup in preparation for Saturday

inspection. (MD SAM WEA)

field fire USMC (1980s) rifle practice under simulated battle conditions, with live rounds.

field first USA (1960s) an unofficial non-commissioned officer's rank conferred on the sergeant who oversaw the unit when the first sergeant was absent. No increase in pay was connected with such a promotion. (*see* NCO)

field grade USA/USMC (1960s) the rankings of officers between captain and brigadier general. (AFS) (*see also* field officer)

Field Grey BrA (WWI) a German soldier, from his grey-green uniform. A far less popular term than Jerry. (*see also* Jerry)

field marshal BrA (1640s) title created to distinguish a commander of troops in the field from a marshal of the courts. A field marshal commanded all of the troops on a battlefield. In the twentieth century, the field marshal is the equivalent of a five-star general in the United States Army.

field music USMC (WWII) music supplied by the bugler. (SAM)

field officer BrA (1768) the commander of a regiment, usually a colonel. USA/USMC (1861–WWI) an officer with the rank of major, lieutenant colonel, or colonel. Prior to WWI, field officers were mounted on horseback so they could see and be seen by their troops; this enhanced the officers' effectiveness and bolstered troop morale. (WWI–present) an officer from the rank of second lieutenant to colonel who commands troops in a combat situation. (ASC ATK EMP MD MDB MMD)

field of fire USA/USMC (1960s–present) an area of ground covered by fire from weapons.

field phone USA/USMC (WWI–1960s) a hand-cranked, battery-powered mobile telephone used in such stationary positions as headquarters, outposts, and fortifications and connected to a switchboard system by heavy-duty insulated wire. (PAT SAM)

field scarf USMC (1930s–70s) a regulation

necktie. (SAM)

field strip USA/USMC (WWII–present) to destroy cigarette butts by reducing them to unrecognizable components so that the enemy cannot determine the number of troops in an area by the remnants of smokes found there; to take apart a weapon in the field in order to clean or repair it. (PAT)

field works CSA/USA/USMC (1860s–present) temporary fortifications built in the field for the protection of troops; also spelled fieldworks. (MD MMD)

fife Swiss>Br>USA (16th c.–present) [Swiss German *Schweizerpfeiff*, Swiss pipe>English *phyfe*, *fyfe*, or *fife*] a pipe first used by Swiss mercenaries fighting in the service of Milan and brought to England by the Germans in the sixteenth century. Its sharp note can be heard above the din of battle. (CWO)

fife rail MM (17th c.) [possibly from English *fife*, belaying pin] a stoutly made collar around the base of each mast, at about waist height, with belaying pins for the securing of lines set into it. BrN (17th c.) a gathering point for Marine fifers during drill or combat. (OST TON)

fifinella (fee•fee•NELL•ah) USAAF>USAF (WWII–1960s) the female version of a gremlin. (AFS) (*see* gremlin)

fifteen and two USA/USMC (1960s) a punishment that entailed fifteen days' restriction to barracks and two hours of extra duty per day.

fifty-hour inspection USAF (1950s) mandatory check of aircraft after fifty hours of flight time. (AFS)

fifty mission cap USAAF>USAF (WWII–Korean War) a brimmed service cap from which the crown grommet had been removed in order to permit the comfortable use of a radio headset. The cap had a crushed look that was popularized by experienced pilots during WWII. (1950s) a hat that would not pass inspection. (AFS) (*see* service cap)

fighting hole USA/USMC/USN/USAF (1960s–70s) a Vietcong foxhole. (*see* foxhole)

fighting the war in triplicate USA (WWII) a nasty reference to the responsibilities of an office clerk. (SID)

fighting tools USMC/USA (WWII) government-issue eating utensils. (PAT SAM)

figurehead MM/BrN (16th c.–1900)>USN (1790–1890) a carved figure of a human, usually a woman, or a mythical beast that was secured to the bow of the ship beneath the bowsprit. The figure often was carved to reflect the name of the ship. (*see* bowsprit)

FIIGMO (FIG•mo) USA/USMC/USAF (1960s–70s) Fuck it! I've got my orders!

file Br>USA (18th–19th c.)>USAAF>USAF (20th c.) a pickpocket; an individual soldier; one who stands in line directly behind the person in front of him, like a pickpocket approaching his prey from behind. In 1768, the British army's formation was two soldiers, one in the front rank or row and one directly behind, in the second rank. (20th c.) at least three soldiers standing one behind the other. (AFR ATK DVT MCT) USA (WWI–present) a wastepaper basket in which one "files" paper; aka File 13, File 17. (AFR MCT) (1861–1960s) the keeping of papers and documents in an orderly manner and place for ready use and reference. (WWII–present) an officer on the promotion list. (AFR ATK DVT MCT)

file a flight plan USAAF (WWII) to request leave from a commander. (SID)

file boner USA (WWII) one who works hard to become a professional military man. He studied (boned up on) what he needed to know. (MCT) (*see also* bone up)

filer FrA>USA [French *filer*, to run, spin, slip] a hurried exit; a panicked retreat. *The whole unit took a filer.* (WWW)

File 17 *See* File 13

File 13 USA/USMC/USAAF (WWII) a wastepaper basket. USA (WWII) aka file, File 17. (AFS) (*see also* file)

filibuster MM (18th c.) [Dutch *vrjbuiter*, freebooter] a freebooter or pirate from the West Indies; an Englishman who preyed on Spaniards in the West Indies. (1851) an American who ran contraband and/or freedom fighters ashore to support a rebellion in South America. (DVT SLA)

fill away MM (19th c.) to turn a ship from the wind, enabling the sails to fill and the ship to sail. (BMO)

fillet of mule tool *See* horse cock

fin BrN>USN (18th–20th c.) a human arm. USN (WWII) a vertical stabilizer on an aircraft. USN (1960s) an unflattering name for one who is not SCUBA trained. (DVT MMD) (*see* guppy, SCUBA)

find out the score USA (WWII) to obtain accurate information. (MMD)

finger charge USA/USMC (1960s–70s) a booby trap that was about the size and shape of a human finger.

fire a bale of hay USN (19th c.) to fire a ship's gun without having placed shot in the barrel. The result was much noise, fire, and smoke—but no damage to the enemy. (RAS)

fire and lights USN (19th c.) a nickname for the master-at-arms, the head of security aboard ship. He and his assistants were responsible for finding illegal lights and fires and enforcing lights-out. (RAS) (*see also* Jimmy Legs, master-at-arms)

fire away USN (19th c.) to speak one's mind. (ANE)

fireball USA/USMC (1960s–70s) firepower concentrated on a specific target.

fire base USA (1960s–70s) an artillery base in the boondocks. (*see* boondocks)

fire chief MM (19th c.) a Chinese coolie on a Western ship in the Far East, many of whom had a habit of venting their anger with one of the ship's fire axes. (TON) (*see* coolie)

firecracker USN (WWII) a bomb or torpedo.

fire fight USA/USMC (WWII) a struggle for fire or small arms supremacy. (1960s) the brink; a heavy engagement between forces armed with light infantry weapons. (MMD)

firefly USA (WWII) an OSS explosive device placed in gas tanks and set to go off within twenty-four hours. (*see* OSS)

fire in the hole USA/USMC (WWII–present) a warning call that an explosive charge is about to be set off. (PAT)

firemaster BrA (1768) the officer in charge

of mixing materials for fireworks or explosives. (MDB) (*see* fireworker, fireworks)

fire ship BrN>USN (16th–20th c.) a ship filled with combustibles, set afire, and permitted to drift into the enemy fleet. (18th–19th c.) a prostitute with venereal disease. (DVT SLA)

fire team USMC (1960s) a basic rifle team of four men—team leader, rifleman or scout, automatic rifleman, and assistant automatic rifleman.

fire track USA/USMC (1960s–70s) a flame-throwing armored vehicle.

fire up USAAF (WWII) to start aircraft engines.

fireworker BrA (1768) one of the youngest commissioned officers in a company of artillery, who worked under the direction of the firemaster. (DVT) (*see* firemaster, fireworks)

fireworks BrA (1768) explosives made by fireworkers and used for war and festivities. (WWI) night bombardment. (AGE DVT) (*see* firemaster, fireworker)

firing squad USA/USMC (19th c.–present) a group of men assigned to execute one condemned to death by court-martial; a squad of men assigned to honor a fallen comrade by firing a specific number of volleys over his grave. (AGE ASC)

first and last chance USA (WWI) the saloon nearest camp—the first stop upon leaving camp and the last stop before returning. (EMP)

First Army Division *See* Big Red One

first chop MM (18th c.) said of an item of highest quality, first-rate. Borrowed from the Chinese by British and American sailors who served in the Far East. (SLA)

first class volunteers BrN (1750s) boys who went aboard English men-of-war as fledgling midshipmen. They were required to serve as first class volunteers for one year and to pass an exam at the end of that year in order to become midshipmen. (*see* middy, midshipman, reefers, snot-nosed brats)

first duty sergeant USA (WWI) the highest-ranking line sergeant in an infantry company. (EMP) (*see* line officer)

first grader USAAF (WWII) a squadron's master sergeant. (AFS)

first John USA/USMC (WWII–1970s) first lieutenant. (SAM) (*see* first lieutenant)

first lieutenant USA/USMC (18th–19th c.) the officer in command of a company. (1900–present) the commander of a platoon within a company. USN (18th–late-19th c.) the formal title of the officer who was the second in command on a man-of-war; aka first luff. He was responsible for the overall physical condition of the ship and her crew. By the 1880s, these had become the responsibility of the executive officer, aka exec. (EMP PAT) (*see also* exec, first John, first louie)

first louie USA (1960s) first lieutenant. (SAM) (*see* first lieutenant)

first luff *See* exec, first lieutenant

first pig USA (1960s) first sergeant of the company.

first pilot USAF (1950s) a senior flight officer in command aboard an aircraft. (AFS)

fiscal year USA/USN/USMC/USAF (1950–present) July 1 through June 30. (AFS)

fish MM (18th c.–present) an ordinary sailor. USN (WWI–present) a torpedo. (DVT SAM)

fish eyes USA/USMC/USN/USAF (WWI–present) tapioca pudding. (MCT)

fishhook USN (1970s) the jagged end of a frayed rope or metal cable. (MAN)

fishtail USAAF (WWII) to swing a plane's tail from side to side during a landing in an attempt to reduce air speed. (MMD)

FIST (fist) USA (1970s) fire support team.

fit as a fiddle CSA/USA (1860s) healthy, in fine physical condition. (LRY)

fitness report USNA (WWII) a report concerning the behavior and qualifications of an officer. An officer's fitness report followed him throughout his career. (AFR)

fit to be tied CSA/USA (1860s) extremely angry. (LRY)

five by five *See* six by four

five o'clock follies USA (1960s) daily official report of allied forces victories and enemy body counts, considered by many to be largely fictional.

five-star general USA (WWII) a general of the army. (ASC) (*see* general of the army)

fixed bayonets BrA (WWI) booze made from potatoes by British POWs in Germany.

fix him a sandwich USA (WWII) to get even. Phrase was directed primarily at the enemy. (SID)

flag officer USN (title created January 16, 1857) a naval captain in command of a squadron. (WWII–1990s) a naval officer with the rank of rear admiral, vice-admiral, or admiral. (NCT)

Flags BrA>USA (WWI) nickname for one who used signal flags, or semaphores, to communicate; aka flag-wagger. (AGE)

flag-wagger *See* Flags

flak Gr>Br>USA (WWII) [German *Flieger Abwher Kanone,* antiflier cannon] antiaircraft fire; an assault of words, comments, or complaints. (ATK IHA) (*see also* Archies)

flake USA/USMC (1960s) someone proven to be a foul-up, a Jonah, or mentally off-balance. (*see* Jonah)

flake out USN (WWII) to lie down, sleep, or rest. (PAT)

flaky USA/USMC (1960s) said of a flake. (*see* flake)

flameout USAF (1950s) total burnout of a jet engine's flame. (AFS)

flamer BrA (WWI) a plane that crashes in flames.

flaming horse turd USA (1960s) insignia of the U.S. Army Ordnance Corps, a flaming bomb or old-style, hand-lit hand grenade; aka flaming onion, flaming piss pot.

U.S. Army Ordnance Corps insignia

Flander's sea lion BrA (WWI) a veteran of France's wet winter of 1914–15. (FFF)

flange head USAAF (WWII) an insulting name for an Oriental person, especially a Chinese.

flanker USA (1860s) a tall man placed on the end, or flank, of a line. His height made him highly visible, which helped to keep the battle line in order. (MCT)

flap BrN (1900) an organized, well-rehearsed action initiated in response to the sounding of an alarm. Br>USA (WWI–Korean War) an air raid; a crisis, emergency, or storm; a state of confusion. BrAF>USA/USAAF (WWI–WWII) an air raid; panic during an emergency. (MCT MMD)

flapjack USA/USMC (1990s, Somalia) a bandit or looter.

flapper Br (1770) a duckling too young to fly. Br (1880s–WWI) a girl who had not yet cut her hair but tied it up in a bun like a grown woman. US (1880s) a prostitute. (1910) an early supporter of women's rights. (1914) a French prostitute. (1920s) a wild or reckless woman. (IHA)

flapper's delight BrA (WWI) a young, inexperienced sublieutenant.

flash gun USAAF (WWII) a machine gun used in training that registered hits with beams of light rather than live ammunition. (AFR)

flash in the pan Br>USA/USMC (1768–present) the going off of the priming in a gun's pan but not the charge in the barrel; a much-heralded event that doesn't meet expectations.

flash packet MM (1820s–early 20th c.) a fast, good-looking ship; a good-looking woman; a prostitute, the implication being that she had a "packet" of venereal disease. (SFS SLA)

flash ship USN (19th c.) a ship or a person who looked great on the outside but whose interior or personality was disappointing. (ANE)

flatfoot USMC (WWII) a derogatory name for a coastguardsman; aka anchor clanker, anchorhead. (PAT) (*see also* deck ape, seaweed, swab jockey)

flat-hat USAAF/USNA>USAF (1940s–60s) to fly dangerously and with unnecessary stunts, including but not limited to flying too close to the ground. (AFS)

flat spin USAAF/USNA (WWII) descriptive of a confused state of mind. (AFR MMD)

flat tire USA (WWII) a failure. (MMD)

flattop USN/USMC (WWII–present) an aircraft carrier. USMC (1980s) an extremely short crewcut. (AFR BJM)

flea bag USA (WWII) a regulation army mattress. (GWD) (*see also* rack)

fledgling USAF (1950s) a newly trained and commissioned officer-pilot. (AFS) (*see* commission)

fleet BrN>USN (16th–18th c.) [Anglo-Saxon *fleot*, fleet] a mixed group of ships, both merchant and men-of-war. (19th c.–present) a large group of warships on a specific mission. (TWW)

Flemish accounts USN (19th c.) fiscal accounts that come up short. (ANE)

flic FrA (WWI) a civilian police detective. (WWW)

flight USAAF (WWII) a small group of aircraft of the same type, usually no more than three or four. (MMD) (*see also* wing)

flight cap See overseas cap

flight jacket USNA (WWII) a log in which a pilot's successes and failures were recorded by a superior. (AFR)

flight line See line

flight line driver USAF (1980s) one who towed aircraft into position on the flight line and removed supplies from the runways; aka Seven Level Turns. (*see line,* seven level turns)

flight pay USAF (1950s) payment beyond base pay for actual flight time; aka flying pay. (AFS) USMC (1980s–90s) money illegally borrowed from boots by the drill instructors. (*see* boot)

flight plan USNA (WWII) a written itinerary filed with the flight tower prior to takeoff. (AFR)

flimsy USAF (1950s) a thin sheet of paper on which orders were typed. (AFS)

flip USN (19th c.) a drink made from beer, hard liquor, and sugar. (ANE)

flipper USN (19th c.) a human arm or hand. (ANE)

floating Bethel USN (19th c.) an old ship fitted out as a church for sailors. Bethels were established in many ports by well-meaning gospel grinders intent upon saving poor Jack from booze and girls. (ANE) (*see* gospel grinder, Jack)

flog BrN>USN (16th c.–1915) to whip. (1915) to gain the upper hand in a bargain. (DVT RAS) USA (WWII) to sell oneself or an item in an overly aggressive manner, the implication being that the seller is beating his victim into submission. (GWD)

flogging through the fleet BrN>USN (18th–19th c.) an especially harsh punishment awarded by court-martial for offenses such as severe disrespect to a superior, striking a superior, or endangering the safety of the ship and crew. The recipient, in the company of the surgeon, the chaplain, and two boatswain's mates, was placed in the ship's boat and rowed from ship to ship. At each he was given a set number of strokes. (BMO RSC) (*see also* four cartridges of gunpowder and a bottle of brandy)

flog the clock USN (mid-19th–20th c.) to move the hands of a clock in an effort to shorten watch. (TON) (*see also* sweat the glass)

flop USA (WWII) a false alarm; a failure. (GWD)

flotsam MM (18th c.) floating debris. (MAN)

flowerpot USAAF (WWII) an aircraft's turret. (ATK MMD)

fluff off USNA (WWII) to goof off, goldbrick. (AFR) (*see* goldbrick)

flustered BrN (1607) excited by drinking alcohol. BrN>USN (19th c.) excited or worried. (ANE DVT)

fly boy BrA (WWI) a refugee. Br>US (WWI–present) an airman. (DVT PAT SAM)

fly by the seat of your pants USAAF> USAF (WWII–present) to fly by instinct or as if untrained; to be guided by instinct in any endeavor. (ATK GWD)

flying boxcar USAAF (WWII) a large bomber, named for its size. (AFR)

flying butterknife USA (1960s) the winged bayonet on a paratrooper's patch.

flying camp BrA (1768) troops on the move. Flying camps screened the movement of an army on the march or protected a garrison from an approaching enemy force. (MDB)

flying coffin USAAF (WWII) a transport plane, especially a glider made of lacquered canvas over a light wood frame. Used chiefly among airborne glider troops.

flying elephant USA (WWII) gas-filled military observation balloon; aka fat friend. (MMD)

flying gadget USAAF (WWII) an air cadet. (SID)

flying on instruments USNA (WWII) having a rough night socially. (AFR) (*see also* on instruments)

flying pay See flight pay

flying pig Br>USA (WWI–WWII) a German 9.5-inch trench mortar shell that resembled a pig in flight. (GWD)

flying shotgun USA (WWII) shrapnel. (MMD) (*see* shrapnel)

flying streamer USA (WWII) a flaming aircraft in a dive toward Earth. (MMD)

fly low USNA (WWII) to drive a vehicle at extremely high speeds. (AFR)

fly-shit water USA/USMC (1990s, Somalia) water bottled in Somalia, which had a very high fly-part content.

flyslicer USA (WWII) a mounted cavalryman armed with a sabre, from a comparison of sabres to flyswatters. (MMD)

fly solo See solo

fly the iron beam USAAF (WWII) to navigate an aircraft by following railroad tracks to the destination. (AFR MMD)

fly the wet beam USAAF (WWII) to navigate an aircraft by following a river. (AFR MMD)

fly trap BrA (WWI) an entanglement of barbed wire, especially concertina wire.

FM USA (WWI–present) field manual. (WWII) radio frequency modulation.

FMF USMC (WWII) fleet Marine force; fucking mother fuckers; free man forever. (SAM) (*see* free man forever)

FN USAF (1950s) flight nurse, a registered nurse who tended to the sick and injured aboard medical transport planes. (AFS)

FNG USA/USN/USMC/USAF (1960s–present) fucking new guy; fucking no good; fucking national guard.

FO *See* forward observer

foc'sul *See* forecastle

FOD USA (1950s) field officer of the day. (ASC) (*see* field grade officer, field officer, OD)

fogey Br>USA/USMC (18th c.) [French *féroce*, fierce, a fierce warrior; invalid soldier] (1885) a person old-fashioned in actions and dress; an old soldier; also spelled fogy, fogie. To be called an old fogey was a compliment. (WWI) an increase in an enlisted man's pay made every two years as a reward for long military service. (1918) a ten percent pay increase awarded to officers every five years. (AFS ASC BJM DVT MCT MMD)

fog off USNA (WWII) to dope off, fade out, or goof off. (AFR) (*see* dope off)

fogy stripes *See* hash marks

foo-fighter USAAF (WWII) an unidentified flying object. The first UFOs reported were glowing balls of greenish light two feet in diameter that darted about, apparently observing the aircraft that were observing them.

foot cavalry CSA (1860s) infantry noted for its ability to march quickly and fight immediately upon completion of the march.

footing USN (19th c.) a fine levied on landsmen or greenhorn by old hands, usually in the form of smuggled booze; a greenhorn's first time aloft. A greenhorn was expected to pay his footing the first time he climbed into the rigging. (ANE) (*see* aloft, greenhorn, old hand, rigging)

footlocker USA/USMC/USN/USAF (1930s–present) a trunk or chest in which personal belongings and clothes are stored. (ATK)

footlocker cocktail USA (WWII) lemon extract, which contains some alcohol. (SID)

foot pounder USA/USMC (1960s–70s) an infantryman.

foot slogger Br>USA (WWI–1960s) an infantryman. (AFR ATK DVT)

foot warbler BrA (18th c.) a cavalryman's name for an infantryman. (DVT)

forage[1] Fr>Br>USA (14th c.–WWII) [Old French *forage*, fodder, food for animals] corn, hay, or other feed for mules, horses, and cattle. (MD MMD)

forage[2] Fr>Br>USA (14th c.–WWII) [Old French *forage*, fodder, food for animals] to gather food for men and animals. USA/USMC (1840s–present) to steal food or goods. (MCT MD MMD)

forager Br>USA (14th c.–present) one assigned to gather food and supplies for men and animals. (MD)

force USA/USMC (1860–present) any large body of troops. (MD)

force a safeguard USA (WWI) to force one's way through troops guarding a person, building, or other property. (*see also* safeguard)

forced landing USAAF (WWII) a slip and fall while walking. (MMD)

fore and aft hat USN (19th–early 20th c.) an officer's dress hat with brims in front and in back. (WEA)

forecastle (FOLK•sul) MM (13th–16th c.) a raised platform resembling a castle keep in ship's bow, from which soldiers fired down on the decks of enemy ships; also spelled foc'sul. (17th–20th c.) below decks in the bow area of a merchant ship, where sailors slept. BrN/USN (17th–20th c.) the spar deck forward of the ship's bell, where enlisted men were permitted to relax in off-duty hours; the bow area of the spar deck. (OST TON) (*see* spar deck)

forecastle joke USN (19th c.) one of several rough practical jokes that sailors played on one another; also spelled foc'sul joke. (ANE)

foreign service USA/USMC/USN/USAF (1940s–present) military service outside the boundaries of the United States. (AFS)

for it Br>USA (WWI–WWII) tired; in serious trouble; scheduled for punishment, "it" being the punishment itself. British usage: *He's for it.* American usage: *He's in for it.* (AGE MMD)

forlorn hope D>Br>USA (18th–20th c.) [Dutch *verloren hoop*, lost troop] a lost company of men. When the British first heard the term, in the early-eighteenth-century wars with the Dutch, they thought the Dutch were saying "hope." BrA (1768) the troops assigned to make the first assault on the enemy, as theirs was a highly dangerous honor. USA (1861) a group of men and officers who volunteer for a seemingly hopeless mission. (20th c.) a lost cause, a hopeless mission; aka rat fuck. (ANE DVT MDB MMD)

form 6A USNA (WWII) a legal form on which an aviation cadet logged his reasons for having committed a specific misdemeanor. Alibis were not accepted. (AFR)

form 66 USA (1950s) an army officer's personal record. (ASC)

for the good of the service USA (WWI) a company commander's rationale for issuing an order not covered by general orders or regulations. (EMP)

forty-eight USMC (1930s–Korean War) forty-eight hours free from duty. (SAM)

forward observer USA (WWI–present) a soldier who observed enemy positions from a spot near the enemy and called in accurate artillery fire upon him; aka FO. (ASC)

fougas (FOO•gaz) USA (1860s) a concealed hole filled with explosives that were detonated by an electrical charge when enemy troops passed overhead. An early version of the antipersonnel mine. (MD)

foul MM (18th c.) bad, confused, or entangled: *a foul line*. (SLA)

foul ball USA (WWII) a company screwball or clown. (SAM)

foul-up USMC (1930s–present) one who gets into trouble or makes stupid mistakes. (PAT SAM)

foul up USMC (1930s–present) to get into trouble, make a mistake, or get confused. (PAT SAM)

found a home, you have See you have found a home

founder MM (17th c.–present) [Old French *effondrir*, to sink, and *engulflu*, a wave>Old English *foundereu*] to sink, especially as a result of wind and waves. (MAN OST)

four cartridges of gunpowder and a bottle of brandy USN (19th c.) a mixture taken by a sailor prior to being flogged through the fleet, the belief being that the gunpowder would give one the strength to take the flog-

ging. (BMO) (*see* flogging through the fleet)

four-deuce USA (1960s) a 4.2-inch mortar.

400 W USA (WWII) maple syrup, from a comparison of its consistency with that of four-hundred-weight motor oil. (GWD)

four-oh USN (1960s) a perfect or outstanding item or person, noted with great admiration; aka four-point. From the highest possible score (4.0) on the navy fitness test.

four-oh sailor USN (WWII–present) one who scores perfectly on a navy fitness test. (*see also* four-oh)

fourragère USAF (1950s) a French or Belgian unit award. The braided cord was worn from the left shoulder of the honorees' service uniforms. (AFS)

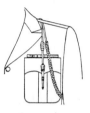

fourragère

four-star general USA (18th c.–WWII) the general of the army. (ASC) (*see* general of the army)

four-striper USN (WWII–1960s) a naval captain, so named for the four gold stripes on the cuffs of his service uniform.

four-way check USA (1950s) a security check on an individual by several different agencies. (ASC)

foxhole BrA>USA/USMC (WWI–present) a shallow, one-man rifle pit dug in haste and meant to provide temporary shelter. The British called such pits shelter trenches. (WWI) aka shelter pits or Belgian pits. (ATK IHA MMD) (*see also* fighting hole)

fox oscar USN (1980s–present) fuck off.

foxtail USMC (1980s) in boot camp, a short-handled brush used with a dustpan.

foxtrot USA/USMC (1960s–70s) a Vietnamese woman.

Foyer de Soldat (foy•AY deh sol•DOT) FrA (WWI) the French equivalent of the Young Men's Christian Association. (WWW)

FPFT USMC (1980s) final physical fitness test, given in the tenth week of basic training.

frag[1] USA/USMC (1960s) a fragmentation grenade.

frag² USA/USMC (1960s) to kill, especially with a hand grenade.

a fragmentation grenade fitted into a rifle grenade launcher

frat¹ BrA (1940, North Africa) a woman. (DRA) (*see also* bint, skirt)

frat² BrA (1940, North Africa) to fraternize with a female. (DRA) (*see also* bint, frat¹, skirt)

freak USA (1960s) radio frequency.

freckles USMC/USN (WWII) tobacco specially cut for making cigarettes.

FRED (fred) USAF (1970s) frigging ridiculous economic disaster.

freebooter BrN>USN (18th–19th c.) a robber; a pirate; a soldier who volunteered to serve without pay. (ANE DVT)

freedom bird USA/USAF/USMC/USN (1960s–70s) any plane that carried troops home to America from Vietnam.

free man forever USMC (WWII) one who has been discharged from the US Marine Corps; aka FMF.

free trader BrN>USN (19th c.) a ship not owned by the East India Company that engaged in trade with India; a prostitute. (ANE)

freeze USAAF (WWII) a muscle spasm. (AFR)

French fever USA/CSA (1860s) venereal disease, especially syphilis; aka pox.

French leave Br>USA/USMC/USN (18th–20th c.) absence without leave or permission. (ANE ASC DVT EMP) (*see also* absent without leave)

Frenchy MM (18th–20th c.) a person from Spain, Italy, or France. (ANE)

French 75 *See* soixante quinze

fresh fish USA/USMC/USN (18th c.–present) a new recruit or a new man in a unit; a newly captured enemy soldier; a green regiment; aka fresh hand. (ANE LRY) (*see also* greenhorn)

fresh grub USN (19th c.) unspoiled provisions. (ANE)

fresh hand *See* fresh fish

freshman USAAF (WWII) a new air recruit. (AFR)

fresh water king USN (20th c.) one responsible for making fresh water with the ship's saltwater evaporators. (TON)

freshwater navy *See* United States Coast Guard

fret¹ USN (19th c.) a narrow patch of sea. (ANE)

fret² USN (19th c.) to worry or chafe. (ANE)

friendly USA (1960s) an ally, military or civilian.

frigate BrN>USN (16th c.) a ship powered by both sails and oars. (18th–20th c.) a ship with twenty-four to forty-four guns mounted on two gun decks. (NCT)

frigging BrN>USN (18th–20th c.) masturbating. (RAS)

Fritz Br>USA/USMC (WWI) a German person or thing. (AGE MMD) (*see also* on the fritz) USA/USN/USMC/USAF (1980s) the Kevlar (plastic) helmet issued to United States military forces. Its shape is similar to that of the WWII-issue German helmet.

frog BrA>USA/USMC/USN (14th c.–present) disparaging name for a Frenchman, from his supposed fondness for frog legs and/or the three frogs on the coat of arms for the city of Paris; aka frog eater, froggie. BrA (17th c.)>USN (19th c.) a term of insult for a Dutchman. (ANE IHA SSD)

frog eater *See* frog

froggie *See* frog

frog hair USA (1960s) an imaginary, very small unit of measure; aka red cunt hair.

frogskin USA (WWII) a United States dollar bill; aka greenback. (GWD)

frog sticker USA/USMC (WWI–WWII) a bayonet. Most likely from the British-origin "frog," meaning Frenchman. French soldiers were highly trained in the use of bayonets. (AFR ATK) (*see also* cheese toaster, Josephine, paring knife, pig sticker, Rosalie)

front Rus>Br>USA (WWI) theater of operations: *the western front.* (IHA)

front porch *See* truck

Frozen Chosen USMC (Korean War) Chosin Reservoir. During a campaign there in mid-

December 1950, the weather was as harsh an enemy as the Chinese. (SAM)

fruit salad USMC/USAAF>USAF (1930s–present) a mass of ribbon bars worn on the left breast of the service uniform. (AFS SAM) (*see* ribbon bars)

FS Coord USA (1970s) fire support coordinator.

FSO USA (1970s) fire support officer.

FTA USA (1960s) fuck the army!

FTN USN (1980s–present) fuck the navy.

FUBAR (FOO•bar) USMC/USN (WWII–present) fucked up beyond all recognition. (PAT SAM)

fuck up USA/USMC/USN/USAF/USCG (1960s) to kill.

fucking mother fuckers *See* FMF

fuck the duck USA/USMC (1960s) to goof off, go to sleep.

fuck-you lizard USA/USMC (1960s) a Vietnamese gecko whose cry sounds like "Fuck you!"

fudge USA (WWII) government-issue bar soap, dark brown in color. (GWD)

fu-fu USN (19th c.) a sailor's dish of barley and molasses. (ANE)

FUJIBAR (FOO•gee•bar) USN (1980s–present) "Fuck you, buddy, I'm just a reservist."

full feather USN (19th c.) best clothes; full dress uniform; aka glad rags. *He's in full feather for the admiral's soiree.* (ANE) (*see also* full fig)

full fig USN (1880s) full dress uniform, for officers, or glad rags, for sailors. (ANE) (*see* dress uniform, full feather, glad rags)

full marching order *See* Christmas tree order

full of feathers USA (WWII) said of someone who was smiling and lying at the same time. (GWD)

full pack slum USA (WWI) a meat stew enclosed in a crust. (EMP) (*see* slum)

FUMTU (fum•TU) USA/USMC (WWII) fucked up more than usual. (PAT SAM)

funeral glide USAAF (WWII) crash dive. (AFR GWD)

funk hole BrA (WWI) dugout. (AGE)

fun meter USAF (1980s) a figurative gauge of one's enjoyment level: *What's your fun meter reading?*

funny money USA/USMC/USAF (1960s) military currency issued to troops in lieu of United States dollars.

funny papers USA (1960s) military maps, from the colored paper and/or inks used to print the maps and their not-infrequent inaccuracies.

furl Br>USA/USMC (18th c.–present) [Old English *fardle>furdle*, to fold into a bundle] to fold or roll in a prescribed manner, as a flag. (NCT) MM (17th c.) [Old French *ferlier*, to bind] to roll and secure a sail to a yard. (20th c.–present) to roll and secure, as a flag or sail. (MAN OST)

furlough D>Br>USA/USMC (1861) [Dutch *verlos*, leave of absence, or *verlof*, leave of absence with permission] a leave of absence granted to noncommissioned officers and enlisted men. USA (18th c.–present) a military leave of absence. (19th c.) a leave from one's employment or a place of incarceration. USMC (1930s) thirty-day leave granted for a family visit. (WWII) a leave granted to an enlisted man for a set period of time, usually thirty days. (MCT MD MMD SAM)

fusil FrA>BrA (1760s–1815) originally, a short, smooth-bore, flintlock musket; later, any musket. (MDB)

fusilier FrA>BrA (1760s–1815) a soldier armed with a fusil; also spelled fusileer, fuzileer. (*see* fusil)

futtock shrouds MM (13th c.) [Middle English *futtaker*, foot hooks] a short section of shrouds and rat lines used by sailors to climb up to the next level of the ship's mast. (NCT OST TON) (*see* rat lines, shrouds)

fuze lighter USA (1960s) an artilleryman.

fuzileer *See* fusilier

fuzzie-wuzzies USA (WWII) heavy wool trousers issued for winter wear. (SID)

fuzzy USN (19th c.) unsound in body and/or mind. (ANE)

G

gab USN (19th c.) [Anglo-Irish *gob*, mouth] human mouth; aka gob. Likely came into use via Irish serving aboard United States ships. (ANE)

gabardine Br>USA (16th–19th c.) a long overcoat made from coarse material. (20th c.) fabric made from a mixture of fibers. (DWO)

gabion (gab•ee•on) FrA>BrA>USA (1760s–present) an open-ended cylinder, approximately five feet, six inches high and three feet in diameter, fashioned from wicker, brush, and/or sticks and used as a reinforcement for field fortifications or as

gabion

a fortification itself. Once in place, the gabion was filled with packed earth and rocks. (*see also* gabionnade) (WWI) metal bands woven around metal rods. (MD MMD) (*see also* picket)

gabionnade (gab•ee•on•ADE) USA (1860s) a field fortification made from gabions. (MD) (*see* gabion)

gack *See* G and C

gadget MM (19th c.) [French *gâchette*, catch of lock] a hook used as a latch on a door or hatch. (20th c.) any mechanical object whose name cannot be recalled; a small, handy tool. (SAM TON WEA) USA (WWII) a ticket to a show, play, movie, or other performance; a corporal. An acting corporal was called an acting gadget; aka little wolf. (SID)

gaffe FrA (WWI) [French *gaffe*, blunder] a

goof, a blunder. (WWW)

gaggle USAAF/USNA (WWII–1960s) a group of planes, not necessarily from the same military unit, in flight. From gaggle of geese.

gale MM (16th c.) [Old Norse *galem* or Old Dutch *gal*, furious] a strong, continuous wind of thirty-five to sixty-five knots. (NCT OST) (*see* knot)

gall USN (19th c.) to irritate, rub the wrong way. (ANE)

galley USN>USMC (18th c.–present) on old sailing ships, the cast-iron range that held the iron pots in which food was cooked. USMC (20th c.) a kitchen. (ANE BJM SAM) (*see* copper)

galley growler USN (19th c.) one who constantly complained about the ship's food. (ANE) (*see* galley)

galley news USN (19th c.) unfounded rumors started by galley growlers and galley stokers; aka galley yarns. (ANE) (*see* galley, galley growler, galley stoker)

galley pepper USN (19th c.) soot from old-style galley smokestack that fell into food in coppers. (ANE) (*see* copper, galley)

galley stoker USN (19th c.) a slacker, one frequently found in or near the galley and said to be tending the fires. The galley stoker is the naval version of the army's "beat." (ANE) (*see* beat, galley)

galley west *See* knocked galley west

galloné (gal•o•NAY) FrA (WWI) [French *gallon*, braid] a braided cord on an officer's sleeve that identified his rank. (WWW)

galloping dominoes USA/USMC (WWII) a crap game; aka shooting dice, parlor dice. (GWD)

galore USN (19th c.) available in great quantity. (ANE)

galvanized Guernsey USA (WWII) government-issue canned milk; aka canned cow, city cow, tin titty. (SID)

game BrA (WWI) unreal, a lie: *it's all a game, it's absurd.*

game warden USN (1960s) a naval patrol boat operator in the Mekong Delta who kept watch over the activities of the Vietcong; the patrol boat itself.

G and C (gack) USAF (1980s) guidance and control; also spelled gack.

gang BrN>USN (1657–present) a herd of animals; a group of men under the supervision of a petty officer. US (1823) a group of dishonest politicians. (ANE IHA) (*see* petty officer)

gangplank MM (16th c.–present) a narrow board or ramp that bridges the dock and an opening in the side of a ship, used to board and disembark the vessel. (OST TON) (*see also* gangway)

gangplank fever USN (1950s) nervousness often observed in those about to be shipped overseas. (MCT)

Gang way! BrN>USN (18th c.–present) an order to clear a path, get out of the way. (BJM SEA)

gangway BrN>USN (16th c.–present) [Anglo-Saxon *weg*, way or opening] originally, a narrow plank or passageway down the center of a slave ship from which the slave master kept an eye on his charges. Later, an opening in a ship's side through which one could enter or leave the vessel. (BJM OST SAM TON) (*see also* gangplank, Gang way!)

Gang way for a navy officer BrN (WWI) call to clear a path to the surgeon's area.

gaol Br>USA (17th–18th c.) jail. By 1775, the spelling "jail" predominated in the United States. (IHA) (*see* jail)

GAPSALS (GAP•sals) US (WWII) Give-a-Pint,-Save-a-Life Society, a civilian organization that collected blood for military use.

GAR USA (1862–66) Grand Army of the Republic, the Union army. (1866) an organization for veterans of the Union army. (IHA)

Garand rifle USA/USMC/USAAF/USCG (WWII–1960s) an eight-round, semi-automatic rifle invented by John Garand in 1930; aka M1. The Garand was adopted by the army in 1936 but was not general issue until 1942. (IHA)

garbage can USN (WWII) an old, worn out destroyer, like the fifty given to Britain under the Lend-Lease program of 1941.

garrison[1] USA (18th c.–WWII) [French *guérir,* to preserve] a fort or other structure designed to preserve the security of the surrounding countryside. (1861–WWII) fortifications and the troops within them. (MCT MD MMD)

garrison[2] USA (WWII) to place troops inside a fortification. (MCT MD MMD)

garrison cap *See* overseas cap

garrison flag USA (WWI–present) a national flag measuring thirty-eight feet by twenty feet and flown only on important posts during important occasions. (ASC MMD)

garrison prisoner USA (WWI) a soldier sentenced to six months in the guardhouse. (EMP)

garrison shoes USA (WWII) army dress shoes worn only for duty in rear areas. (AFR) (*see also* brown shoe army, garrison)

garrison trooper USA (WWII) an infantryman assigned to the rear. (*see also* garrison, garritrooper)

garritrooper USA (WWII–present) a soldier who can hear gunfire but is not near enough action to risk getting shot; one who talks a good fight but never sees real action. Coined by cartoonist Bill Mauldin, the creator of Willie and Joe of WWII fame. (*see also* garrison, garrison trooper)

garters USN (19th c.) leg irons. (ANE) (*see also* irons)

gas[1] BrA (WWI) idle chatter. (AGE)

gas[2] BrA (WWI) to shoot the breeze, kill time. (AGE)

gas bag BrA (WWI) a gas-filled observation balloon; aka maiden's prayer, virgin's dream, virgin's prayer. (*see also* flying elephant)

gas house USA (WWII) a beer joint; aka gas hangar. (GWD)

gas house gang USA (WWII) chemical warfare instructors. (GWD)

gas mask BrA>USA/ USMC (WWI–present) a respirator used to filter out poison gas. (MLS)

gasoline cowboy USA (WWII) one who

WWII gas mask

100

served in mechanized armor. (GWD)

gasper USA/USMC (WWI) a bad-tasting, foul-smelling cigarette. (EMP) (*see also* fag)

gassed BrA (WWI) said of one exposed to poison gas, bored by a talkative friend, or drunk.

gate ghetto USA (1960s) a bar and house of ill repute near the gate of a base or camp.

gauntlet *See* run the gauntlet

gaw-gaw USN (19th c.) one who was clumsy or simpleminded. (ANE)

gawpus (GAW•pus) USN (19th c.) one who was stupid or idle. (ANE)

GCA USAF (1950s) ground control approach, an aircraft landing guided by a radio operator on the ground. (AFS)

GCI USA (1960s–present) ground control intercept station, which may be a building, tent, or tower.

GCM USA (19th c.–present) general court-martial. (ASC) (*see* general court-martial)

GCO USA (1960s) general counteroffensive of the Chinese communists. According to Chairman Mao, revolution entailed three steps: placing the enemy on the defensive, demoralizing the enemy, and launching a GCO to obtain final victory.

gear USA/USMC/USN (18th c.–present) equipment. (AFR DWO PAT SAM) (*see* 782 gear, that's the gear)

gear locker USMC (1980s) a broom or storage closet.

gedunk (GEE•dunk) USMC/USN (WWII–present) sweets and desserts, especially ice cream or pudding; also spelled geedunk.

geese USAAF (WWII) an enemy bomber formation, from its resemblance to geese in flight. (MMD)

Gen BrA (WWII) an intelligence officer. (*see* gen)

gen BrA (WWII) information, from "general information all ranks," which was the subject of many wartime memos. (*see also* duff gen, pukka gen, secret gen)

general Fr>Br>USA/USMC/USAF (16th c.–present) [French *capitaine generale*, captain general>English *captain general*] a senior military officer who commands an army

or large military force. (DWO)

general court-martial USA (WWI–present) the highest military court-martial. Since 1948, it has been responsible for hearing all cases under the Uniform Code of Military Justice. (ASC WWW) (*see also* Uniform Code of Military Justice)

general muster BrN>USN (1794–1914) a practice in which a sailor reported his name and rate, or the rank for which he was trained, upon enlistment. The general muster ensured that enlisted men would be paid fair wages. It was abolished in 1914, when the USN began a training camp system that assured that all sailors had learned the basics before taking a ship assignment. (NCT) (*see also* open muster)

general officer USA/USAF/USMC (WWI–present) an officer above the rank of colonel. (AFS ASC)

general officer of the air force USAF (1950s) the highest ranking general in the air force. (AFS)

general officer's efficiency report USAF (1950s) an official evaluation of an air force officer with the rank of brigadier or major general. (AFS) (*see also* effectiveness report)

general of the army USA (1860s–present) the highest ranking officer in the army. Ulysses S. Grant was the first to bear the title. The general of the army became a four-star general when that rank was created prior to WWII. (ASC IHA)

general orders USA/USMC (1900–present) eleven commandments that every Marine and soldier must memorize and be able to recite at any time. (EMP GFM PAT SAM) (see box on next page)

general quarters USN (WWII–present) the order for all hands to report to battle stations. (MAN)

general's car USA (WWII) a wheelbarrow, an example of enlisted men's sarcasm. (GWD)

general staff USA/USN/USMC/USAF (WWII–present) the officers who assist the commanding general in the control, coordination, planning, and execution of military operations assigned to a specific unit. The general staff includes the G1, G2, G3, G4, S1, S2, S3, and S4 sections. (ASC) (*see also* commanding general, G1, G2, G3, G4, S1, S2, S3, S4)

gen merchant BrA (WWII) a reliable source of information. (*see* gen, pukka gen)

gentleman by an act of congress USA (WWII) a derisive reference to an officer who wears his rank for all to see and admire. (GWD)

Georgia ice cream USA (WWII) grits. Soldiers from northern states said that southerners liked grits better than ice cream. (GWD)

Georgia pine *See* higher than a Georgia pine

German of, relating to, or characteristic of Germany or the German-speaking people. Military monikers for Germans are legion and include boche, Hans Wurdt, Heine, hun, Jerry, Katzenjammer Kid, kraut, moffer, and Ted; see specific entries for details.

germ bird USA (WWII) one who was quarantined because of a contagious disease. (GWD)

Gertrude USA (WWII) one assigned to office duty. In civilian life, office duty was a woman's job. USN (1960s) a telephone used in underwater communications between submarines. (GWD)

get a check BrA (WWI) to receive one's discharge, especially for medical reasons; to get killed; to pay one's bill. (EMP)

get a crow USN (1960s–present) to be promoted to the rank of petty officer, from the eagle (crow) that is a part of the insignia for that rank. (*see* petty officer)

get a sub BrA (WWI) to get a loan against future pay from a subaltern, the lowest ranking lieutenant. (AGE) (*see* subaltern)

get back in the rack USA (WWII) to crawl back into bed. (GWD) (*see* rack)

get eager USA (WWII) to strive to do more work than anyone else; to be too anxious to work. (AFR)

get it on USMC (1960s) to get into a fight; to have sex.

get off the ground USAAF (WWII) to influence a woman with a line of gab. (SID)

get on the ball USA (WWII) to move faster; to be more attentive to work; to get on with the business at hand. (GWD)

get short USA (1960s) to be near the end of a tour of duty in Vietnam.

get some USA/USMC (1960s–90s) to kill an enemy. (1990s) to have sex.

get the chop *See* chop

get the crown BrA (WWI) to be promoted to the rank of sergeant major, the insignia of which bore a royal crown. (AGE) (*see* sergeant major)

get the drop USA/CSA (1860s) to draw a sight with one's weapon before an opponent can do the same; to have the upper hand. (CWO)

get the drift MM (19th c.–present) to understand what has been said; to pick up recent gossip.

get the point BrN (19th c.) to be found guilty. When a British court-martial rendered a verdict in a case involving a naval officer, the head of the court placed the officer's sword on a table before him to signify the ruling. If the sword's hilt lay toward the accused, he had been found not guilty; if the point of the weapon was toward the accused, he had been found guilty. (TON)

get the score USA (WWII–1970s) originally, to learn one's score on a rifle range; later, to get accurate information. (SID)

get the sparks BrA (WWI) to cut barbed wire with machine gun fire. When the bullets struck the wire, blue sparks were created. (AGE)

get wet USA/USMC (1960s) to kill with an edged weapon, such as a knife or bayonet.

G-force USAF (1950s) a unit of measure equal to the acceleration of gravity; the force of gravity on an object as it accelerates or decelerates through the atmosphere. (AFS)

G4 USA (WWI–present) the officer of the general staff who is responsible for supplies, logistics, plans, and policy. (ASC) (*see* general staff, S4)

ghost USA (1960s) among special forces/ Green Berets, to avoid work; aka sandbag. (*see also* dodge the column, goldbrick, leadswinger)

ghost of Joan BrA (WWI) a nursing sister (British term for nurse), named for Joan of Arc. (EMP)

ghost time USA (1960s) among special forces/Green Berets, off-duty time, especially if time was spent avoiding any kind of early recall to duty or work. (*see* ghost)

ghost walks today, the USA (pre-WWI) today is payday. (EMP) (*see also* eagle day, eagle farts)

Ghot, the (gote) BrA (1940, North Africa) a British soldier's name for the North African desert; aka the Blue. (DRA)

GHQ Br>USA/USMC (WWI–present) general headquarters, where the commanding general sets up shop. USA (WWII–present) supreme headquarters for a theater of operations. (AFS WWW) (*see* commanding general)

GI USA/USMC/USAF/USN/USCG (1920s) galvanized iron, from which trash cans and barracks' roofs were made. (1935) general issue, said of items distributed to most of those in military. (1940–1960s) government issue; to Marines and sailors, an ordinary soldier, aka GI Joe. (WWII–present) one who lives and works strictly by the book of army regulations, keeping all in perfect order, preparing for inspection by cleaning thoroughly with soap and water, and so forth. (AFR AFS ATK IHA MCT PAT SAM) (*see also* GI Joe)

GIB USA/USMC/USN/USAF (1960s) guy in the backseat, the radio operator of a Phantom jet, who occupied the cockpit's rear seat.

GI Bill USA/USMC/USAF/USN/USCG (1944–1980s) Service Readjustment Act of 1944, which entitled military personnel to home loans, unemployment insurance after discharge, and partial payment for college or vocational school. (IHA) (*see* GI)

GI bucket USA (WWII) a government-issue water bucket. (ATK)

GI can USA/USMC (WWII–1960s) a galvanized iron trash can. (GWD SAM)

GI cocktail USA (WWII) medicinal salts that relieved constipation. (SID) (*see* GI)

gig BrN>USN (18th–20th c.) a ship captain's personal vessel, a lightly built boat. West Point (WWII–present) a demerit for committing an offense. (GWD NCT)

gig

gigged West Point (WWII–present) said of one whose leave was cancelled for infractions of military regulations. (GWD)

gig getter West Point (WWII–present) an infraction of rules and regulations that results in demerits. (SID) (*see* gig)

GI haircut USA (WWII) a regulation haircut that left the hair no more than one inch long. (AFR GWD) (*see* GI)

GI hop USA (WWII) a chaperoned dance held on base; aka GI struggle. (AFR GWD) (*see* GI)

GI Jesus USA (WWII) an army chaplain. (SID) (*see also* chaplain, GI, gospel grinder, Holy Joe, padre, sky pilot, sky scout)

GI Joe USA (WWII–1960s) an ordinary soldier, especially an infantryman. The term first appeared in *Yank* magazine on June 17, 1942, but it had been in limited use since at least 1940. (IHA) (*see* GI)

GI lemonade USA (WWII) plain water. (SID) (*see* GI)

gimp USA (1960s) a poor excuse for a soldier.

gimper-goofer USAAF (WWII) a highly skilled pilot. (MMD)

ginger BrA (WWI–WWII) energy, courage. (EMP)

Ginger BrA/BrN (WWI–WWII) nickname for a redhead. (AGE)

gink USA/USMC (1960s) a derogatory term for a Vietnamese person.

gin mill USA (WWII) a place that sold alcoholic drinks. (SAM)

GI sky pilot USAAF (WWII) a chaplain. (AFR) (*see also* chaplain, gospel grinder, Holy Joe, padre, sky pilot, sky scout)

GI struggle *See* GI hop

Gitmo USN/USMC (1960s) Guantanamo Bay, Cuba, where the United States Navy maintains a large base.

GI turkey USA (WWII) government-issue corned beef. (SID)

give a berth MM (17th c.) to give a ship sufficient space to maneuver at sea. (DWO MAN)

give chocolate BrA (18th c.) to give a good, sound chewing out that's bitter to taste, like unsweetened chocolate. (DVT) (*see* chew out)

give it the gun USA (WWII) to step on the gas. (MMD)

give it to the Belgians BrA (WWI) a response to complaints about food, equipment, or treatment. The implication was that the Belgians, who had lost all in the war, would be more than happy to have even supposedly inferior items. (AGE)

given one's bowler BrA (WWI) sacked; demobilized; sent back to England in disgrace, with hat in hand.

give the oil USA (WWII) to do some smooth talking in an attempt to get out of trouble or a difficult situation. (GWD)

give the wind the chance USA (WWI) a command to be quiet. (EMP)

GI war USA (WWII) field maneuvers held in the United States. (AFR GWD) (*see* GI)

gizmo USMC (1930s–1960s) an unidentified item. The term was often applied in haste to an object whose name could not be readily recalled. (SAM)

GL USA (1970s) grenade launcher. (*see also* blooper, elephant gun, thumper, thump gun)

glad bag USA/USMC (1960s) a heavy-duty, zippered, plastic body bag, so named after Glad brand sandwich bags.

glad rags MM/USMC/USN (19th c.) dress clothes worn on shore liberty by sailors in the merchant marine and navy. In the navy, it was common practice for the men to embroider designs on cuffs, collars, shirt fronts, trouser cuffs and fronts, hats, and neckerchiefs. (BJM) (*see also* go ashores, liberty)

glass MM>BrN>USN (18th c.) a spyglass used by ship's officers or, in the navy, by quartermasters. (19th c.–present) a barometer. (MAN) (*see* quartermaster)

glasses USA/USN/USMC (mid-19th c.–present) a pair of binoculars. (MAN)

glasshouse USAAF (WWII) a steel-framed, electric-powered bomber turret that resembled a conservatory or greenhouse; aka conservatory. (MMD)

globe ranger USN/USMC (19th c.) a member of the United States Marine Corps. (ANE)

glory hole MM (18th c.–1960s) a holding cell for prisoners aboard ship; the place where gold or silver was kept. (20th c.) on a merchant or passenger ship, the quarters for the captain's steward. USN (20th c.) shipboard quarters for chief petty officers. (AST

OST) (*see* petty officer)

G-man USA (WWII) one assigned to garbage detail. (GWD)

GO USA (WWI–present) a general order, one that applies to all personnel, not a specific person or unit. Usually, a general order concerns a matter of importance and gives directives concerning the handling of the situation. It applies to everyone and is permanent. Also, an order given to all sentries posted on interior security. (MMD WWW)

go about BrN>USN (18th c.) to place a ship on the opposite tack. (TWW)

go-around *See* landing circle

go ashore MM/BrN>USN>USMC (16th c.–present) to leave the ship; to be stranded, as a vessel, on a beach, sandbar, or shoals. (SLA) USMC (19th c.–present) to go on liberty. (SAM) USN/USMC (18th c.–WWII) to go into town for liberty; to go on a spree. (AFR) (*see* ashore, liberty)

go-ashores USN (19th c.) a sailor's best uniform. The term was not commonly used. (ANE) (*see also* glad rags)

goat USA/West Point (1860s) one who graduated at the very bottom of his class. USA (WWI) the most recently commissioned junior officer in the unit. (WWII) the lowest ranking enlisted man; an army horse. Often used derisively by infantrymen towards cavalry mounts. (GWD MMD SID) USAAF (WWII) the aviation cadet with the lowest academic standing; the most junior officer on the base or post. (AFR)

goaty USA/USAAF (WWI–WWII) awkward, ignorant. (AFR MMD)

gob USN (19th c.) [Anglo-Irish *gob*, mouth] human mouth; aka gab. Likely came into use via Irish serving aboard United States ships. (ANE) USN/USCG (1890s–1960s) originally, a term of insult used by navy men for a coastguardsman. Later, any enlisted sailor. In the 1950s, gob was commonly used by United States civilians as an insulting name for a sailor. (IHA WEA) (*see also* bluejacket, swab, swabbie)

gobbledygook USA (WWII) meaningless words; too many words; red tape. (SAM)

gob hat USN (1890s–WWII) a round white cap worn with work and service uniforms; aka dixie cup. (*see* dixie cup)

go boom boom USA (WWII) to go to a rifle range. (GWD)

go by the boards MM (15th c.–present) to be a complete loss or total ruin. Originally, the phrase was meant literally. Masts and spars washed overboard as a result of an accident or storm were said to have gone by the boards. (SLA)

God botherer BrN (1980s–present) the ship's chaplain.

Goddam FrA (1600s–1815) French soldier's nickname for a British soldier because of the Brit's frequent use of the word.

go-fasters USMC (1980s) tennis shoes.

go-fer *See* goofer

go home BrA (WWI) to die.

go into a tailspin USAAF (WWII) to lose one's temper. (GWD MMD)

go-juice USAF (1950s) jet fuel. (AFS)

gold brick USA/USMC (1853) a bar of gold. (1880) a fake gold brick. (1914) an army lieutenant fresh from civilian life with little or no military training; an unattractive female. (1918) a soldier on special duty who did not have to stand formations; one who faked illness to avoid duty; also spelled goldbrick. (WWII) a lazy person; an ugly woman. (BJM EMP IHA MMD PAT SAM) (*see also* dodge the column, ghost, lead-swinger)

goldbrick USA/USMC/USN (WWI–1960s) to goof off; to go out of one's way to avoid work. (BJM EMP IHA PAT SAM)

golden BB USA/USAF (1960s) a bullet that kills a man.

goldfish USA (WWI–WWII) canned salmon. (AFR ATK)

gold hands USAF (1980s) said of a pilot with excellent skills.

gold lace candidate USA (1910–WWII) an enlisted man who had passed his first exam as an officer candidate and was entitled to be saluted as an officer. (EMP)

golf balls and bullets USA/USMC (1960s) C rations that contained meatballs and beans. (*see* C rations)

go like a bat out of hell BrA (WWI) to go about in a panic. BrAF (1915) to fly at a very high speed.

go like blue murder BrA (WWI) to move with great haste, especially in retreat.

Gomer (GO•mer) USA (1960s) a derogatory name for a Marine, from the popular television comedy *Gomer Pyle, USMC.*

go native USA/USN/USMC (1898–Vietnam) to live among the local people and adopt their customs. The term and the practice were most common in the Pacific theater of operations. (PAT SAM)

G1 USA (WWI–present) the officer of the general staff who is responsible for personnel plans and policy. (ASC) (*see also* general staff, S1)

gone goose USN (19th c.) a deserted ship; a ship abandoned in anticipation of its imminent demise. (ANE)

gone up *See* SNAFU

gone west *See* go west

goney bird *See* goony bird

gongs Br>USA/USMC (WWI–1960s) decorations, military medals. (*see also* chest gongs)

gony bird *See* goony bird

goober CSA (1860s) peanut; aka goober pea. (LRY)

goodie USA (1960s) a trap or ambush left behind for an unsuspecting enemy.

good kit BrA (1940, North Africa) someone or something that is nice, good, pretty, fine, or excellent. (DRA)

Good night, nurse! BrA (WWI) an expression of surprise or disgust, depending on the mood of the moment. (AGE) (*see also* Carry me out, let me die!; that's torn it)

good 'til the last drop USA (WWII) said by infantrymen of paratroopers. (GWD)

goof burner USA (WWII) one who smokes dope. (GWD)

goofer USA (WWII) an unreliable paper match; also spelled go-fer, because as soon as a soldier struck one, he immediately had to "go fer" another. (GWD)

goof off¹ USA/USMC/USN (WWII) a lazy person, especially one who makes frequent mistakes. (AFR GWD MMD PAT) (*see* gold brick)

goof off² USA/USMC/USN (WWII) to loaf or evade work. (AFR GWD MMD PAT) (*see* goldbrick)

goofy discharge USA (WWII) a discharge for mental instability; aka Section 8. (GWD) (*see* Section 8)

goo-goo USA/USN/USMC/USAF (1898–WWII, Far East) a disrespectful name for a native of the Philippine Islands; aka gook.

gook USA/USMC (1898) [Korean *gook*, person] an uncomplimentary name for a native of the Philippine Islands. (*see also* goo-goo) USA/USMC/USN/USAF (1950–53) a derogatory nickname for a North Korean. (1960s) a derogatory term for an Oriental, especially a Vietnamese. (IHA MCT) (*see also* slant, slope, wickerhead, zip)

gook sore USA/USMC (1960s) any skin rash or infection.

goolies BrN/BrA>USA (18th c.–WWII) [Urdu/Hindustani *goli*, ball or bullet] testicles. (TBS)

goon BrA>USA (WWII) a prison camp guard in Europe. USA/USMC/USAAF/USN (WWII) a slow-witted person, so named for the cartoon character Alice the Goon; a guard at a POW camp. (IHA TOC) (*see* POW)

go on a bender *See* bender

gooner USA/USMC (1960s) a North Vietnamese soldier.

goony bird (GOO•nee burd) MM/USA/USMC (18th–19th c.) an albatross, a bird graceful in flight but very awkward on the ground; an awkward, slow, and/or stupid person; a DC3 cargo plane; also spelled goney bird, gony bird. (AST IHA)

gooseneck BrN (1750s) a mobile wooden beam on which the tiller rested. The gooseneck was located in the gunroom and swung with the movement of the ship's wheel. (*see* gunroom, tiller)

goose the wind USA (WWII) to hitchhike, from the thumb and arm motion used to flag down a ride. (GWD)

go over the hill USA (1920) to desert. (GWD)

USMC (1930s–60s) to desert one's unit; to take unauthorized leave. (PAT SAM) (*see also* adrift, AOL, AWOL, deserter, dicky leave)

gorblimey (gore•BLYE•mee) BrA (WWI) a brimmed service cap with the stiff grommet removed; a soft winter cap with ear flaps that were tied under the chin or, when not in use, on top of the head. (*see* grommet, service cap)

gork USA (1960s) one who appears to be brain dead.

go south USMC (1960s) to ship from Okinawa to Vietnam.

gospel grinder CSA/USA (1860s–WWI) a chaplain or preacher; a holier-than-thou soldier; a zealot; one who was constantly talking about God. (PAT) (*see also* chaplain, GI sky pilot, Holy Joe, padre, sky pilot, sky scout)

gosse FrA (WWI) a youngster; a new soldier. (WWW)

got a packet *See* cop a packet

go tell it to the chaplain USA (WWII) a brush-off used when the speaker did not wish to be bothered by someone else's problems. (IHA)

go tell it to the Marines Br>USA (1820s) an expression of total disbelief, used especially in response to a tall tale. The suggestion was that, while the listener certainly isn't dumb enough to believe such a yarn, the Marines may be. USMC (WWI) slogan on a Marine recruiting poster designed by James Montgomery Flagg. (IHA)

Gotha (GAH•tha) BrA (WWI) any German bomber, from a German bomber by that name.

got his buzzard USA (WWI) said of one who had received a military discharge, from the eagle stamped on the document. (EMP)

go through the mill CSA/USA (1860s) to suffer a rough time emotionally, physically, or mentally; to do many different things. (LRY)

go-to-hell cap *See* overseas cap

go to pieces MM/BrN>USN (19th c.–present) to be broken into bits, as a wooden ship, by the sea and reefs. (20th c.) civilian usage:

to be in a state of extremely nervous upset. (SLA)

gouge¹ USNA (WWII) to con, cheat, or overcharge. (AFR) USN (1960s) to defraud or cheat.

gouge² USNA (WWII) to aviation cadets, a cheat sheet for an exam. (AFR) USN (1960s) a solution to a problem.

go up USAAF (WWII) to take off. (AFR)

go up the pole USA (WWII) to refrain from drinking alcoholic beverages. (GWD) (*see also* go on the tack)

government bouquet USA (WWI–WWII) government-issue laundry soap. (EMP)

government straight USA (WWI–WWII) goverment-issue food. (EMP) (*see also* canned Willie, can of worms, C rations)

gowed up *See* hopped up

go west MM>BrA (9th c.–WWI) to die. Most often used in the past tense, as in *Murphy's gone west.* (AGE IHA MMD) (*see also* knocked galley west)

GOYA USA (1960s) get off your ass.

GPF 155 FrA (WWI) a long-range, 155-mm field gun with caterpillar tracks. It was designed by a Colonel Filleux of the French army. (WWW)

GQG FrA (WWI) [French *Grand Quartier Général*, General Headquarters] the French version of the British and United States GHQ. (WWW) (*see* GHQ)

grab a root CSA/USA (1860s) to eat, as to take a potato. (*see also* gun the potatoes)

grab leather USA (19th c.–WWII) to hold onto the saddle for dear life to avoid being thrown. (EMP)

grandma USA (WWII) one who drives a vehicle slowly and timidly. (AFR) (*see also* grannie)

grandpa USA (WWI–early WWII) large-caliber German artillery piece. (MMD)

grand skedaddle CSA/USA (1860s) the flight of an entire army from the field of battle.

grannie BrN (1980s–present) a person or thing that is old, slow, or indecisive. (*see also* grandma)

granny BrA (WWI) any large-caliber

artillery piece. (*see also* grandpa)

grape *See* grapeshot

grapeshot USN (18th–19th c.) a stand of cast-iron balls; aka grape. Three or more layers of shot were bunched like grapes around a metal core at the center of the stand, separated by pieces of wood; the

grapeshot

entire stand was then wrapped in tarred cloth and twine. (*see also* canister)

grapevine CSA/USA (1860s–present) a source of unofficial, unsubstantiated information, rumors, and/or hearsay that is part of every organization; aka grapevine telegraph. (MMD)

grapevine telegraph *See* grapevine

grass USAAF (WWII) green vegetables, salad. (AFR)

grass-cutter USA (WWII) a small air-dropped antipersonnel bomb said to explode so close to the ground that it cut the grass. (MMD)

grasshoppers FrA (1790s–1815) British riflemen, possibly from their green uniforms and their role as skirmishers, the men who advanced in open order ahead of the main battle formation.

grassed USA (1870s) said by cavalrymen of someone thrown from his horse.

gravel agitator *See* infantryman

gravel crusher *See* infantryman

graveyard shift US (19th c.) a watch from midnight to 4 A.M. meant to deter body snatching and grave robbing. MM>USN (19th c.–present) watch aboard a ship from midnight to 4 A.M.; aka churchyard watch, graveyard watch, gravy-eye watch. (SLA)

graveyard watch *See* graveyard shift

gravy-eye watch *See* graveyard shift

grayback USA (1860s) a Confederate soldier; a body louse; Confederate money, from the color of the paper; also spelled greyback. (IHA) BrA (WWI) a German soldier, from his gray-green uniform. (MMD) (*see also* louse, Federal)

grease[1] USA/USMC (WWI–1960s) table butter; aka axle grease. (1960s) C rations. (AET AFR) (*see also* C rations)

grease[2] (1960s–present) to kill; aka waste, wax. (AET AFR)

grease gun USA/USMC (WWII–1960s) an M1 submachine gun, a .45-caliber automatic weapon made from stamped metal parts. (*see also* Garand rifle)

grease monkey USAAF (WWII) an assistant aircraft mechanic. (AFR)

greenback USA (1862–present) paper money. On February 25, 1862, the first national currency printed on green paper was issued by the United States government. (IHA) (*see also* funny money)

green bait USA/USMC (1960s) a cash bonus for reenlistment, especially for another term in Vietnam.

green banana USA (WWII) an early name for a Dear John letter, used by those serving in the Pacific. Supposedly, a comparison between the pain caused by eating green fruit and the pain of losing a girlfriend. (*see* Dear John)

green beanies USA/USMC (1960s) special forces, known for their distinctive green berets. (*see also* Green Berets, open mess operators, SEALS)

green belt USMC (1980s) a boot camp term for an assistant drill instructor.

Green Beret USA (1952–present) a member of the United States Army Special Forces, from the distinctive green beret they wear. The mission of the Green Berets includes but is not limited to the training of regular and paramilitary troops of allied nations for internal armed conflict, special reconnaissance, and antiterrorist assignments. Each member of the unit is trained in at least two specialties. Their counterparts in the United States Navy are the SEALS. (*see also* green beanies, open mess operators, SEALS)

Green Cross Society BrA (WWI) the women's reserve ambulance society, which saw service only in England. The Green Cross Society helped the wounded once they had been evacuated to Britain.

green dragon USA (1960s) an M113 armored personnel carrier; aka ACSV.

green envelope BrA (WWI) an envelope whose green color signaled that it was not to be opened by the army censor. Such envelopes were used only by specified officers and government officials.

greenhead *See* greenhorn

greenhorn MM (17th c.–present) an inexperienced hand; aka greenhead. (17th–18th c.) one who was ignorant or as inexperienced as a calf growing a set of green horns. The term also came from the color of the skin after a severe bout of seasickness. US (19th c., West) one new to the life and therefore slow and ignorant. (1917) an immigrant. (IHA SLA)

green machine USA (1960s) the entire army, from the color of its uniforms.

green oil and whistle steam MM (19th c.) the elements of a practical joke. Greenhorns were sent to the bosun's locker for green oil for the starboard running light, red oil for the port running light, or a bucket of steam for the whistle. (TON) (*see* boatswain, greenhorn)

greens USMC (WWII) an olive drab, wool winter uniform. (PAT SAM) (*see also* OD)

green slime BrN (1970s–present) a sailor's derogatory name for a member of the Army Intelligence Service, for the color of their uniforms.

grego USN (19th c.) a greatcoat, a long, heavy, woolen overcoat worn by sailors in cold weather. (AST)

gremlin USAAF>USAF (WWII–1960s) a mythical creature thought to be male and blamed for unusual or inexplicable problems in aircraft. (AFS) (*see also* fifinella)

grenade Sp>Br>USA (15th c.–present) [Spanish *granada,* pomegranate, a fruit full of seeds] originally, an explosive made from clay. (1594) a hollow metal shell filled with gunpowder and set off by a hand-lit fuse. (1861) a shell thrown by hand or fired by the basketload from mortars; aka bomb, cricket ball, hand frag, hand grenade, pineapple, potato masher, short put. (WWI–present) a hand grenade. (MCT MD MMD) (*see also* grenadier, jam pot, Mill's spud, pineapple)

grenadier Fr>Br>USA/USMC (17th c.–present) [French *grenadier*, grenade thrower] a man chosen to throw hand grenades because of his size and accuracy. The first companies of grenadiers were formed in European armies in 1660. (1770s) a soldier in an elite shock troop of a major European army who seldom used grenades. (WWI) a volunteer who carried sacks of grenades on a trench raid, called a bomber by British and United States troops. USA (WWII) one trained in the use of a rifle grenade, sometimes called a rifle grenadier. (MCT MD MMD) (*see* grenade)

Grey Funnel Line BrN (1900–present) the Royal Navy, from the paint used on her ships.

greyhound USN (19th c.) a hammock without a mattress and often without a blanket, from a comparison to a thin greyhound dog. (ANE)

griff Br>USA (1942, North Africa) news, as in *What's the griff?* (*see also* dope)

grin and bear it MM (18th c.–present) to take things with a smile; to make the best of a bad situation. An old sailor's comment on a long bout of filthy weather. (CWO)

grinder USMC (WWII–present) a parade ground on which troops are drilled until they feel as if they have been put through a meat grinder.

grinders Br>USA/USMC/USN (18th c.–WWII) teeth. (WWII) severe radio static that sounded like grinding teeth. (AFR DVT MMD)

grins and shakes USMC (1960s–present) the reception given VIPs as they tour the front, from the inordinate amount of smiling and handshaking that takes place.

gripe¹ USA (WWII) a complaint about something bothersome. (AFR GWD MMD)

gripe² USA (WWII) to anger or complain: *that gripes me.* (AFR GWD MMD)

grocer's shop MM (19th c.) a pub or a grog shop. (BMO) (*see* grog)

grog BrN (1791–1861) [British *groggam,* cloth that is fifty percent silk and fifty percent wool] a mixture of three parts water and two parts rum that was issued daily. Admiral William Vernon, or Old Grog, began the practice to save money on straight spirits. USN (1791–1861) one part alcohol and one part water (until 1842, four ounces each; beginning in August 1842, two ounces each) issued to men over age twenty-one. Underage men were paid three cents more per day, while men twenty-one or older who did not drink were paid five cents more per day. Grog issue stopped for enlisted men in September 1862; officers' issue stopped in 1914, when the United States Navy went totally dry. (NCT RAS TON)

grommet USA/USMC/USN/USAF (WWI–present) wire and cloth placed in the crown of a brimmed service cap to maintain its neat, round shape. (AFS ASC) (*see* campaign hat)

gronk BrN (1980s–present) an unattractive female.

gros legumes FrA (WWI) [French *gros légumes*, large or bulky vegetables and herbs] the top military brass; staff officers; aka les huiles (pronounced wheels). (WWW)

grounded USAAF>USAF (WWII–present) ordered to remain on the ground, not permitted to fly as a passenger or pilot. (AFS)

groundhog USAAF (WWII) a nonflying member of the army air force; aka kiwi. (MMD)

ground loop USAAF (WWII) a sloppy landing. (GWD)

ground pounder USA/USMC (1950s–60s) a nonflying officer of the air force. (AFS) (*see* infantryman)

ground school pilot USAAF (WWII) an air cadet with theory and textbook experience but no actual flight time. (AFR ATK MMD)

grouse[1] USA (1860s–WWII) to complain constantly in a nonthreatening manner. (AGE GWD MMD)

grouse[2] USA (1860s–WWII) one who complained constantly in a nonthreatening manner. (AGE GWD MMD)

growl MM>USA/USMC/USN (1830s–1960s) to complain or to find fault, a privilege allowed to veterans but not to new recruits. (EMP)

growler CSA/USA (1860s) a complainer, one who sees no hope or no good in any situation.

grub USA/USMC/USN (19th c.–present) [British *grub*, slang for food, from act of birds digging for grubs or larva] food. The term was first used by United States civilians in 1807, and United States military usage began in 1856. (19th c.) a child who was dirty from digging in the dirt. (DWO IHA)

grubber USA (WWII) a new recruit who did very little work. (GWD)

grub trap USN (1850s) mouth. (ANE) (*see* grub)

grub wagon USA (1884) a provisions wagon used by troops serving in the West. (*see* grub)

grungey AusA (1815–1918) a stew made from water, salt, bully beef, onion, and broken biscuits, supposed to be eaten warm. (*see* bully beef)

grunt USA/USMC (WWII) a slightly insulting name for a Marine; an electrician's helper. (AFR) USA/USMC (1960s–80s) a combat soldier or Marine. Several possible origins for the term exist: one veteran asserts that it arose from the sound one makes when hit by a round or shell fragment. According to Flexner in *I Hear America Talking*, it refers to the constant underbreath grumbling of a foot soldier. A third possibility is that it came from the sharp exhaling sound made by an infantryman who carries a heavy load on his back in the field. (IHA)

GS USA (1970s) general support.

GSR USA (1970s) ground support radar.

GTA USA (1970s) graphic training aid, a visual teaching aid.

G3 USA (WWI–present) the officer of the general staff who is in charge of operations and training. (ASC) (*see also* general staff, S3)

G-tolerance USAF (1950s) the amount of G-force one can tolerate before passing out. (AFS) (*see* G-force)

G2 USA (WWI–present) the second section of the general staff. The G2 is responsible for military intelligence. (ASC ATK WWW) (*see also* general staff, S2)

Guadalcanal Island *See* 'Canal

guardhouse USA (1890s) a military jail, found on all army posts. (*see also* jail)

guardhouse lawyer USA (1890s–present) an enlisted man who is a self-proclaimed expert on military law. He likely has little knowledge and a big mouth. (ASC)

guardo USN (19th c.) a receiving ship for new recruits noted for its lax discipline and corruption. Ashore: a house of vice. (ANE)

guardo move USN (19th c.) an action or maneuver employed by a sailor to avoid the clutches of the master-at-arms. (ANE) (*see* master-at-arms)

guard shack USMC (1930s–Korean War) a room or building in which the guard on duty remains. (SAM)

guard the flagpole USA (1890s) to be restricted to camp or post as punishment. (ATK)

guerrilla Sp>Br>USA (1800–present) [Spanish *guerra*, little war, first used by Spanish in 1880 war with Napoleon] a member of paramilitary or irregular troops that operate in small units and generally conduct hit-and-run attacks against enemy forces. (IHA) (*see also* partisan)

guide USA (1860s–WWI) a man, usually a local civilian, who supplied the army with information about an area's terrain. (MD MMD)

Gulf War US (1990–91) the war that began when the forces of Iraq under Saddam Hussein invaded Kuwait and threatened to invade Saudi Arabia. The United States and twenty-six allied nations formed a coalition that forced the Army of Iraq to give up its occupied territories in February 1991.

gull¹ USN (WWII) a prostitute who follows the fleet from port to port.

gull² USN (WWII) to fly in an aircraft.

gum boots USA (WWI) rubber boots. (AGE)

gummer's mate USN (1960s) a dental assistant.

gum shoe US>USA (WWI–Korean War) a military policeman. In civilian use, a private

detective, who was said to wear rubber-soled shoes so as to carry out his work in silence. USA (WWII) one assigned to G2 or another army intelligence section. (ATK) (*see* G2)

gum the game BrA (WWI) to foul up, as a plan; to interfere in business that is not one's own. (AGE)

gun¹ USAAF>USAF (WWI–1950s) the throttle of an aircraft. (*see also* joystick)

gun² USAAF (WWII) to have the mess attendant fetch more food, as in *Hey, Jack! Gun us some more food!* (AFR) (*see* mess)

gun ape USA/USMC (1960s) an artilleryman; aka gun bunny.

gunboats USA (1860s) heavy army boots or shoes. (*see also* mud hooks)

gun bunny *See* gun ape

gun-bus BrA (WWI) an aircraft armed with machine guns.

gundeck USN (1860s–1900) to vent anger and frustration. Upon entering the gun deck, sailors coming off liberty were permitted to use any manner of foul language short of cursing the officers of the ship, who were held to be above God. (1970s–present) to mark an assignment as completed when in reality it was not attempted; aka radio in. (*see also* pencil whip)

gundecker USN (1800s–WWII) a midshipman who lounged around the gun deck in an effort to dodge his assigned duties.

gundecking *See* gundeck

gun fire BrA (WWI) tea served before morning parade or assembly, before the morning gun marked the beginning of the soldier's day. (*see* morning gun)

gungey (GUN•jee) USMC (1960s) an overly enthusiastic Marine. (*see also* gung ho Marine)

gung ho¹ USA/USMC (19th c.–present) [Chinese *keng ho*, more fiery, more spirit] eager and spirited.

gung ho² USMC (WWII) a war cry. (PAT SAM)

gung ho Marine USMC (WWII–present) one who has all the positive qualities expected of a Marine. (IHA PAT SAM) (*see* gung ho¹)

gunlock BrN (1750s) the flintlock firing

mechanism on some naval cannon.

gun mount USN (20th c.) a lightly armored ship's emplacement of one to four guns. The guns in a mount are not larger than five inches in diameter. (MAN)

gunner's daughter BrN>USN (18th–19th c.) the breech of a gun, to which a victim was sometimes secured for flogging. (AST) (*see also* black Monday, blue Monday, boy's cat, cat-o'-nine-tails, earn your stripes, flog, man's cat, marry the gunner's daughter, thieves' cat)

gunner's tailor BrN>USN (18th–19th c.) the sailor who made cloth cartridges for the ship's powder charges. (ANE)

gunnery sergeant USMC (19th c.–present) originally, the Marine sergeant in charge of the gun crew. In the twentieth century, the Marine gunnery sergeant was equivalent to an E-7 or army master sergeant. (SAM)

Gunney *See* Gunny

Gunny USMC (19th c.–present) nickname for a gunnery sergeant; aka Guns. Also spelled Gunney. (SAM) (*see also* gunnery sergeant)

gunpowder tea BrA (1800–WWI) fine green or mild tea, from the texture of the dried leaves, which resembled that of gunpowder. (1860s) a coarse or strong tea of the run-of-the-mill variety. (*see also* chai, char)

gunroom BrN (1750s) a very small storage room on the orlop deck, in the very stern of the ship. (*see* orlop deck, stern)

Guns *See* Gunny

gunship USA/USMC (1960s) a heavily armed helicopter used in a ground support role. (IHA)

gun the potatoes USA (WWII) to pass the potatoes. (GWD) (*see also* grab a root)

gunwale (GUN•ell) MM (15th c.–present) the upper edge of a ship's side or railing. (MAN OST)

guppy USN (1960s) an unkind name for one who was not SCUBA trained; aka fin, straightfin.

Gurkha BrA (1815–present) a native of Nepal in service with the British army. Since 1815, the Gurkhas have been among the most renowned and highly decorated British troops.

guy USN (18th–20th c.) [Middle English *gye* and Old French *guie*, to guide] a tackle or line used to support or steady an object, yard, or sail. (MAN OST)

GVN USA/USMC/USN/USAF (1960s) the government of South Vietnam.

gyppo (JI•poe) BrA (1940, North Africa) a derogatory name for an Egyptian; aka nigger, wog. (DRA)

gyrene USMC (WWII–present) a Marine, possibly from a combination of GI and Marine. (PAT SAM) (*see* GI)

GZ USAF (1950s) ground zero, ground level. (AFS)

H

hack it USA (1960s) to bear strain or stress; to do one's assigned task despite great difficulties.

had it Br>USA (WWI–WWII) done for; out of luck; dying. (MCT)

hair trigger USN (19th c.) a gun trigger adjusted so that it fires at the slightest pressure; an easily flared temper. (ANE)

HAL (hal) USA (1960s) helicopter attack squadron.

half gone USA (WWII) hungry. (GWD)

half mast USA/USAF/USMC/USN (1930s–present) said of the national flag flown at the midpoint of the flagpole as a sign of mourning; aka half staff. (SAM)

half seas over MM (18th c.) partially drunk. (SLA)

half staff *See* half mast

halt and freeze USAAF (WWII) to stop and snap to attention immediately. (AFR)

halyard MM (18th c.–present) [French *haler* or Saxon *halar*, to haul, and Saxon *gerd*, yard or spar] a rope used to hoist yards and sails into place; also spelled halliard. (OST)

ham USAAF (WWII) a shortwave radio operator. (AFR)

ham and motherfuckers USA/USMC (1960s) ham and lima beans served in C rations. (*see also* C rations)

hammock Sp>Br>USN (16th c.–present) [Taino language of West Indies>Spanish *hamaca*>English *hamaca* or *hammaker*] a bed suspended above the ground. Hammocks were first seen by the Spanish when they conquered the Arawakan people of the West Indies and were quickly adopted by European sailors, who until that time had slept wherever they could find space. (DWO NCT TON)

hand[1] MM (13th c.–present) [Old English/Saxon *hand*, hired person] a sailor or any member of a ship's crew; a member of a work gang. (OST SLA) USA (19th c.) a unit of measure equal to four inches (the width of the average human hand) used to measure the height of horses from hoof to shoulder. (MD)

hand[2] MM (16th c.) to take in and furl sail. (OST SLA)

handbarrow Br>USA (1768–present) a lightly made, single-wheel cart used to transport earth; aka wheelbarrow. (MDB)

handcart artillery *See* Stokes trench mortar

handcuff volunteer USA (WWII) one who had been drafted. (SID)

hand frag USA/USMC (1960s) a fragmentation hand grenade. (*see* grenade)

hand grenade BrA (WWI) a government-issue water bottle. USA (WWII) a government-issue hamburger. (GWD MMD)

hand-me-down MM>Br>US (19th–20th c.) a clothing store found at docks and selling both new and used clothes, which hung from nails in the ceiling beams and were taken down by customers using poles with hooks on the ends; a secondhand article of cloth-

ing, especially one passed from an older to a younger generation.

hand over fist[1] MM (18th c.) a method by which sailors hauled in line or climbed rigging; aka hand over hand. (CWO) (*see* rigging)

hand over fist[2] US (early 19th c.) at a fast clip, used especially to refer to the intake of money; aka hand over hand. (CWO)

hand-rolled USA (WWI–WWII) handmade, in reference to a cigarette. (*see also* tailor mades)

handshaker USA (WWI–WWII) one who kisses up to superiors and appears to be too friendly with them. (EMP)

handsomely USN (19th c.) in a slow, steady, and cautious manner. (ANE BJM)

handspike USN (18th–19th c.) a strong pole used as a lever to move or elevate heavy items. (AST)

handspike hash USN (18th–19th c.) the resultant wounds when corporal punishment was applied with a handspike. (AST) (*see* handspike)

hangar USAAF (WWII) a bar, pub, or saloon. (GWD)

hangar pilot USAAF (WWII) a pilot who bragged, exaggerated, or lied about his talents as a flier. (GWD)

hangfire USN/USMC (WWII–present) a charge of gunpowder or a round that does not explode immediately upon ignition. This delay can occur in any type of ammunition and is usually due to faulty production. (MAN)

hanging on its props USNA (WWII) said of a propeller-driven aircraft flying barely fast enough to stay aloft. (BCD)

hanging on the wire BrA (WWI) said casually of one whose whereabouts were unknown. (AGE)

hang out the laundry USA (WWII) to drop paratroopers from a plane.

Hanoi Hilton USA/USMC/USN (1960s) Hos Lo Prison in Hanoi, North Vietnam.

happy-go-lucky USN (19th c.) said of one who recklessly places his faith in luck rather than ability, thought, and preparation. (ANE)

happy hour USN/USAF/USMC/USA (WWI–1950s) a period of time during which those not assigned to duty stations were allowed to relax. (1950s) a cocktail party; a set period of time each day when nightclubs and bars sell drinks at a reduced price. (AFS ASC OST) (*see* duty station)

hard and fast MM (18th–19th c.) said of a vessel that is firmly aground. (AST)

hard-boiled USA (WWII) tough, strictly disciplined, seasoned. (MMD)

hard case CSA/USA/USN (1860s) a very tough, hardened man. (LRY)

hard cash USA/USMC/USN (early 19th c.–WWII) minted coins; aka hard money. (AFR) (*see also* cabbage, lettuce, toot)

hard charger USMC (WWII–Korean War) a good, seasoned combat Marine. (SAM)

hard fish MM (18th–19th c.) hard, extremely salty fish that had been too long in the salt barrel. (AST)

hard hat USAF/USA/USMC (1950s–60s) a crash helmet specially designed for jet pilots. USA/USMC (1960s) a member of the Vietcong who served on a full-time basis.

hard horse USN (19th c.) a cruel, tyrannical officer. (ANE)

hard knocks CSA/USA (1860s) a beating. (LRY)

hard money *See* hard cash

hard rice USA (1960s) weapons and munitions supplied to Vietnamese allies. Military goods were considered as vital to survival as rice, the staple food of the region.

hard-rolled USA (WWI–WWII) machine-made, in reference to a cigarette; aka tailor made. (AFR ATK) (*see also* hand-rolled)

hard-skin BrA (WWI) a ruffian, one who is rough and wild.

hardtack MM (16th–20th c.) a cracker or biscuit made of salt, water, and flour and noted for its hardness; aka worm castle. Properly made and stored, hardtack could outlive many people. It was said to supply fresh meat in the form of weevils and ants. (EMP) (*see also* ANZAC wafer, tea cakes)

hard tail Br/USA (19th–20th c.) a mule. (AGE EMP GWD) (*see also* mule)

hard target *See* soft target

hardware BrA (WWI) ammunition, especially artillery ammunition.

harker BrA (WWI) [Scottish *harken*, to listen] one assigned to a listening post in no man's land. (*see* no man's land)

Harpoon missile USAF/USN (1977–present) a turbojet-powered cruise missile that carries a conventional warhead of five hundred pounds and has an effective range of more than fifty miles. It is an antiship missile that can be launched from a submerged submarine or an airborne aircraft. (*see* cruise missile)

Harriet Lane *See* Lane, Harriet

hash *See* sixty-second

hash burner USA (WWII) a cook. (AFR)

hash marks USA/USMC/USAAF (WWI–present) stripes worn on the cuffs of a dress uniform or class As that indicate length of service (one stripe for every four years). During and between WWI and WWII, the army's hash marks were color coded by branch: red for artillery, light blue for infantry, and yellow for cavalry. USMC (WWII) aka stupidity stripes, on the assumption that anyone who reenlisted had to be stupid. USAF (1950s) aka fogy stripes. (AFR AFS ATK EMP SAM)

hasty pudding BrN>USN (18th–19th c.) a batter made of flour and oatmeal and stirred into a pot of boiling water. The result was served with sugar and/or molasses. (ANE DVT)

hat, the USMC (1980s–90s) a boot camp term for a drill instructor; aka DI.

hatch USMC (1890s–present) a doorway; an opening between compartments on a modern, metal ship. (SAM)

hat cord USA (WWI–WWII) braided cord worn on the campaign hat or piping on the overseas cap that denoted the wearer's army branch. In 1944, the colors were as follows: infantry, light blue; artillery, red; signal corps, orange and white; engineers, red and white; medical corps, maroon and white; ordnance, red and yellow; quartermaster corps, buff; air corps, blue and golden orange; chemical warfare, cobalt blue and orange; tanks, green and white; military police, yellow and green; finance department, silver gray and yellow; detached enlisted men, green; tank destroyer, golden orange and black; transportation, brick red and golden yellow; women's army corps, old gold and moss. (CAM MSH) (*see* campaign hat)

hate BrA (WWI) a severe bombardment, from a German song entitled the "Hymn of Hate." (*see also* stir up a little hate)

hatrack *See* horse, mule

haul MM (16th c.–present) [French *haler*, to pull or to haul] to pull. Ashore: to carry a load for a distance; to carry merchandise from one point to another. (AST OST)

haul ass USA (WWII) to leave a position as quickly as possible yet in an orderly manner. When communicating by field telephone, haul ass was rendered as "how able." (MCT)

haul off BrN>USN (17th c.–present) to increase the distance between opposing ships by sailing to the windward. (OST TWW)

haul yards MM (13th–17th c.) to pull on ropes to raise yards or spars into position on a mast. (OST TON) (*see also* halyard)

have a doss BrA (WWI) to get some sleep.

haversack Gr>Fr>Br>USA/USMC (18th c.–1830s) [German *habersack*, oat bag> French *havresac*, oat bag for horses] a cloth bag in which a soldier carried his personal belongings, daily food rations, and souvenirs (war booty). (DWO) (*see also* knapsack)

have the wind up *See* windy

havoc Gr>Fr>Br>USA (15th c.–present) [German war cry or signal to begin plundering> Old French *criet havot*>English *shout havot*] total destruction and confusion. (DWO)

hawks *See* war hawks

hawse hole MM (ancient Greece) originally, human eyes painted on a ship's bow to fend off evil spirits. (16th c.–present) an opening in the bow of a ship through which anchor hawsers or cables pass. (TON) (*see* hawser)

hawser MM (14th c.–present) [Anglo-Norman *haucer*, heavy rope] a heavy line,

five inches or more in diameter, to which the anchor is attached. (20th c.) any heavy mooring line. (OST TON)

hay USA (WWII) sauerkraut. (SID)

hayburner *See* horse, mule

hay shaker USA (1860s) a farmer; aka hen wrangler.

hazardous duty USA/USMC/USAAF/USN (WWII–present) duty, such as demolitions and parachuting, considered to be dangerous. Those accepting such assignments receive hazardous duty pay in addition to regular salary. (AFS)

haze MM>USA/USMC/USN/USAF (19th c.) to hit, strike, or beat. (19th–20th c.) to harrass or assign extremely difficult or demeaning work, especially to an underclassman at a military academy. Hazing frequently was carried to an extreme and is now discouraged or forbidden. (AST SLA)

HE Br>USA (WWI–present) high explosives, such as those used in artillery shells. (MMD)

head Br>USN/USMC/USA (15th c.–present) [Old English *heden*, head] the bow of a ship, which was the location of the sailors' toilet. On the best ships, the toilet consisted of planks on either side of the bowsprit with a few convenient holes cut into them and a line overhead for users to take hold of while using the contraption. USA (1960s) a compass heading. Br>USN/USMC (20th c.) any bathroom or toilet. (BJM OST SAM SLA) (*see* bowsprit)

head and gun money BrN>USN (18th–19th c.) reward money paid to captor(s) for every prisoner rescued from a pirate ship. (ANE)

head bucket USA (WWII) an M2 helmet, which consisted of a steel outer shell and a fiberboard liner. It replaced the flat British-style helmet of the WWI–WWII era. (ATK)

head call USMC (WWI–present) a need to answer nature's call. (PAT SAM) (*see* head)

head honcho *See* honcho

head reach BrN>USN (18th c.) to sail with the wind under shortened sail. (SLA)

headroom USN (19th c.–present) the distance between a deck and its overhead, or ceiling. (MAN)

headstone USA (WWII) a hard, government-issue pillow. (GWD)

heap *See* airplane

hearse USN (WWII) a German submarine, as so many of them carried their crews to rest at the bottom of the sea; aka crapper, iron coffin.

heart *See* purple heart

heartburn USMC (1980s) a complaint, gripe, or objection.

heart trouble USA (WWII) a girlfriend.

HEAT (heet) USA/USMC/USAF/USN (1970s) high explosives used against tanks.

heat can USAF (1950s) a jet plane, whose exhaust resembles a can of burning Sterno. (AFS)

heat up USA (1860s) to run a horse until it is overheated.

heave MM/BrN>USN (17th–20th c.) [Anglo-Saxon *hebban*, to pull] to pull. Ashore: to pull, throw, or toss. (AST OST)

heave the lead MM/BrN>USN (15th c.–present) to take a depth sounding with a line and lead weight. (OST SLA)

heave to MM/BrN>USN (18th c.–present) to stop.

heave up anchor MM (18th–20th c.) to die. (AST)

heavier metal USN (1960s) a ship that is larger and more powerful than other ships in the fleet.

heavy A USMC (1980s) the assistant drill instructor who is in charge of the physical training of recruits.

heavy duty USA/USMC/USN/USAF (1960s) very serious or intense.

hedgehog USN (19th c.) a vessel powered by many oars. (WWII) a depth charge launched in a high arc from a vessel's deck. (ANE) Fr>USA/USMC (1950s–70s) an isolated post established by the French during the 1950s' Indochina War in Vietnam. Similar posts were established later by United States troops.

hedge hop Br>USAAF (WWI–WWII) to fly an aircraft at treetop or hedgetop level in an attempt to surprise the enemy or avoid

detection. (AFR GWD)

HEDP USA (1970s) high explosive, dual purpose.

heel MM (16th c.) to lean to one side, as a ship, as a result of the wind; to fall over. (MAN OST)

Heine (HIGH•nee) US>USA/USMC/USN (1890–WWII) [German *Heinrich,* Henry] nickname for a German. (AGE IHA MMD) (*see also* boche, hun, Jerry, Katzenjammer Kid, kraut, moffer, Ted)

HEIT (hite) USA (1970s) high explosive incendiary tracer rounds.

helicopter Fr>Br>USA/USMC (19th c.) [French *hélicoptère*>English *helicoptere*] (1861) a crude, less-than-successful aircraft that relied on human muscle power to turn rotating, spiral-shaped wings, or aerofoils. Fr (1930s) a rotor- and propeller-driven, one-man, open-frame aircraft. (DWO) (*see also* chopper, Huey, whirlybird, windmill)

heliport USA (1950s) an area set aside as a landing pad and hangar for helicopters. (ASC)

hell buggy USA (WWII) a tank. (GWD MMD)

hell ship MM (19th c.) a ship commanded by cruel, brutal officers. (AST)

helm MM>BrN>USN (18th c.–present) the steering mechanism of a vessel. (OST)

helmsman MM>BrN>USN (18th c.–present) the man who steers the vessel. (SEA) (*see* steersman)

hen buttons CSA (1860s) Union uniform buttons, which bore a representation of an eagle.

hen fruit USA (WWII) a chicken egg. (GWD)

hen wrangler USA (1860s) a farmer; aka hay shaker.

HEP USA (1970s) high explosive plastics.

herd USA (WWI–WWII) to drive, escort, or direct, as a group of people (especially POWs), to a specific location. (AFR GWD)

herdbound USA (WWI–WWII) said of a soldier unfit for further military service. (AFR)

here's how USA (WWI–WWII) a traditional drinking salute. (MMD)

hershey bar USA (WWII) a gold-brown stripe worn on the sleeve cuffs of the brown service dress uniform; aka overseas stripe. One stripe was issued for every six months spent overseas. (1942) a cheap prostitute, who could be bought for the price of a chocolate bar. (MSH)

HFDF USN (1960s) high-frequency direction finder; aka huff duff.

HHC USA (1970s) headquarters and headquarters company.

hide USN (19th c.) to beat or flog. (ANE) (*see* flog)

hidey-hole USA (1960s) a hastily dug hole in which one could seek shelter.

high and dry MM (18th c.) said of a ship that was hung up on rocks or reefs and could not be dislodged by the tide. Ashore: stranded, powerless, deserted. (SLA)

high and tight USMC (1980s) a military hairstyle in which the hair is cut to about a quarter inch in length.

highball[1] USA/USN/USMC/USAF (1890s) a railroad signal flag with a red ball at its center. When the flag was raised, the engineer could continue moving down the track. USA/USN/USMC/USAF (WWI–present) a hand salute; the act of saluting a superior. (ASC EMP IHA)

highball[2] USA/USMC/USAAF/USN (1930) to drive a vehicle at full speed. (ASC EMP IHA)

highbrow USA (WWII) an officer of the general staff, typically of good breeding; an enlisted man or junior officer who put on airs. (MMD) (*see* general staff)

higher than a Georgia pine USA (WWII) overly excited, ecstatic. (MMD)

high jump USA (WWII) a knee-jerk response to being called on the carpet by the commander. Probably from drill instructors' oft-heard order: "When I say 'jump,' you say, 'how high?'!" (AGE EMP)

high point USA/Central Intelligence Agency (1960s) a period, usually several days, of increased enemy activity.

hike USA/USMC (1860s) a practice march, a long march intended to toughen soldiers. (MSH)

hike off *See* take a hike

hike up USN (19th c.) to kidnap or carry off

by force. (ANE)

hip flask USA (WWII) a .45-caliber pistol in its holster. (SID)

hip shooting *See* shoot and scoot

His Majesty's bad bargain BrA (18th c.) one who is totally useless. (DVT)

hist *See* hoist

hit USMC (1930s–present) wounded. (SAM)

hit between the wind and the water BrN>USN (18th c.) to strike a ship with shot or shell at or below the waterline; to strike in the stomach. (SLA)

hitch USA/USMC/USAAF/USN (19th c.–present) duration of enlistment; the enlistment itself. May have arisen from the civilian phrase "to get hitched," to get married, as one is "married" to the service for the duration of his contract. (AFR MCT PAT)

hitching post *See* sailor's hitching post

hit the beach USMC/USN (19th c.–present) to make an armed landing on an enemy shore; to go ashore or into town on liberty. (AST SAM)

hit the deck USMC/USN (19th c.) to get out of a bed or hammock; to hit the ground to avoid enemy fire; to land an aircraft. The cry *Hit the deck!* alerts sailors and Marines to danger. (MMD PAT SAM)

hit the dirt USA/USMC (WWI–present) to take cover immediately. (ATK PAT)

hit the hay USA (WWII) to go to bed. (MMD)

hit the sack USA/USMC/USAAF/USN (WWII–present) to go to bed, most widely used by United States servicemen during WWII. (IHA SAM)

hit the silk USAAF (WWII) to jump from an airplane with a parachute. (ATK GWD)

hit the white fluff USA (WWII) to sleep in a clean, soft civilian bed. (MMD)

hive USA (WWI–WWII) to discover, catch, or capture. (AFR)

HMFIC (HEM•fick) USAF (1960s) head motherfucker in charge.

HMFWIC (HEM•fwick) USAF (1960s) head motherfucker who's in charge.

hog USA (1960s) a Huey helicopter gunship; an A10 Thunderbolt II; aka warthog. (*see also* Huey)

hog board USMC (1980s) a boot camp term for a bulletin board in the barracks, near the drill instructor's quarters, where recruits' photographs of family and friends were posted.

hoggie USA (WWII) a one dollar bill, United States currency. (GWD)

hog in armor USN (1870s) an ironclad ship. (ANE)

hog–60 USA (1960s) an M60 machine gun.

hoist (hoyst) MM (16th c.–present) [Dutch *hyssen*, to lift] to lift or raise up, especially with a block and tackle; to be thrown into the air, as by an explosion; aka hist. (OST SLA) (*see also* hoisted by one's own petard)

hoisted by one's own petard MM>BrN> USN (16th c.–present) to have been thrown in the air by the explosion of one's own demolition charge. (*see* hoist)

hold-all BrA (WWI) a canvas roll that held a soldier's razor, comb, soap, knife, fork, spoon, mirror, and toothbrush. (AGE)

holders USN (19th c.) men assigned to work in the ship's hold, at the very bottom of the ship. (AST)

hold it down USA/USAAF (WWII) to quiet down. (AFR)

holiday USN (1960s) a flaw in a piece of equipment or other item; a spot missed during cleaning or painting.

Hollywood corporal USA (WWII) an acting corporal. (GWD)

Hollywood shower USN (1960s) a long, luxurious shower with unlimited warm water, the opposite of a navy shower. (*see* navy shower)

holsters USA (1861) leather pistol holders affixed to the saddles of cavalrymen. (WWI–WWII) webbed canvas or leather cases for carrying revolvers or automatic pistols. (MD MMD)

holy ground USN (19th–20th c.) the parts of a ship off limits to enlisted men unless they were assigned to a duty station or given special permission by an authorized officer. Such areas included the officers' wardroom, the captain's quarters, and the quarterdeck. (AST NCT RAS)

Holy Joe USA>USN>BrA (1840s–WWII) a chaplain. Possibly so named after Joseph Smith, who in the 1830s founded Mormonism, noted for the armed enforcement and defense of its faith. Smith was considered a heretic by many Christians because of his belief in polygamy and his theory that Native Americans were the lost tribes of Israel. Therefore, in the 1840s, to call a preacher a Holy Joe was to imply that he was a heretic. (AGE EMP TON WEA) (*see also* chaplain, GI sky pilot, gospel grinder, padre, sky pilot, sky scout)

holystone MM/BrN>USN (18th c.–1931) a block of sandstone used to scour the decks of British and United States warships for more than one hundred years. Larger blocks were also called bibles; smaller, worn blocks were also called prayer books. Scrubbing was done on hands and knees, like a person in devout prayer, and legend has it that sailors of the British navy once used fragments of gravestones. On March 5, 1931, the United States Navy banned holystones with General Order No. 215. (OST TON)

hombre USA (ca.1836) [Spanish *hombre*, man] man. First used by soldiers and civilians on the southwestern frontier but eventually common throughout the army and Marine corps as a result of the Spanish-American War. (ATK)

home NZA (WWI) one's frontline dugout.

homesteader USA (1960s) a United States serviceman who remained in Vietnam for five years or more. Many homesteaders married Vietnamese women and had families.

homeward bound stitches MM (18th–19th c.) poorly executed and usually self-sewn repairs to one's clothing that were expected to last only until one was paid off at the end of a voyage. (AST)

homing device USA/USAAF (WWII) a weekend pass or long furlough. (AFR GWD) (*see* furlough)

homme forty Br>USA (WWI) [French *homme*, man] a French railroad car with a capacity of forty men or eight horses. The standard speed of an homme forty was 1fi mph.

honcho USA/USN/USMC/USAF/Viet (1950s–70s) [Japanese *honcho*, squad leader, corporal] leader; supervisor; boss; aka head honcho. (ASC IHA MCT) (*see* NCO)

Honey BrA (1940, North Africa) United States M3 light cavalry tank; aka the Stuart, after Confederate general J. E. B. Stuart. The M3 had a 37-mm gun. (BRC)

honey barge USMC/USN (WWII–Korean War) a garbage barge. (PAT SAM)

honey bucket CA (WWI) a bucket used to empty latrines. (*see* honey dipper, latrine)

honey dipper USMC (Korean War) a Korean laborer who emptied military latrines and the village cesspool; aka honey bucket man. (PAT SAM) (*see* honey bucket, latrine)

honey wagon USA (WWI–WWII) a garbage truck or the tank truck used to haul human waste. (GWD)

Hong Kong haircut USN (1980s–present) oral sex; aka blow job.

hooch USA (19th c.) [Eskimo *hoochino*, home-brewed liquor] strong home-brewed liquor. Hooch was in widespread use during the Alaskan gold rush of 1898, both by miners and by the soldiers sent to protect them. (ATK MCT) BrA (1940s, North Africa) a home-brewed tonic that was ninety-five percent wood alcohol; aka RSM's milk, stromboli, zbib (ZEE•bib). (DRA)

hoodlum MM (18th–19th c.) a sailor who lied about his rating when signing on, implying a level of skill he didn't have; aka hoosier. Hoodlums were treated poorly by the rest of the crew because it took two or more sailors to do the job that he had claimed he could do. (AST)

hook USA (WWII) a medical injection. USN (1940s–present) a ship's anchor. (GWD)

hooker Br (18th c.) [Dutch *hoeker*, small round-bottomed, slow-moving coastal and fishing craft>Persian *hooak*, water pipe] a small Dutch merchant craft that plied its trade between England and Holland. MM (18th c.) a short clay pipe favored by British and United States sailors; a prostitute, from

a comparison of a woman's shape and attributes to those of Dutch coastal craft. USN (19th c.) a term of affection for one's ship. (ANE SLA)

hooks USA (19th c.) spurs. (EMP)

hooligan navy USN (WWII–1960s) the United States Coast Guard; aka baby navy, bucket brigade, freshwater navy, muddy water sailors.

hoosegow US>USA (1860s–WWII) [Spanish *juzgado,* to be sentenced to jail] jail. The term came to the army via cowboys of the Southwest. (AFR IHA) (*see also* jail)

hoosier *See* hoodlum

hootch USA/USMC (1960s–present) a basic shelter of any sort; a military barracks; a Vietnamese home or hut. USMC (1980s–90s) a pup tent. (*see* pup tent)

hop USA (WWI–WWII) an informal dance. (GWD)

hopped up USN (WWI) drunk, smashed; aka gowed up.

hop tac USA/USMC (1964) [Vietnamese *hop tac*, cooperation] a program designed to counteract the influences of the Communist forces operating in seven provinces surrounding Saigon. United States troops were sent into the villages, where they provided medical assistance and educational programs as well as training for local anticommunist militia units. In the end, the program was not considered a success due to the strong Communist and antigovernment influences that were firmly entrenched there.

horizontal pleasure USA (WWII) sleep. (GWD)

hornet CSA/USA (1860s) a bullet. USA/USAAF (WWII) a USAAF dive bomber. (GWD MMD)

hors de combat Fr>Br>USA (18th c.) [French *hors de combat*, out of the battle] wounded and unable to continue to fight.

horse USA (18th c.–present) an animal ridden in combat by cavalrymen and mounted infantry; aka hatrack, hayburner. (GWD)

horse cock USN (WWII–present) unidentifiable meat, especially luncheon meat; aka cylindrical sirloin, fillet of mule tool, tube steak.

horse marine USN (18th c.) one who is out of his place or element; a lubberly sailor; a soldier. Usually, an insult hurled by sailors at a Marine or another sailor. (ANE RAS) (*see* landlubber)

horse potato USN (19th c.) a yam or sweet potato. (ANE)

horse salts USN (19th c.) salts and/or other purgatives used to cleanse the body of "evil fluids" believed to cause illness. (AST)

horse sense CSA/USA (1860s) common sense, intelligence. (LRY)

horseshit man USA (Vietnam) among special forces, a nickname for Ho Chi Minh City.

hose USA/USMC (1960s) to clear, as a targeted area, with automatic weapons fire; aka hose down.

hot USAAF (WWII) fast, as an airplane. (AFR) (*see also* hot crate)

hot bunk USN (WWII–present) a bunk shared with another in rotation. A hot bunk is always warm because someone is always in it.

hot cat *See* Chauchat automatic assault rifle

hot cock USMC (Korean War) a hot dog. (PAT SAM)

hot copper USN (1860s) a headache brought on by drinking alcohol. (RAS)

hot crate USAAF (WWII) a fast fighter plane. (GWD) (*see* hot)

hot dog USA/USMC (1960s) a big shot; a braggart; a show-off.

hotel de ginks USAF (1950s) barracks reserved for the use of men in transit between bases. (AFS)

hot LZ USA/USMC (1960s) a helicopter landing zone under direct enemy attack.

hot pilot USAAF>USAF/USNA (WWII–1960s) an exceptionally skilled flier; aka hot shot. (GWD)

hot rock USAF (1950s) a skilled pilot, especially one who was daring or reckless. (AFS)

hots USA (1960s) a hot meal or hot food in general, a rarity for those in the field.

hot seat USAF (1950s) the automatic ejection seat of a jet aircraft, aka panic rack; the center of controversy. (AFS)

hot shot Br>USA/USN (18th–19th c.) solid shot heated in a furnace prior to firing, designed to set its target afire. (MMD) USAAF (WWII) a man who excelled at his work. (AFR) USAF (1960s) a person of great ability; an expert flier; aka hot pilot, ace of the base. (1980s) an unsafe or dangerous pilot.

Hot SOP USMC (1980s) Hot Standard Operating Procedure, which was in effect between April 15 and October 15, when heat precaution techniques were followed during training in hot weather.

hot stuff BrA (WWI) heavy shelling by enemy artillery.

house mouse USA/USMC/USAF (1960s) a Vietnamese cleaning girl; a mistress.

housewife BrA/USA/USN/USMC (19th–20th c.) a sewing kit containing thread, buttons, and needles. (AGE ASC GWD)

hover USN (19th c.) to hang about, like a seagull that drifts around a ship or port; to pace. (ANE)

HOW (how) BrA (WWI) an artillery howitzer.

how USA (1815) [Lakota *hao* and Omaha *hau*, greeting] a greeting adopted from Native Americans, often spoken in a tone of voice that rang with impatience. (IHA)

how able *See* haul ass

howker USN (1860s) [Dutch *howker*, two-masted ship] a sailor with two girls on shore. (ANE)

HP USAAF (WWII) hot pilot, a good flier, especially a self-proclaimed one. (AFR GWD) USNA (WWII) hot pilot; a man who was too self-important. (AFR) (*see* hot pilot)

Huey USA/USMC/USN/USAF (1960s) a nickname for the Bell UH1, a universal duty helicopter.

huff duff USN (1960s) high-frequency direction finder; aka HFDF.

huffed BrA>USAAF (1915–WWII) killed as a result of a fall or jump from an aircraft in flight. (MMD)

Hugh Williams *See* Williams, Hugh

huiles (wheels) FrA (WWI) [French *les huiles*, the gray ones] the top brass; general staff officers; political top dogs; aka gros legumes. (WWW) (*see* general staff, top brass)

hull down MM (18th c.) said of a vessel at a distance, with only its upper works (sails or smokestacks) visible. (MAN OST)

hull thumper USA (WWII) the shell ejector inside a tank or armored vehicle, which threw empty shell casings against the hull. (GWD)

hump¹ USA/USMC (WWII) the midpoint of an enlistment period; an obstacle. (1960s) a combat soldier's or Marine's twenty-five-day rotation in the field. (MCT)

hump² USA/USMC (1960s) to do heavy work; to walk or hike; to carry a heavy load. An infantryman who carried his gear in the field was said to be *humping the bush*. (MCT)

hun Br>USA/USMC/USN (1908–WWII) a German, from Attila the Hun. This nickname was popular with civilians and newspapers but not with frontline soldiers. (AGE) (*see also* boche, Heine, Jerry, Katzenjammer Kid, kraut, moffer, Ted)

hundred and worst USA (1960s) a nickname for the 101st Airborne Division.

hungry hill USA (WWI) living quarters on post for married NCOs and their families, a reflection of the low pay and large families that were typical. USA (1870s–WWII) aka soap suds row, because many wives took in laundry to help support their families. (ATK) (*see* NCO)

hungry hundred BrN (1890s) Royal Navy reserve officers, who were few in number and poorly paid. (TON)

hunky-dory CSA/USA>USN (1860s–1945) [Japanese *Honkidori*, street in Yokohama where one could fulfill nearly every wish and desire] fantastic, great; aka bully. (LRY TON)

hun pinch Br>USA/USMC (WWI) to capture German prisoners: *The 355th did some hun pinching*. (AGE) (*see* hun)

Hüren-Känne (HOO•ren-KAH•neh) GrA (1940, North Africa) a whore's bed; the Hurricane, a British fighter plane noted for its effectiveness at ground attack and tank killing. (WID)

Hurricane *See* Huren-Kanne

hurtin' USA/USMC (1960s) wounded; dead.

hush-hush Br>USA/USN/USMC/USAF (WWI–present) [English *hush* (14th c.), to be quiet] said of top secret military plans.

hussar Hun>Br>FrA (15th–18th c.) [Old Serbian *husar*, plunderer, and Hungarian *huszar*, plunderer] a lightly armed horseman uniformed in imitation of Hungarian light cavalry. (MMD)

hypo happy USAAF (WWII) said of an enthusiastic photographer. (AFR) (*see also* shutterbug)

I

I and I USA (1960s) intelligence and interdiction, the use of artillery fire at night to disrupt enemy movement; intercourse and intoxication.

IC USA/USMC/USN (WWI) inspected and condemned. The initials were painted or stenciled on items unfit for further military service. (ATK MMD)

ICBM USA/USAF/USMC/USN (1950s–present) intercontinental ballistic missile.

ICC USA/USAF/USMC/USN (1950s–70s) International Control Commission, established by the United Nations in 1954 to oversee agreements that dealt with Vietnam. The member states of the commission were Poland, Canada, and India.

ice wagon *See* truck

ichi ban USA/USMC (Korean War) [Japanese *ichi ban*, one] top notch, of finest quality, perfect. (MCT)

I Corps USA/USMC (1960s) the first allied tactical zone established in South Vietnam. It consisted of South Vietnam's five northernmost provinces.

ICP Vietminh (1930–present) Indo-Chinese Communist Party, founded by Ho Chi Minh in 1930 as a replacement for the Vietnamese Communist Party.

IDA USA (1960s) Institute for Defense Analysis, a nonprofit group that conducted research for the Department of Defense.

ID card USMC (WWII) an identification card displaying a photograph of the holder. (SAM)

iddy-umpty USA (WWI) a man in the army Signal Corps; aka buzzer. (*see* Signal Corps)

identification disc See dog tags

idiot seat USAF (1950s) seat occupied by the copilot in a two-seater fighter aircraft. (AFS)

idler USN (18th–19th c.) one who did not stand watch aboard ship, including the surgeon, cook, barber, officer of Marines, and captain. (OST) USN (WWI) one who stood the morning watch, from midnight to 4 A.M. (OST)

If I hadn't been born a bloody fool, I wouldn't have joined the Navy—fire! BrN>USN (18th–19th c.) a chant taken up by gun captains in order to time the firing of a salute. A similar chant went: "My mother never raised me to be a bloody gunner—fire!" (AST)

IFR USAF (1950s) instrument flight rules. (AFS)

if that don't beat the Dutch Br>USA/USN (17th–18th c.) a remark denoting amazement or surprise and reflecting admiration for the toughness and resourcefulness of the Dutch during wars with England. (IHA)

IG USA/USMC/USN/USAF (1960s) inspector general.

IIR USA/USMC (1960s) infrared imaging radar, used by gunships that hunt the enemy at night. (*see* gunship)

illum (il•UME) USA (1960s) an illumination flare.

impressment BrN (17th–mid-19th c.) the act of forcing men into naval service. The term arises from the placement of a king's shilling into the hand of the man being pressed into service. Having "accepted" the money, the impressed man was then officially in the navy. The shilling was then taken back "to purchase the pressed man's kit." Of course the poor soul never saw the shilling again or the kit. (NCT TWW) (*see* press gang)

in a spin USAAF/USN (WWII) mentally confused or unsettled; abed; napping. USN (WWII) said of one landing a plane in an out-of-control manner on the deck of carrier; said of one who fell face down on the deck as a result of drinking too much. (AFR ATK MMD)

in a storm USA/USAAF (WWII) a condition of agitation or excitement in which the sufferer didn't know what he was doing. (AFR GWD)

incentive pay USA (1950s) additional money paid to military personnel for specialty ratings, length of service, or hazardous duty. (ASC) (*see* hazardous duty, rating)

INCOC (IN•cock) USA (1960s) infantry non-commissioned officer's course. (*see also* instant NCO)

in country USA/USMC (1960s) said of one assigned to duty in an area outside of the United States and its territories.

Indian Sp>Br>USA (15th–20th c.) a native of the Americas. So named by early European explorers who believed that they had discovered islands off the coast of India. (IHA)

Indian country USA/USMC (1960s) the central highlands of South Vietnam, an area controlled by the Vietcong or North Vietnamese; aka Injun country.

Indian file BrA>USA (1756–WWII) single file. (ATK IHA)

indirect fire USA/USMC/USN/USAF (1960s–present) mortar and artillery fire used against targets not directly visible to gunners. The shells are fired at a high trajectory, or arc.

sounded at the flag-lowering ceremony held each day at sunset on all military posts. (AFS MCT MD MMD) (*see also* skedaddle)

retreat gun BrA>USA (19th c.–present) the artillery piece that is fired to signal the beginning of the evening flag-lowering ceremony. (ASC)

return USA (WWII) a wounded man sent to the rear for medical treatment. (MMD) (*see* rear)

re-up USA/USMC/USN (WWI–present) to reenlist. (ASC EMP MCT) (*see also* reenlistment leave)

reveille BrA>USA/USMC/USN/USAF/ USCG (17th c.–present) [French *reveiller* (17th c.), to wake up] a drum roll, bugle call, or gun shot sounded at daybreak to awaken troops. (DWO MCT MD MMD)

reveille gun BrA>USA (19th c.–present) an artillery piece fired at sunrise to mark the beginning of the military day; aka morning gun. (ASC) (*see also* retreat gun, reveille)

Revenue Cutter Service *See* Revenue Marines, United States Coast Guard

Revenue Marines US (1790–1915) the forerunner of the United States Coast Guard, established August 4, 1790. In 1915, the RMs and the Life Saving Service were combined to become the United States Coast Guard. (NCT) (*see* United States Coast Guard)

review BrA (1768) inspection by the commanding general to ensure that regiments were fit for service—properly uniformed and equipped. Unfit men were discharged. USA (1833 c.–present) formal parade of troops passing person[s] of importance; careful examination of records, accounts, equipment, or troops. (AFS MD MDB MMD TLL)

reviewing party USA (WWII) the commander and his staff, whose duty it is to observe a parade; the VIPs being honored by the parade. (ASC) (*see* review, VIPs)

reward USA (1860s) money paid for capture of a deserter. (MD)

rhino BrA/BrN (1920–present) money, cash or coin. USN (1925–WWII) a state of being totally broke, without money, cash or coin,

as in *Jones hoped to avoid being rhino.*

RHIO USA/USAAF>USAF (WWII–1960s) rank hath its obligations. (AFS ASC)

RHIP USA/USMC/USN/USAF (WWII–present) rank hath its privilege. (AFS ASC PAT)

ribbon bars USA/USMC/USN/USAF (20th c.) the bars of miniature ribbons that are worn on the left breast of the service uniform in lieu of full-size ribbons or medals. Each multicolored miniature represents a full-sized military medal. (AFS SAM) (*see also* rosette)

ricco BrA (WWI) ricochet bullet. (AGE)

rice bill USA (1945–58) monthly expense of keeping a native girl in the Orient. (MCT)

ricocheted off too many bulkheads USMC (WWII) descriptive of an odd character with strange habits, slightly off in the head; aka rock happy, two cans shy of a six-pack. (SAM)

ride the beam USAAF (WWII) to pretend innocence by gazing intently at the ceiling, as if studying a course or beam, in order to ignore someone or something. (AFR)

ride the bear USN (19th c.) to drag a wooden box filled with holystones up and down the deck to increase the deck's shine. (TON) (*see* holystone)

ride the bow gun USN (19th c.) to be punished by having to sit astride a gun barrel with the feet tied together underneath for three to seven days. (BMO)

ride the sick boot USA (WWII) to fake illness in order to avoid duty. (GWD SID)

ride you down USN (19th c.) to break a man's spirit, a threat from an officer to an enlisted man. (AST)

ridge runner *See* plow jockey

rien à signaler FrA (WWI) "No news today."

rifle USA (1960s) infantryman, whose main weapon is a rifle.

rifle grenade BrA>USA/USMC (WWI–present) a grenade specially designed to be fired from a rifle. (*see also* grenadier)

rig¹ MM (15th c.) [Norse *rigge*, to prepare or arrange] the spar and sail arrangement of a vessel; sailor's clothing. (BJM OST)

rig² MM (15th c.) [Norse *rigge*, to prepare or

arrange] to equip a vessel. (BJM OST)

rigging MM>BrN>USN (15th c.–present) lines and chains used aboard a ship, especially in working sail and supporting masts and spars. (*see* spar)

right drill USA (WWII) something done right, as in *Jamison finally got the right drill.* (MMD)

RIP BrA (WWI) rest in pieces, said especially after a heavy artillery barrage. A pun on rest in piece.

rip cords USA (1960s) paratroopers' name for loose threads.

ripple USN (WWII) noncommissioned officer in the WAVES. (*see* WAVES)

rise and shine USA/USMC (WWI–present) call to get up and get out of bed. (AFR EMP) (*see* roll out)

RO USA (WWI) a regimental order, which concerned everyone in the unit. (EMP)

roach wagon USA (1960s) mobile snack bar, kitchen, or canteen.

ROAD sergeant USAF (1980s) a retired, on-active-duty sergeant.

Robincrotch, Suzie *See* Suzie

ROC USA (1970s–present) rules of confrontation.

Roc USA/USMC (1950–present) a native of the Republic of South Korea.

rock an' roll USA/USMC (1960s–present) to fire a weapon on full automatic. (AET)

rocket city USA (1960s) a base under heavy and/or constant rocket attack.

rock happy *See* ricocheted off too many bulkheads

rocks and shoals USN/USMC (1799–WWII) naval rules and regulations. The term arose with old sailors and Marines who were always caught between a rock and a hard place. (RAS SAM)

rock slinger USA (WWII) mortar man.

ROE USA (1970s–present) rules of engagement.

roger USAAF>USAF (WWII–present) radio reply meaning "OK," "all right," "understood." (AFR)

roller skate USA (WWII) tank or other armored vehicle. (MMD)

rollings USAAF (WWII) the papers and tobacco for making cigarettes. (AFR)

roll out USA (1960s) an order to get up and get moving.

roll up your flaps USAAF (WWII) an order to be silent. (AFR)

Rome plow USA (1960s) a high-bladed plow mounted on the front of a tank and used to clear a path through the jungle.

RON USAF (1950s) remaining overnight. This stamp on a pass indicated that the holder had permission to be away from the base overnight. (AFS)

Ronson GrA (WWII) a German nickname for a United States Sherman tank, which used aircraft fuel and, when hit in the right place, lit up like a Ronson-brand cigarette lighter. (FOD)

rookie *See* recruit

room to swing a cat BrN>USN (17th–late 19th c.) enough room for the bosun's mate to swing a cat-o'-nine-tails without fouling it in the ship's rigging. (RAS) (*see* cat-o'-nine-tails, rigging)

rooty BrA (WWI) bread. (AGE)

ropey USA (WWII) foul or filthy. Usually said of weather. (MMD)

rope yarn Sunday *See* make and mend day

Rosalie FrA (WWI) the beloved bayonet. (WWW) (*see also* cheese toaster, frog sticker, Josephine, paring knife, pig sticker)

rosette USA (WWII) a miniature of a military award worn on the lapel of a civilian suit coat to denote that the wearer had earned the award. (ASC) (*see also* ribbon bar)

rosewater sailor USN (1860s) an incompetent, unsailorlike officer, a dandy. Because officers bathed in hot, fresh water and used scented soap and cologne, they smelled of rosewater. Sailors were forbidden to have cologne since it was a favored drink. (RAS)

rotate USA (1960s) to return to the United States after service overseas. (TON)

ROTC USA (1920s–present) Reserve Officer Training Corps, a four-year college-level program that requires its members to become second lieutenants in the army upon graduation. (AFS) (*see also* Rot Corps)

Rot Corps USA (1960s) nickname for Reserve Officer Training Corps; aka Rotsey.

rotor head USA (1991) helicopter crew member. (AET)

Rotsey *See* Rot Corps

Rottencrotch, Suzie *See* Suzie

rough as bags BrA (WWI) as tough (uncouth) as burlap bags.

rough riding *See* monkey drill

round-bottomed chest USN (19th c.) sailor's seabag. (TON) (*see* seabag)

round dozen USN (1794–1850s) thirteen strokes of the cat-o'-nine-tails as punishment for an offense, the naval version of a baker's dozen. (ANE)

round eyes USA (1960s) white woman (as opposed to an Oriental woman, whose eyes were slanted).

roundhouse BrN (1750s) a round, enclosed cubicle at the bow of a ship that served as the junior officer's head. (*see* bow, head, junior officer)

roundly USN (19th c.) quickly. (ANE)

round robin BrN>USN (18th–19th c.) a petition with signatures arranged in a circular pattern from the center outwards, begun as a means of protest by sailors in the British navy in the 1790s. The finished product resembled a target. Its rings made it very difficult for authorities to figure out who had signed the paper first and thereby to determine the ringleader. (ANE)

rouse and shine USN (18th–mid-19th c.) call to get troops out of their hammocks. (ANE)

route march USA (WWI) march used to exercise troops or to move them from point A to point B. In a route march, the troops were permitted to get out of step and to talk. (EMP MMD)

rover MM (18th–19th c.) ship's rigger who moved, or roved, from port to port to seek employment. (19th c.) pirate or brigand. (TON)

RPG USA (1960s–present) rocket-propelled grenade.

RSM BrA (WWI) regimental sergeant major.

RSM's Milk BrA>North Africa (1940) the regimental sergeant major's milk, a strong, home-brewed alcoholic beverage. (DRA) (*see also* hooch, stromboli)

RTO USA/USMC (1960s) radio telephone operator.

rubber duckie USN (1960s) inflatable boat sometimes towed behind a ship in an attempt to confuse enemy radar. (ASL)

rubber sock USN (1960s) new recruit.

rub out USA (WWII) to kill.

rucksack Gr>USA (WWII–present) [German *Rucksack*, back pack] infantry backpack.

ruffles USA (18th c.–present) the slow, steady drumbeat that accompanies the rendering of military honors. Ruffles are quieter than a drumroll. (ASC MDB MMD)

Ruff Puffs USA (1960s) regional and popular forces of South Vietnam, the local militia.

rug dance USN (1980s–present) what one does when one is chewed out by a superior. (*see* called on the carpet)

rugged USA (1960s) dangerous, tough, unpleasant, or difficult.

run amok *See* amok

rum hound USA (WWII) one who likes to drink too much alcohol. (MMD)

run ashore BrN>USN (18th c.) to take a day on shore leave, to go ashore. (TWW)

run money USN (19th c.) reward paid to anyone who returned a deserter to ship. (ANE)

runner USA/USMC (WWI–WWII) unit messenger. (AFR SAM)

running fire USA (WWII) rapid and continuous fire. (MMD)

running gear USAAF (WWII) human legs; aka landing gear. (AFR) (*see also* exercise the landing gear)

runt USA (WWII) shortest man in the unit, often slightly under the height requirement. (MCT)

run the gauntlet Sweden>Fr>Gr>D>Br> USA/USN (15th–late 18th c.) [Swedish *gatlopp*, passageway>English *gauntlet*, gloved course (to strike with glove)] to run, as a punishment, between parallel rows of captors and sometimes comrades armed with lengths of knotted ropes and sticks. (CWO DOC DWO)

ruptured duck USA/USMC/USN/USCG (WWII) an award, in the form of a cloth patch or a brass lapel pin, issued to those who had been honorably discharged from the military. The patch and pin depicted an eagle with spread wings sitting in the center of a wreath of oak leaves. (PAT SAM)

Russian sap BrA>USA/USMC (WWI–WWII) trenching technique that employed subterranean powder charges, including tubes filled with explosives, instead of shovels. (MMD)

rust bucket USN (WWII) old, worn out destroyer.

S

saber strength BrA>USA (WWI) number of troopers in a cavalry unit.

SAC (sac) USAF (1950s–present) Strategic Air Command. (AFS)

sack[1] BrA>USA (16th c.–present) [French *sac*, to plunder] to pillage and plunder. (AFR DWO IHA MCT MD MMD SAM TLL) USA/USMC (1950s–present) to dismiss or fire from an assignment. (PAT)

sack[2] USMC>USA (WWI–present) bed; aka rack, bunk. (PAT) (*see also* bed sack)

sack drill USMC (WWII–present) time spent sleeping; aka sack duty, sack time. (SAM)

sack duty *See* sack drill

sack out USN/USMC (WWI–WWII) to sleep soundly. (AFR IHA SAM) (*see* rack, sack)

sack out artist USMC (WWII) one who

sleeps whenever the opportunity presents itself; aka sack time artist. (SAM)

sack time *See* sack drill

Saddam USA (1991) a lie, pure and utter garbage, the truth stretched to the limit. From Saddam Hussein, who rarely spoke the plain truth. (AET)

Saddam happens USA/USMC (1991) the unexpected occurs, a play on the civilian phrase "shit happens." (AET)

Saddamist USA/USMC (1991) Saddam Hussein, who "sodomized" the areas he conquered. (AET)

Saddamy USA (1991) Saddam Hussein. (AET)

Sad Sack USA (WWII) unkempt soldier, from a cartoon character by the same name who was depicted as a well-intentioned goof-off. (CWO SAM)

SAF USAF (1950s) Secretary of the Air Force. (AFS)

safeguard USA (WWI) a select body of troops assigned the duty of protecting a person, building, or other property. (*see also* force a safeguard)

sailor's blessing MM (19th c.) good sound cursing. (AST)

sailor's hitching post USN (19th c.) one of the Marines who customarily dragged sailors on liberty back to the ship. (*see also* marine)

sailor's pleasure MM (19th c.) relaxation. (AST)

sailor's weather MM (19th c.) fair weather with a steady wind. (AST)

Sails MM (19th c.) ship's sailmaker. (AST)

sail under false colors MM/USN (17th–20th c.) to fly, as pirates, the colors or flag of an intended victim in order to get close enough to launch a surprise attack. Ships of warring nations sometimes employed this trick. Ashore: to pretend, to misrepresent oneself, to lie. (TON)

Sakdalisata and Gunaps USA/USMC/USN (WWII, Philippines) names of traitor groups in the Pacific Islands; aka fifth columns. (TOC)

salavate USA (WWII) to knock another person out. (AFR GWD)

sally[1] Fr>Br>USA (1768–1860s) [Latin *salire*, to jump>Old French *salir* or *sallir*, sudden breakout from defensive position> English *sally*, launch attack upon defensive position] an assault made by defenders of a besieged fortification upon enemy siege lines with the purpose of destroying those works and possibly forcing the enemy to lift the siege. (DWO MD MMD TLL)

sally[2] MM (16th c.–present) to work a ship loose from a sandbar by rocking it from side to side as the crew shifts the weight aboard by rushing en masse from one side of the open deck to the other. (20th c.) aka sally ship. (16th c.) to leave, especially to go to sea, as in "to sally forth." (MAN OST)

sally port Fr>Br>USA (16th–19th c.) a strongly fortified gate that permitted the defenders of a besieged fort to exit, or sally forth, against the besieging forces of the enemy. (MD MDB MMD)

salt horse BrN>USN (17th–19th c.) salt beef or pork. Dishonest contractors cut up horses or mules and put them in beef or pork barrels, and bits and pieces of harness and horseshoes supposedly were sometimes found in with the meat.

salt water soap *See* soap, salt water

salt water stripes USA (WWI–WWII) temporary rank of corporal or sergeant, often conferred aboard transport ships en route to Europe or the South Pacific. (MCT)

salty USMC (WWII) said of a cocky or seasoned Marine. (SAM)

saluting gun USA (WWI) an artillery piece that was fired as a sign of respect. (ASC)

salvation army BrA (WWI) nickname for the Salvage Corps, which was responsible for cleaning up the battlefield. Members salvaged military gear as the Salvation Army salvaged souls.

salve USA (WWII) butter. (GWD)

salvo BrA (WWI) Salvation Army rest and recreation hut.

SAM (sam) USA (1960s) surface-to-air missile.

Sam Browne USA/USMC (WWI) any army

officer, for the Sam Browne belt worn as part of his uniform. (*see* Sam Browne belt)

Sam Browne belt BrA>FrA>USA/USMC (1878) a belt designed by Sir Basil Montgomery to give extra support for heavy items carried on the waist, based on a belt of similar design that had been in use among British cavalry and dragoons since the 1750s. A cross strap ran from the right shoulder across the chest to the left hip. In 1900, the belt was adopted by the British and copied by the French. In 1901, British army officer Sir Samuel James Browne improved Montgomery's design so that despite having only one arm, he could use his saber effectively. Although US troops disliked both the belt and the name, US forces adopted and wore a similarly designed belt between 1917 and 1940. (ATK MCT)

sammies USA (WWI) newspaper term for United States soldiers, who hated the name. USA/USMC (1991, Somalia) Somalians; aka skippies.

samshoo MM (19th c.) pidgin English for strong booze of any kind. (SLA)

sand USA/USMC/USN (1915) granulated sugar. (1930) table salt. (SAM)

sand and specks USA (WWII) salt and pepper. (SID)

sandbag[1] USNA (WWII) a student pilot's first passenger. (AFR)

sandbag[2] USA (1960s) among special forces, to avoid work; aka ghost. (*see also* dodge the column, goldbrick, lead swinger)

sandbox USA/USMC (1991) a desert in a Gulf War state. (AET)

S and D USA (1960s) search and destroy mission.

sandpaper USA (1960s) army-issue toilet paper.

sand-pounder USN (WWII) sailor assigned to shore duty.

sand rat USA (WWI–Korean War) enlisted man or officer assigned to work in the butts of the rifle pits during small arms practice. (EMP PAT SAM)

san fairy ann BrA (WWI) [French *ça ne fait*

rein, it doesn't matter, it makes no difference] it doesn't matter; it makes no difference, a mispronunciation of the French term; aka san fairy.

sanitary fatigue BrA (WWI) work duty consisting of removing buckets of human waste from trenches or covering unburied dead with lime.

sanitation engineer USA (WWII) mocking name for a latrine orderly. (SID) (*see* latrine)

Santa Claus in the pits USA (WWII) one who made a perfect score on the rifle range. (GWD)

sap It>Fr>Br>USA (16th–20th c.) [Italian *zappare*>French *saper*, to undermine>English *sap*, to dig tunnel or trench in order to attack enemy] narrow trench running toward the enemy. (DWO MD MDB MMD TLL)

sappers BrA>USA (18th–20th c.) those of besieging army who dug trenches in siege lines. (mid-19th c.) military engineers. (WWI–1960s) those who dug trenches or saps. USA (1960s) Vietcong or North Vietnamese army commandos equipped with explosives; enemy infiltrators. (MD MMD) (*see* sap)

sardine box CSA/USA (1860s) leather cap box that carried the copper caps needed to fire muskets. (LRY)

sarkan (sahr•kan) BrA (1940, North Africa) "What time is it?" (DRA)

SAT USNA (WWII) Supervisor Aviation Training. (AFR)

satchel charge USA/USMC (WWII–present) a canvas pack filled with explosives (dynamite in WWII) to produce a powerful blast. The fuses on the homemade charges were lighted by hand and the satchel thrown by hand into an enemy position, bunker, or cave. (PAT)

Saturday night soldier *See* terrier

save one's bacon BrA (17th c.) to escape a dangerous situation with one's hide intact. (DVT)

savvy Sp>Br>USMM (18th c.–present) [Span-ish *saber*, to know; West African pidgin English>English *savvy*, to understand or know] shrewd, astute. (DWO)

sawbones MM/BrA>USA (18th c.–WWII) nickname for a doctor or surgeon whose main job was to amputate; any doctor; aka bones.

sawmill BrA (WWI) operating theater of a military hospital.

scag USA (WWII) cigarette. (MMD)

scandal sheet USAAF (WWII) the monthly payroll sheet, as pay was so pitifully low. (AFR) (*see* eagle farts)

scarce as hen's teeth CSA/USA (1860s) said of an item that was hard to find and extremely rare. (LRY)

scarf USA (1950s–60s) a scarf or ascot worn with the class A uniform. The color of the scarf corresponded to the branch of service (infantry, light blue; armored cavalry, yellow; artillery, red; and so on). (ASC)

scatter gun USAAF (WWII) machine gun. (AFR)

SCD USA (WWI) army discharge based on Surgeon's Certificate of Disability. This paper was a medical discharge issued for various reasons. It was often applied to benzined officers who were unfit emotionally, physically, or mentally to hold a command. An SCD saved them the embarrassment of being court-martialed or cashiered from the service. (MMD WWW) (*see* benzined, bobtail, cashiered)

schemes and dreams USAF (1980s) plans and scheduling.

schlappen BrA (1940s) [German *schlaffen*, to sleep] to sleep, a British mispronunciation of the German; aka kip, schlaap-n. (DRA)

schooner MM (18th c.–present) originally, any shallow drafted vessel that skipped, or schooned, over the water. (late 18th c.) a fore-and-aft-rigged vessel. (OST TON)

Schwarze Maria GrA (WWI) [German *Schwarze Maria*, Black Mary] a heavy artillery shell used by the Allied Forces that created huge black columns of smoke.

SCM USA (WWI) summary court-martial. (EMP)

scoff USN (19th c.) to eat, especially to eat hurriedly. (AST)

scoop USA (1940) news, fresh information,

supposedly official; information that was leaked before its intended release.

'scope USN (1935–present) periscope.

scopehead USA (1960s) radar operator.

scout USA (1833–WWI) [Old French *escouter*, to listen>English *scout*, to spy or look upon>(15th c.) one who looks upon enemy] mounted soldier sent out ahead of and on the flanks of a body of troops to locate enemy forces. USA/USMC (WWII) one who was sent out to locate enemy forces; the act of conducting reconnaissance. (DWO MD MMD TLL)

scramble BrAF (WWII) aerial combat between planes of opposing armies. USAAF>USAF (WWII–present) call for all pilots to man their planes and get airborne. (AFS GWD)

scrambled eggs USN/USA (1940s–60s) gold oak leaves found on the visors of senior military officers' service hats. (WEA) (*see also* brass hat)

scraper *See* lawnmower

screamers USA (1860s) severe diarrhea or dysentery.

screaming meemies USMC/USA (WWII– Korean War) truck-mounted, multiple-barrel rocket launchers. When fired, the sound of these rockets was shrill and nerve wracking. The phrase also describes a person's visible jitters and/or shakes. (PAT SAM)

screechers BrAF (WWII) blind, raving drunk: *He's screechers.*

scribe USMC (1980s) boot camp term for a recruit assigned to help the drill instructor with his paperwork.

scrip BrA>USA/USN/USMC/USAF (18th c.–present) a written receipt indicating the bearer was entitled to receive something. In the United States, scrip also referred to a military coupon or promissory note issued in place of government currency. (*see* canteen checks)

script USAAF (WWII) special orders to be followed to the letter, not unlike a movie script. (AFR)

scrounge BrA>USA/USMC/USN (WWII) to steal, borrow, or mooch; to seek out a par-ticular item; to borrow money; to look for a person in hopes of getting free drinks or money; aka scrounge around. (GWD PAT SAM)

SCUBA (SKOO•ba) USN (1960s–present) self-contained underwater breathing apparatus, the air tanks and regulators that permit divers to remain underwater for extended periods of time without being tethered to a ship or other source of oxygen.

scudbusters USA (1991) Patriot missiles that shot down Soviet-made Iraqi SCUD missiles, a play on the movie title *Ghostbusters*. (AET)

scurvy MM (16th c.–present) disease caused by lack of vitamin C. (*see also* limeys)

scurvy trick MM (18th–20th c.) low, mean, nasty trick.

scuttle[1] MM (15th c.) large container, such as a coal scuttle. (17th c.) opening or hole in a barrel; hatch in a deck. (DWO OST) (18th– 19th c.) opening in a deck through which ammunition was passed from the magazine to the decks above.

scuttle[2] MM (17th c) to sink a ship, especially with malice; to hurry along; also spelled scuddle. (DWO OST)

scuttlebutt MM (18th–20th c.) water barrel (butt) with a hole, or scuttle, to which several tin cups were chained to prevent sailors from stealing them. Sailors shot the breeze while awaiting their turn to drink water, thus giving the name scuttlebutt to news, rumors, and gossip. USMC/USN (1935) electric water fountain or bucket of water. (PAT RAS SAM TON)

scuz rag USMC (1980s) boot camp term for a scrubbing or cleaning rag.

SD USA (WWI) special duty. (EMP)

SDC USA/USAF (1960s) Special Defense Corps, local South Vietnamese militia.

SDI USMC (1980s) senior drill instructor.

SDO USNA (WWII) squadron duty officer. USAF (1950s) special duty only. (AFR AFS)

seabag USN (18th c.–present) canvas bag used by sailors to carry clothing and belongings. During the eighteenth and nineteenth centuries, seabags were often tarred to keep their contents safe from dampness and mice.

Seabees USN (WWII) naval construction battalions. At first, they were civilian construction workers or engineers under naval contract, but by 1943 they had been absorbed by the navy.

SEAC USA/USMC/USN (WWII) Southeast Asian Command; aka Save England's Asiatic Colonies.

sea-cock USN (WWII) valve located in the bottom of a ship which when opened would permit the ship to fill with water and sink so as to avoid capture by the enemy.

SEAD USA (1970s) suppression of enemy air defenses.

sea dog MM (1570s) Spanish term (adopted by the British) for English privateer Sir Francis Drake and his crew, who wreaked havoc in the Spanish West Indies. (17th–20th c.) nickname for a crusty or old sailor, an insult or compliment according to the tone of voice used. USN (19th c.) common seal; old sailor. (ANE TON)

sea-going bellhop USA/USN (WWI–present) insulting term used by sailors and soldiers for a Marine assigned to duty as a naval officer's orderly at sea.

sea-grocer BrN (1750s) kindly nickname for the ship's purser. (*see* nip-cheese, purser)

seagull Naval Academy>USMC (1925) chicken or turkey, especially the canned variety. USAAF (WWII) government-issue chicken. USN/USMC (WWII) member of a sailor's family who followed him from base to base; one with a hearty appetite, like the bird. (AFR SAM)

sea lawyer USN/USMC (1850s–present) self-appointed expert on naval law; one who questions all military regulations, generally considered an agitator by officers. (PAT RAS SAM) (*see also* barracks lawyer, lower deck lawyer)

sealed orders USA (WWII) confidential orders that were delivered in a sealed envelope and opened at a specific time or place by an authorized person. (ASC)

sea legs USN (19th c.) surefootedness on the rolling deck of a ship at sea; ability to walk when intoxicated. (ANE)

SEALs USN (1962–present) Sea and Land, the land operation unit of the United States Navy, which was created to work with the navy's Underwater Demolition Teams (UDTs). In 1983, the two units were reorganized, and the UDTs became an arm of the SEALs. SEAL teams are responsible for preassault reconnaissance of hostile beach positions, harbors, coasts, and waterways. They train allied naval troops in couterterrorism and operate as antiterrorist combat teams. As of 1989, there were six active teams with a complement of 175 men each-supported by five SEAL reserve units. (*see also* Green Berets, open mess operators)

Seaman Jones *See* Joe Shit, the ragman

seam squirrel *See* louse

Sears & Roebuck lieutenant USA (WWII) a newly commissioned second lieutenant, who supposedly had ordered his commission from a Sears catalog. (GWD)

seat of ease BrN (1750s) a hole in the planks at the bow of the ship that served as the sailor's head. (*see* head, roundhouse)

seaweed USN (WWII–present) government-issue spinach. USMC (WWII–present) Marine's derogatory name for a sailor; aka deck ape, squid, swab jockey. (SAM) (*see also* anchor clanker, flatfoot, popeye)

secesh CSA/USA (1860s) said of anything relating to the Confederate States of America, from the word secession.

second balloon USA (1960s) second lieutenant.

second grader USAAF (WWII) the rank of technical, or tech, sergeant, who wore two stripes with the letter T below them. (AFR)

second hat USMC (1980s) boot camp term for assistant drill instructor. (*see* hat)

second John USMC (WWII–Korean War) second lieutenant. (SAM)

second lieutenant USA/USMC (1800–1898) the third officer in line of command of a company. (1898–present) the officer who is second in line of command of a platoon within a company. (EMP SAW)

second pilot USAF (1950s) copilot. (AFS)

second John USMC (WWII–Korean War) second lieutenant. (SAM)

second lieutenant USA/USMC (1800–1898) the third officer in line of command of a company. (1898–present) the officer who is second in line of command of a platoon within a company. (EMP SAW)

second pilot USAF (1950s) copilot. (AFS)

seconds USA (WWI–present) additional helping of food. (EMP)

secret gen BrA (WWII) secret information. (*see* gen)

section USA (WWI–present) a military unit smaller than a platoon but larger than a squad. (ASC) (*see also* army, brigade, battalion, company, corps, division, platoon, regiment, squad)

Section 8 USA/USMC/USN (WWII–present) discharge based on ineptitude or inability to function in the military; one who is mentally imbalanced or neurotic. This general term was officially replaced by more clinical ones in 1954 and 1955. (*see also* goofy discharge)

section whore USN (1980s) jack-of-all-trades assigned to the ship's repair shop who does everything related to running the ship.

secure BrN>USN (17th c.–present) to tie down or make fast; to complete or finish; to cease working; to put away in the proper place. (AFR OST SAM)

secure the butts USMC (WWII) to cease or terminate all types of activity. (SAM)

security USA (WWI) the measures taken for the protection of property, personnel, defenses, earthworks, and more from observation, sabotage, or surprise attack by a hostile force; the protection provided by taking such measures. (ASC MMD)

security clearance USAF (1950s) special permit allowing access to classified material. (AFS)

see cum saw USA (WWII) pidgin English for "I know how. And I know what to do." (GWD) (*see* pidgin English)

seep USN (WWII) a jeep made waterproof for amphibious operations.

see the elephant USA (1840s–60s, 1960s) to experience battle. The term originated during the Mexican War, was used throughout the Civil War, and was revived during the Vietnam War. (*see* combat)

seize MM (18th–20th c.) to secure with a small line. (MAN)

semaphore CSA/USA/USMC/USN (1860s–WWII) a signaling system that used hand-held flags to transmit messages via a letter system, usually the Morse code.

semper fi USMC (WWII) from the USMC motto *Semper Fidelis,* meaning "always faithful," this term could mean anything from "bug off" to "everything's okay," depending on the tone of voice used. (SAM)

senior pilot USAF (1950s) next to highest possible rating for a flyer. To earn the title, one had to have been a pilot for at least seven years, have logged at least two thousand hours of flight time and hold a green instrument card. (AFS)

sentinel Rome>Br>USA (B.C.–present) [Latin *sentina,* outhouse, hold of ship where bilges were found or *sentire,* to perceive through senses] originally, one stationed in the ship's hold to keep watch on the level of the bilges and issue a call to man the pumps if the level rose; later, a soldier standing guard at a gate or other entryway. The name possibly arose from the resemblance of a military sentry box to an outhouse (*sentina*), but more likely it arose from *sentire,* because one who keeps watch relies on his senses. (DWO MCT)

sentry BrA>USA (16th c.–present) [Latin *centinel,* century, hundred, or number of men in Roman company] one posted to guard duty, one who kept watch; a variant of sentinel. Until the early eighteenth century, a British private was called "private centinel," meaning that he was one of a hundred. (DWO MCT)

sentry box USA (1861–present) a shelter that protects a sentry or guard from the elements. (MD MDB) BrA (1768) also spelled centry box.

sergeant BrA>USA/USMC/USAF (12th c.–present) [Latin *servient,* to serve>Old

French *sergent*, servant>English *sergeant*, servant; became military rank mid-16th c.] troop commander. (18th c.) noncommissioned rank above corporal. In the US Army from 1861 to the 1930s, the various sergeant rankings included, from highest to lowest: sergeant major (assistant to major), quartermaster sergeant (assistant to regimental quartermaster), lead musician, ordnance sergeant (assistant to officer in charge of weapons and munitions), first sergeant (senior NCO of company), and sergeant of line. The number of sergeants in a company depended on the number of platoons it contained. (MCT MD)

sergeant major Br (16th c.) [French *sergeant-major*, staff officer of regiment and second in command] officer second in command either to the colonel or the commander of a regiment. (DWO MCT) USA (1960s–present) an E9, the second highest rank for enlisted personnel in the US Army.

sergeant major general *See* major general

sergeant major of the army USA (1960s–present) an E10, the highest rank for enlisted personnel in the US Army. There is only one sergeant major of the army.

sergeant major's BrA (WWI) of high grade or quality. It was assumed by the rank and file that, because of his high rank, the sergeant major received the best of everything.

serum USA/USAAF (WWII) an alcoholic beverage, especially a strong one. (AFR MMD) (*see also* Anzac shandy, killdevil, lightning, panther blood, stupor juice, swill, tiger piss, white lightning)

serve MM (16th c.–present) [French *servir*, to protect] to repair or protect line or other gear by wrapping it in something small; to be part of a ship's crew. (NSB OST)

service bars USA (WWII) small gold bars worn on the left sleeve of a class A service uniform. Each bar represented six months' overseas duty. These replaced the WWI-era overseas stripes or chevrons. (*see also* Hershey bar, overseas stripes)

service cap USA/USMC/USN/USAF/ USCG (1900–present) a hat with a large, flat

crown, a leather bill or brim, and a chin strap. (*see also* fifty mission cap, gorblimey)

service cap

service dress *See* class A uniform

service hat *See* campaign hat

service jacket USA (WWII–present) class A uniform jacket. (*see also* service record)

service medal USA (WWII) an award for a specific military service. (ASC)

service number USA/USMC/USN (WWI–present) an identification number given to each member of the armed forces. (MCT SAM)

service record USA/USMC/USN/USAF (20th c.) file kept on every member of the armed forces that contained behavior reports and documentation of official business, assignments, duty stations, awards, and type of discharge; aka jacket, service jacket. (AFS ASC MMD SAM)

service ribbon USA (WWI–present) a small, rectangular ribbon worn on the service uniform in lieu of the actual medal. (ASC MMD) (*see* ribbon bars, service medal)

service school service stripe USA (1950s) V-shaped crease that resulted when the seat of service trousers was let out to accommodate the enlarged posterior of one who was desk bound. (MCT)

service stripes *See* hash marks

service uniform USA (WWI–present) the military uniform prescribed for normal military duty (as opposed to the dress uniform, the dress blue uniform, or fatigue uniform). (ASC MMD)

set her down USAAF (WWII) an order to land an aircraft. (MMD)

782 gear USMC (WWII–1980s) Marine's field gear, from a now-obsolete supply form designation.

Seven Level Turns USAF (1980s) a flight line driver who drove in circles due to his excessive workload. (*see* line)

seventy-two USMC (WWII) three-day pass. (SAM)

sewed in a blanket BrA (WWI) dead, from the practice of burying the deceased in his

blanket. (AGE)

sewer trout USA (WWII–1960s) government-issue whitefish. (AFR GWD)

sew-sew boy BrN (1750s) a sailor who was noted for his skill with needle and thread. Sew-sew boys were often employed by the officers to repair their clothing.

S4 USA (WWII) a staff officer of a lower echelon headquarters' staff who was responsible for the logistics—both plans and policy—of the unit. (ASC) (*see* G4)

shack man USA (1900–WWII) married man who lived off base and "shacked up" with his wife. (AFT ATK GWD)

shack rat USAAF (WWII) one who had a girlfriend nearby and saw her almost every night. (AFR)

shack up USA (1900–present) to have sexual relations with a member of the opposite sex, probably from the fact that soldiers visited girls in their huts or shacks. The term is rarely used to refer to sex with a regular girlfriend. (GWD MCT)

shad belly USA (WWI) horse whose belly tapered sharply toward his rear, causing the cinch of the saddle to slide out of place. (EMP)

SHAEF (shaff) USA/USN/USAAF (WWII) Supreme Headquarters, Allied Expeditionary Force (European theater).

shag BrA (WWI) cigarette, from type of tobacco used to make it. (AGE)

shai BrN (1940, North Africa) an extremely sweet mixture of tea, sugar, and milk. (DRA) (*see also* brewed up)

shake BrN (1750s) to break up empty barrels and save the components for future use.

shake a leg USN (18th c.–present) originally, a call to awaken; later, an informal request to get moving or hurry up. (PAT SAM WEA) (*see also* show a leg)

shake and bake USA (1960s) NCO who received stripes via NCO school (as opposed to one who was promoted in the field), from a comparison to a popular coating for oven-fried chicken that was applied by shaking chicken parts together with the coating in a plastic bag. The implication was that such an

NCO had not actually earned his stripes. (1991) use of combined arms fire in air-to-ground or ground-to-air attack. (AET)

shake-down USN>USAF (1940s–60s) trial time in the field to test newly issued material or to get settled into a new position or situation; also spelled shakedown. (AFS WEA)

shake-down cruise USN (1940s–present) first cruise of a newly commissioned ship, designed to test the vessel under operating conditions. (WEA)

shaking *See* shake

shako Hun>Fr>Br>USA/USMC (18th c.) [Hungarian *csako*, peaked hat>French *schako*>English *shako*, tall cylindrical hat with flat crown] pointed, mitre-like headgear worn by grenadier regiments. In the late eighteenth century, the top of the hat was flattened and a plume or pompom added variously to the front or side. (CWO)

shanghai USMC (WWII) to transfer a dud Marine to another unit. (SAM)

Shank USA/USMC (1950s–60s) a Sheridan tank, a medium-sized tank.

shanker mechanic *See* corpsman

sharpshooter GrA>BrA (1750s–present) [German *Scharffschutze*, sharpshooter] a member of an organized regiment of experts with rifles (as opposed to smoothbore muskets). In the USA in 1861, two regiments of sharpshooters were established. Hiram Berdan initially commanded

WWII sharpshooter badge

the first regiment. In 1863, both regiments were combined under his command. USA/USMC (1898–present) classification of one's ability with small arms. The sharpshooter award ranks between that of expert (highest) and marksman (lowest). (MCT MMD)

shavetail USA/USMC (1846) army mule, whose backside was shaved bare in an effort to keep the animal clean; also spelled shave tail. (1899–1960s) newly commissioned second lieutenant, a comparison between the officer's clean-shaven upper lip and the bare backside of a mule. The term also reflected some similarities in behavior. (AFS ASC ATK EMP MCT PAT SAM)

shebang CSA/USA (1860s) crude shelter. The word is believed to have been coined by Irish soldiers in the Union army held at Andersonville Prison in Georgia. US West (1870s) small, crude roadside shack.

sheet iron crackers CSA/USA (1860s) army hardtack. (LRY)

shell BrA (1768) a hollow, cast-iron device filled with gunpowder and fired from a mortar. By the 1800s, shells that could be fired from the artillery pieces were in use in the US army and navy. (MD MDB MMD)

shellback USN (19th–20th c.) sailor who has crossed the equator. (20th c.–present) sailor with experience at sea.

shell hole *See* crump hole

shell shock BrA>USA/USMC (WWI) nervous condition that developed as a result of being exposed to shell fire for an extended period of time. The sufferer might exhibit extreme depression and/or mania. (*see also* battle fatigue, combat fatigue, PTSD, windy)

shell shoveller USA (WWII) a man who shoved shells into the breech of an artillery piece prior to the firing of the gun. (GWD)

shelter pit *See* foxhole

shelter trench *See* foxhole

Sherman's bummers *See* bummer

Sherwood Forest USN (1960s) missile control room on a nuclear-powered submarine.

shimmy pudding USA (WWII) jello, from its consistency; aka shivering Liz. (GWD)

ship[1] Br>USN (8th–17th c.) any large, oceangoing vessel. (18th–19th c.) a three-masted, square-rigged vessel only. (20th c.) any large, seagoing vessel. (OST TWW)

ship[2] MM (18th c.–present) to sign aboard a ship and go to sea. Ashore: to hire or be hired for work. (NSB)

ship a quarterdeck face USN (19th c.) to assume a formal attitude toward crew and/or fellow officers, especially after crew had

been permitted to skylark. When the officer of the deck shipped his quarterdeck face, fun and games were over. (RAS) (*see* skylark)

ship before the mast MM (19th c.) to go to sea as a common sailor, not an officer. On merchant ships, sailors were quartered in the forecastle, the area forward of the main mast, while officers were quartered in the stern. (AST) (*see* forecastle)

ship over USMC/USN (WWII–present) to enlist for another tour of duty. (SAM)

shipping over music USMC (WWII) patriotic, martial music played as troops boarded ships for places unknown. (SAM)

ship's biscuit *See* biscuit

ship's manger *See* manger

shipwright BrN>USN (18th c.) carpenter who worked in the shipbuilding trade. (TWW)

shirk *See* shirker

shirker CSA/USA (1860s) one who ducked his duty, a deadbeat; aka shirk.

shitbird *See* clown

shit coolie USMC (Korean War) one assigned to menial tasks. (SAM)

shithook USA (1960s) a Chinnock helicopter, the CH47, a purposeful mispronunciation.

Shit, Joe *See* Joe Shit, the ragman

shitters USMC (1960s) heads, toilets, latrines. The shitters were fifty-five gallon drums that had been cut in half and had handles welded onto them for easy transport. They were slid under the wooden seats of heads. (*see also* burning the shitters)

shiv *See* chivey

shivering Liz *See* shimmy pudding

shivoo USA (WWI) [French *chez vous*, at your house] a party.

shlaak Vehter (schlahk VEH·ter) BrA (1940s) [Dutch *shlaak Vehter,* bad or evil weather] greeting used on rainy days. (DRA)

shock troops *See* storm troopers

shoestring corporal USA (WWI) lance corporal, who wore only one stripe. During WWII, the rank was renamed private first class. (EMP) (*see also* Pfc)

shoot a line USA (WWII) to brag. (GWD)

shoot and scoot USA (1960s–present) an

artillery tactic involving the movement of an artillery position to a new location after only a few rounds have been fired, designed to prevent the enemy from getting an exact fix on the artillery's position. (Gulf War, 1991) aka hip shooting. (AET)

shoot Charlie Noble BrN>USN (19th c.) to discharge a pistol inside galley's smokestack to loosen accumulated soot in preparation for cleaning. (AST) (*see* Charlie Noble)

shooting dice *See* galloping dominoes

shooting pads *See* collision mats

shoot the breeze USMC/USN (WWI–present) to gossip, spin a yarn, or say much about nothing of importance; to chat or talk idly to pass time; aka bat the breeze. (AFR PAT SAM)

shoot the possible USA (WWII–1950s) to attain the highest possible score on the weapons range. (MCT)

shore bird MM (19th c.) term of mild disrespect for one who lived ashore. (SLA)

shore patrol USMC/USN (WWII–present) naval military police. (PAT SAM)

short arm inspection Br>USA/USMC/USAF/USN (WWI–present) medical inspection for venereal disease. (SAM WWW) (*see also* dingle-dangle parade)

short circuit between the headphones USAAF (WWII) a temporary mental lapse. (AFR)

short discharge USA (WWI–WWII) discharge granted before current enlistment ended, permitting soldier to reenlist with reassignment to special duty or training school. (ATK)

short-legged USAF (1950s) said of an aircraft with limited range of operation. (AFS)

short put USA (WWII) hand grenade, so named because of its relatively short range (thirty to forty yards with a good arm). (GWD)

short stop USA (WWII–Korean War) to interrupt passage of food to another person at table in order to help oneself. (GWD)

short timer USA/USMC/USN (WWI–present) one who has only a short amount of time left in his enlistment; one whose overseas duty is almost over; aka short. (ASC ATK MCT SAM TON)

short timer's disease USAF (1980s) apathetic condition exhibited by one about to retire or be transferred. (*see* short timer)

short timer stick USA (1960s) stick carried by some with less than two months left in Vietnam. Every day a new notch was added.

sho-sho *See* Chauchat automatic assault rifle

shot USA/USMC/USN (18th c.–present) originally, a cast-iron ball fired from an artillery piece; a lead projectile fired from a small arm; a marksman. USA/USMC/USN (17th– 9th c.) act of loading shot into a weapon; act of firing weapon. (MD MMD) USA (WWI–present) medical innoculation. (AFR)

shot down in flames USAAF (WWII) chewed out by a superior. (MMD)

shotgun envelope USA (1960s) a perforated, manila, reusable envelope for interoffice correspondence. The holes revealed whether the envelope was in use or was empty and ready for reuse.

shot his bolt Br (13th c.) originally, said of a crossbowman who had fired his bolt, or arrow, and was trying to reload before being cut down by the enemy. (1225) said of one who was too exhausted to continue fighting; said when the supply of arrows or bolts was exhausted. (CWO) (*see* crossbow)

shot in the locker BrN>USN (17th–19th c.) originally, reserve shot stored in the ship's shot locker; later and less politely, said of one who had not had relations with a woman for a long while. (TON)

shoulder sleeve insignia USA (1950s) a special patch worn on the upper left shoulder to show overseas wartime service with a specific military unit. (ASC)

shoulder strap USA (1860s) insulting name for an officer. (19th c.–1980s) thin strip of cloth worn on the shoulder of a blouse, shirt, or uniform coat to which an insignia of rank (usually officer's insignia) was attached. In the 1980s, all branches of the armed services began to use cloth slipover tabs in distinct colors (olive green, Army; navy blue, Navy; blue, Air Force). The rank insignia was sewn onto the tabs and covered all ranks and ratings. (ASC MMD)

shove off¹ MM/USMC (12th c.–present) [Old English *scufan*, to push off] to push a small boat away from a larger vessel; to go away, get lost. (OST SAM SLA TON)

shove off² MM/USMC (12th–20th c.) [Old English *scufan*, to push off] any departure. (OST SAM SLA TON)

shove an oar in MM (19th c.) to interrupt a conversation. (AST)

show a leg BrN (17th–19th c.) order to wake up and stick a leg out of the hammock. If the exposed leg was that of a female, the hammock's occupants were permitted to stay in for a while. (AST) (*see also* liberty liquor, shake a leg, son of a gun)

shrapnel Br>USA (19th c.–present) lead or iron balls. (ca. 1800) hollow, cast-iron ball invented by Gen. Henry Shrapnel that was filled with gunpowder and lead or iron balls and designed to explode fifty to seventy-five yards above ground level. Upon explosion, its contents rained down upon

shrapnel shell

the troops below. (WWI–WWII) shell and projectiles made of steel. USA (WWII) aka flying shotgun. (MCT MMD)

shroud MM (16th c.) [Old Norse *scruth*, wrapping] one of several heavily tarred lines that support masts from the sides and hide them from view, just as a civilian shroud hides a corpse prior to burial. (OST SLA) (*see also* rat lines)

shufiscope BrA (WWII, North Africa) a medical instrument used to observe the intestines and thus aid in the diagnosis of dysentery. (ADW)

shufty hatch BrA (WWII, North Africa) [Arabic *shufty*, to look] hatch or door in the roof of some trucks in which a person stood to observe enemy aircraft. (ADW)

shufty kite BrA (WWII, North Africa) [Arabic *shufty*, to look] a scout or reconnaissance aircraft. (ADW)

shufty truck BrA (WWII, North Africa)

[Arabic *shufty*, to look] a reconnaissance car. (ADW)

shut-eye USA (WWII) sleep. (MMD)

shutterbug USAAF (WWII) photographer, especially an aerial photographer. (AFR GWD) (*see also* hypo-happy)

shutters USA (WWI–WWII) pills used to treat insomnia. During WWI, camphor or opium was prescribed. (AFR)

shwaya BrA (1940, North Africa) small, from an Arabic word. (DRA)

shwaya mushti BrA (1940, North Africa) small boy, small fellow; aka shwaya wallah. (DRA) (*see* wallah)

SI West Point (WWI–present) Saturday inspection. USA (1960s) seriously ill, notation on sick call roster. (MCT)

sick bay BrN>USN/USMC (18th c.–present) place where the ill are tended, originally in the stern of a warship's lower decks; aka sick berth. US (18th–19th c.) warship's infirmary. Sick bay was generally located in the bow, directly below the galley and manger, in the part of the ship that hit the waves first. With no ventilation, it was always hot and smelly. One had to be ill for twenty-four hours before seeing the surgeon and lost grog ration for the duration of confinement. To leave sick bay alive was considered a miracle; to die was considered God's will. (20th c.) any hospital or dispensary. (AFR SAM TON) (*see also* dispensary, grog)

sick bay commando USMC (WWII–present) one who reported for sick call frequently; aka sick bay soldier. (SAM) (*see* sick bay, sick call)

sick call USA/USAAF>USAF/USMC (1860s–present) daily morning routine during which those who are ill report. USAAF (WWII) aka limp line. (AFR MMD)

sicker BrA (WWI) sick call list or report. (AGE) (*see* sick call)

sidearm USA/USMC/USN (1860s–present) a weapon carried at one's side, on a waist belt, including pistols, knives, and swords; also spelled side arm. (1930s–60s) sugar or cream. (AFR MCT MMD SAM)

side-boy BrN>USN (18th–19th c.) one detailed to handle hoists used to bring an officer aboard ship when rough water or the size of the officer prevented him from using the Jacob's ladder. (18th–20th c.) one stationed on deck to salute officers boarding the ship. (MAN TON) (*see* Jacob's ladder)

sideburns USA (1860s–80s) side-whiskers, a play on the name of Gen. Ambrose Burnside, who sported an extravagant set of muttonchop whiskers. During the Civil War, side-whiskers were called burnsides.

sideslip USAAF (WWII) buttered bread. (MMD)

side swiper USAAF (WWII) speed key on a telegraph set that swung from side to side. (AFR)

Signal Corps USA (1860s–present) the branch of the army that handles communications. (CAM MSH)

signal officer USA (1860s) officer assigned to army headquarters with responsibility for all signal equipment, entitled to rank and rights of a major in the cavalry; one who handled equipment and transmissions. (MD)

silent contempt BrN (1750s) smile or frown on the face of a subordinate that was considered by a superior to be an insult.

silent insolence *See* dumb insolence

silent pianist USA (WWII) a clerk-typist. (GWD)

silent Susan USA (WWI–WWII) high-velocity German artillery shell that, because of its high speed, was difficult to hear until too late. (MMD)

silk USA (1960s) a parachute. (*see also* parachute)

silk stockings, colonel's wife's USAAF (WWII) wind sock, which looked like a lady's silk stocking blowing in the wind. (ATK)

silo sitter USA (1960s) one assigned to duty in one of the underground missile sites scattered around the United States.

sing USN (18th c.–1970s) to cry out; to shout when hauling on a line; aka sing out. (ANE MAN)

singe FrA (WWI) [French *singe*, monkey]

canned beef; aka monkey meat. (WWW) (*see also* bully beef, canned horse, canned Willie, monkey meat)

single-digit fidget USA (1960s) nervous condition observed in soldiers within a combat zone who had fewer than ten days left in their tour of duty.

single-digit midget USA (1960s) one in a combat zone with fewer than ten days left in his tour of duty.

single footer USA (1860s–1942) horse that allowed only one foot to hit the ground at a time. One foot fell right after the other, in a set pattern. (EMP)

sing out *See* sing

sinkers USA (WWI) dumplings.

sinks CSA/USA (1860s) sewage ditches that carried waste away from camp.

SIR USMC (1980s) Serious Incident Report, the official document sent to Marine headquarters in the event of an out-of-the-ordinary occurrence, accident, or injury.

sitmap USA (1960s) military situation map, which details the exact strength and location of units in action.

sitrep USA/USMC (1960s) situation report.

SIW BrA>USA (WWI–1960s) self-inflicted wound. In the British army during WWI, an SIW could result in the victim's being charged with cowardliness in the presence of the enemy and being sent before a firing squad.

six and twenty tootsie USAAF (WWII) woman responsible for a cadet's tardiness in returning from leave, at a cost of six demerits and twenty hours of punishment. (AFR)

six by USA/USMC (WWII–1960s) truck with six-wheel drive. (MCT)

six by four BrA/BrN (WWI) army toilet paper, which was six inches by four inches. Navy paper, known as five by five, was five inches by five inches. (*see also* stocks and bonds)

six for five USA (WWI) the rate at which loans were to be paid back on payday. (EMP)

six, six, and a kick USMC (1980s) punishment of six months' confinement, six months' loss of pay, and a bad conduct discharge.

six-sixty USA (WWI) punishment of six days in the guardhouse and a sixty-dollar fine. (EMP)

sixty-second USA (WWI–WWII) sixty-second article of war, a blanket article that covered every crime not covered by other articles of war; aka hash because, like army hash, it contained every possible ingredient. (EMP)

skag USA (Korean War–1960s) cigarette. (MCT)

skate USA (1960s) an easy job, assignment, or accomplishment.

skedaddle CSA/USA (1860s) to run away in a hurry.

skee USA (WWI) shorthand for whiskey or other booze. (EMP)

skid USN (WWII) rack on a ship's deck used for storage of a boat.

skilly USN (19th c.) an oatmeal broth that contained pieces of meat. (ANE)

skillygallee USA/USN (1860s–1900) hardtack soaked in water and fried in pork fat. USN (19th c.) drink made from broth of skilly. (ANE) (*see* skilly)

skin[1] West Point (WWI–WWII) to report an error or wrongdoing. (MCT)

skin[2] USN (1860s–1900) a receptacle used to hold booze. (MCT) (*see* snake)

skinhead USMC (1960s) a Marine, for closely shaven head. US (1980s–present) a member of a neo-Nazi organization, who usually has a shaven head.

skins USN (1960s) oilskins or other waterproof clothing.

skip-jack USN (1860s) a pushy upstart; an overly fussy, trifling officer. (ANE)

skipper USN (19th c.–present) [Dutch *schipper*, master of small craft] commander of a small craft. US/USA (19th c.–present) pilot or commander of an aircraft. USA/USMC (19th c.–present) a company commander. (AFR SAM SLA TON)

skippies See sammies

skirmish[1] Br>USA (14th c.–present) [Old French *eskermir*>English *skirmish*, sword fight] a brief, sometimes sporadic engagement with the enemy. (WWII) brief encounter with the enemy in which only small elements of the opposing forces are engaged; brief encounter with a member of the opposite sex. (MD MDB MMD)

skirmish[2] USA (WWI–WWII) to search for happiness with a member of the opposite sex. (PAT SAM)

skirt USA/USMC/USN (WWII) young woman, girl. (PAT) (*see also* bint, frat)

skirt patrol USA/USAAF (WWII) a search for girls in town. (AFR MMD)

skivver USN (1860s) dirk or short sword; table fork. (ANE)

skivvies USMC/USN (1930s–present) underwear. (PAT SAM)

skosh USA (1945) [Japanese *sukoski*, some, little] few, some, little bit; aka skoshee. (MCT TON)

skunk USN (1960s) unidentified surface object that appears on submarine radar.

sky hook USA (WWII) an element of a prank played on a raw recruit, who is required to find hooks that will be used to hold targets in the clouds for antiaircraft practice. (GWD)

skylark BrN>USN (18th–19th c.) [Anglo-Saxon *lac*, to play] to play in a ship's rigging, climbing aloft and then sliding down to the deck, like a skylark swooping down to earth. Sailors enjoyed rough and tumble games when permitted by the first lieutenant. Ashore: to play in a carefree manner. (OST SLA TON)

sky out USA (1960s) to depart in a hurry.

sky pilot USN/USMC/USAAF>USAF (19th–20th c.) a chaplain, one who guides souls to heaven just as a harbor pilot guides vessels into safe harbor. (AFS SLA TON) (*see also* chaplain, GI sky pilot, gospel grinder, Holy Joe, padre, sky scout)

sky scout USA (WWI–WWII) chaplain, one who guides souls as a scout guides troops. (AFR MMD) (*see also* chaplain, GI sky pilot, gospel grinder, Holy Joe, padre, sky pilot)

skyscraper MM (18th–19th c.) a small triangular sail located above or in place of the sail at the very upper limits of a mast, so far aloft that it supposedly scraped the heavens. (SLA)

sky winder USAAF (WWII) a member of the United States Army Air Force. (AFR)

sky wire USAAF (WWII) antenna. (AFR)

slack USA (1960s) second man in line on patrol, who took up the slack for the lead man.

slag heap BrA (WWII) garbage or rubbish pile. (AGE)

slant USA (1960s) an insulting name for an Oriental person; aka gook, slope, zip. (*see also* wickerhead)

slap happy USA (WWII) carefree, careless. (ATK)

slap it on USA/USAAF (WWII) to give a soldier a monetary fine. (AFR)

slap jacks USA/USMC/USN (WWI–present) pancakes. (AFR PAT SAM)

slave ship USA/USAF/USMC (1960s) a commercial airliner that ferried soldiers to Vietnam.

slew MM (18th c.–present) [Dutch *slue*, to turn] to change course, as a vessel or person. Ashore: to turn around or move alongside another. (OST SLA)

slick USA/USMC (1960s) Huey Iroquois helicopter (UH1), an unarmed helicopter. Since no guns protruded from its sides, its exterior was smooth, or slick.

slicker CSA/USA (1860s–WWII) rubberized or oilskin raincoat issued to mounted troops. (EMP)

slime USA (1991) to attack with chemical weapons, from the *Ghostbusters* movie, in which a character is attacked by a ghost who covers him with slime. (AET)

sling it over USN/USMC (18th–20th c.) to pass something. (PAT SAM)

sling palsy USMC (1980s) physical condition characterized by weakness, loss of feeling, and muscle spasms induced by securing a rifle sling too snugly.

slingshot USA (WWII) a .45-caliber automatic pistol, possibly from the opinion that it would be more effective to throw bullets at the enemy rather than try to hit him by firing this awkward weapon. (GWD)

sling the language BrA (WWI) to speak a foreign language.

slipping his wind MM (19th c.) said of one who was dying. The wind was leaving his lungs as a dying wind leaves a ship's sails. (AST)

slip one's cable MM (13th–20th c.) to die, a comparison to the loss of a ship's anchor, hawser, or anchor chain in a storm, which leaves the ship prey to fate. (OST TON) (*see also* bitter end)

slip the clutch USAAF (WWII) to criticize.

SLJO USA (1960s) shitty little job officer; aka slow Joe.

slogan Br>USA (18th–20th c.) [Gaelic *slaugh*, host or army, and *gharim*, outcry] battle cry. US (19th c.–present) a catchword or phrase used as the rallying cry of a political party. (MCT)

slop chest MM (17th–20th c.) [Old English *sloppes*, trousers and personal gear, or *ofer-slop*, outer garment] chest on board a ship containing spare cloth or clothing that was sold to sailors by ship's purser. MM (20th c.) ship's store that sold small necessities to crew. (OST TON) (*see* purser)

slop chute USN/USMC/USA (1930s–60s) beer joint; ship's garbage bin; also spelled slopchute. USA (1960s) a beer hall on an army base for the use of enlisted men below the rank of sergeant. (SAM)

slope USA (1960s) insulting name for an Oriental, especially a native of Vietnam; aka gook, slant, wickerhead, zip.

slops MM (18th–20th c.) sailor's clothing purchased from the slop chest. (*see* slop chest)

slow Joe See SLJO

slow leak USAF (1980s) a slow, unenthusiastic worker.

slug USA (1991, Desert Storm) an overweight, slow, and/or lazy soldier.

slum See slumgullion

slum burner USA (19th c.–WWII) a cook; one who enjoys eating slum; a field kitchen. (AFR ATK) (*see* slumgullion)

slum cannon See slum wagon

slum diver USA (WWI–WWII) one who ate

slum on a regular basis. (ATK) (*see* slumgullion)

slumgullion MM>USA/USMC/USN (19th–20th c.) originally, a whaler's term for scrap and intestines of a whale; later, a stew made from pieces of scrap meat; aka slum. USA/USMC/USN (1860s–WWI) meat stew. USA (WWII) hash. (AFR MCT OST)

slum wagon USA (WWI) mobile field kitchen; aka slum cannon. (ATK)

slung his hammock in a bloody hooker MM (19th c.) said of one who went to sea, an expression that conveyed the speaker's disgust for such a desperate and foolish act. (AST) (*see* hooker)

slush BrN>USN (18th–19th c.) residual grease left in a pot after meat had been boiled. (OST SLA)

slush fund USN (18th–19th c.) payment received by the cook from sailors who bought slush, an ingredient in their duff, or pudding. Unused slush was used to lubricate the ship's moving parts and then returned to the cook, who sold the leftovers to supplement his pay. Ashore: graft or funds set aside to be used for bribes and other illegal activities. (OST SLA) (*see* duff, slush)

slush lamp USA (WWI) a sardine can filled with meat grease and using a rag for a wick. (*see* slush)

slush oil USA (WWII) to an artilleryman, to speak nonsense. (ATK)

slushy BrN (1750s) nickname for the ship's cook. (*see* slush, slush fund)

SM BrA (WWI) sergeant major.

smadge USA (1960s) sergeant major.

small arms USA/USMC (1860s–present) hand-carried weapons, such as pistols, rifles, and carbines. (SAM)

small boy USN (WWII–present) a destroyer or frigate.

small fry USN (19th c.) young fish; physically small person. (ANE)

smart USN (19th c.–present) sharp, alert, seamanlike.

smart bombs USA/USMC/USAF/USN (1960s–present) bombs that can be controlled after release, originally LGBs (laser-guided bombs) and now EOGBs (electro-optically guided bombs). (AET)

smart money BrN (19th c.) payment awarded to one who was wounded in action. (ANE)

smart ticket BrN (19th c.) a certificate signed by a chaplain or surgeon that enabled a wounded man to receive smart money. (ANE) (*see* smart money)

smasher *See* carronade

Smiling Jack *See* Jack

smoke USA/USMC (1960s) to shoot down, as an airplane or helicopter.

smoke 'em USA (1991) to get to an assigned destination quickly, ahead of the enemy; to fire on the enemy with every weapon available; aka light 'em up. (AET)

smoke helmet BrA (WWI) gas mask or respirator. (AGE)

smoke stack USMC (1930s) a Marine who imagined or pretended he was drunk. (SAM)

smoke wagons USA (WWI) field artillery, which used black powder that raised huge clouds of smoke. (EMP)

Smokey Bear USA (1960s) army drill sergeant, who wore the old-style campaign hat with the Montana peak crown, the same hat worn by fire prevention character Smokey the Bear. (*see* campaign hat)

smoking lamp is lit BrN>USN (18th c.–present) permission to smoke has been granted. (20th c.) said of an area on board ship where smoking is permitted. In the early part of the century, the smoking lamp was a lantern hung near the ship's galley that was lighted for half an hour at each meal. Sailors were permitted to light their pipes from it and sit by the galley to enjoy their smokes. Officers could smoke anywhere they wished with the exception of the orlop deck, where the powder magazines and liquor locker were located. (ANE SAM)

smoking lamp is out BrN>USN (18th–19th c.) smoking privileges have ended; an order to put out smoking materials. Until the 1860s, when cigarettes became popular, sailors generally smoked pipes and officers smoked cigars. (ANE SAM)

smoko AusA (1915–18) a smoking break.

SMRLH USA (WWII) soldier's mail—rush like hell. (GWD SID)

SNAFU (sna·foo) USA/USMC/USN (1930s–present) situation normal, all fucked up. (AFR ATK PAT SAM) (*see also* it's gone up)

snake USN (19th c.) length of clean animal intestine filled with whiskey or other booze and tied off at each end. Wrapped around a lower leg from ankle to knee and secured with string, it was hard to detect under wide-bottomed trousers. (*see also* skin) USA (1960s) Huey AH–IG Cobra assault helicopter. (RAS)

snake eater USA (1960s–1991) member of special forces or Green Berets. During the Gulf War, the term "tree eater" was used. (AET)

snap in USMC (1930s–present) to fire a rifle without ammunition; to dry fire a rifle. (SAM)

snap-snap USA (WWII) pidgin English for hurry up. (SID)

snap to USAAF (WWII) to come to attention. (AFR)

snatch USA (1960s) a mission to bring in live enemy soldiers; mission to rescue friendly soldiers from the enemy.

sneakers up *See* tits up

sneezing gas *See* tear gas

snipe USN (1960s) sailor assigned to engineering section.

snoop and poop USMC (WWII–1960s) to gather military intelligence; aka creep and crawl. (SAM)

snot nosed brat USN (18th–19th c.) nickname for a midshipman; aka snotty. From the sailors' perspective, midshipmen were the spoiled children of rich families who were sent to sea to become officers and gentlemen. The sailors maintained that it rarely worked, and in many cases they were correct. (RAS RSC SLA) (*see* midshipman)

snotty *See* snot nosed brat

snow USMC/USA (WWII–Korean War) to lie convincingly. (*see also* snow job)

snow drop USAF (1950s) an air force military policeman, who wore a white helmet.

snow job USMC/USA (WWII–Korean War) a con. (AFS GWD SAM)

snow under USAAF (WWII) to exaggerate. (AFS)

SNR USMC (1980s) subject named recruit, the official (not to mention time-wasting) way of saying "he."

snuffy USA (1960s) a new recruit or one of low rank who was not able to perform his duties, was not up to snuff.

snug as a bug CSA/USA (1860s) comfortable, cozy, at ease. (LRY)

So! MM (18th–20th c.) order to stop (work) immediately. (ANE NSB SLA)

soap, saltwater USN (19th c.) soap made from cocoa and palm oil that was seventy-five percent water. (ANE) USMC/USN (WWII) soap that produced a lather in saltwater. (SAM)

soap suds row *See* hungry hill

social security USA (1930s) the garters men wore to keep their socks from falling down and embarrassing them in public. (GWD)

socked in USAF (1950s) said of an air base with zero visibility and zero ceiling. (AFS)

sods opera Br (WWII) among POWs, a camp play or other production in which male actors played female roles. BrA/BrN (1980s–present) a spur-of-the-moment skit, usually of a bawdy nature. (*see* POW)

soft money USA (WWII) paper currency, not coins (hard money). (AFR)

soft tack USN (19th c.) soft bread, especially freshly baked wheat bread; aka soft Tommy. (ANE)

soft target USA (1991) unarmored target, especially a person. Tanks, fortified positions, and buildings were hard targets. (AET)

soft Tommy *See* soft tack

soger (SEW·jeer) USN (19th c.) a native of Port Mahon on the island of Minorca. The island was ceded to England by Spain in 1802, and the natives took pride in robbing sailors in every way possible. For most of the nineteenth century, it was an American base and liberty port. BrN>USN (18th–19th c.) lazy, cowardly sailor who looked fit in his uniform but had not earned the right to wear it; a Marine or soldier, meant insultingly; also spelled sojer. (AST)

soixante quinze Fr>USA/USMC (WWI–early WWII) [French *soixante quinze,* seventy-five] French-designed and built 75-mm, quick-firing field gun; aka Josephine, for Napoleon Bonaparte's elegant wife, a reflection of the grace and beauty of the weapon. United States troops usually called it the French 75 or simply the 75. (MMD)

sojer *See* soger

SOL USA/USMC/USN (WWI–present) shit out of luck. (ATK GWD PAT)

soldier[1] Rome>Fr>Br>USA (13th c.–present) [Latin *solidus,* coin used to pay Roman troops>Old French *soudier,* pay] one employed by a government to fight its wars. (DWO MCT)

soldier[2] USMC/USN (18th c.–present) [Latin *solidus,* coin used to pay Roman troops>Old French *soudier,* pay] to serve in the Marine Corps; to campaign in the field; to dodge one's assigned duty. (PAT SAM TON)

Soldier's Friend BrA (WWI) originally, a specific brand of metal polish that was malleable once one had spit into it; later, any metal polish. (AGE)

soldier's wind MM (19th c.) a wind that enabled a vessel to sail on almost any course. (AST)

solo USAAF (WWII) to fly an airplane without assistance from a trainer or copilot; aka fly solo.

so long MM (18th c.–present) [East Indian *salaam,* farewell] goodbye, see you later, adieu. (TON)

solo the Simmons USNA (WWII) to sleep alone, from the Simmons brand of mattress. (AFR)

S1 USA (WWII) an officer on the headquarters' staff who is responsible for personnel plans and policy. (ASC) (*see also* G1)

son of a farmer *See* Jemmy Ducks

son of a gun BrN (17th–19th c.) anyone conceived or born aboard a man-of-war; aka son of a gunner. Depending on the speaker's tone of voice, it could be a lighthearted jibe or a serious insult. (TON) (*see also* liberty liquor, show a leg)

son of a gunner *See* son of a gun

son of Nipon USN/USMC/USA (WWII) a loyal, dedicated member of the Japanese military; also spelled son-of-Nippon. (BCD)

SOP USMC/USA/USAF (1950s–present) standard operating procedure(s). In the USMC, SOP is an extremely rigid schedule followed by all recruits.

Sopwith Camel *See* Camel

SOQ USAF (1950s) sick officer's quarters, reserved strictly for officers who had reported for sick call. (AFS) (*see* sick call)

SOR USA (WWI) Service of the Rear. The title was changed to the less easily distorted Service of Supply (SOS) in 1917–18. (WWW) (*see also* L of C, SOS)

sortie USAAF>USAF (WWI–present) mission flown by a single aircraft.

SOS BrA/USA (WWI) same old stew, same old shit. USA/USMC (WWI) Service of Supply. In 1942, Service of Supply became a major part of the Communications Zone, which included all branches of the army that were classified as service branches. USA/USMC/USN (WWII) shit on a shingle (creamed chipped beef on toast). (20th c.) call letters for the international distress signal. (ATK GWD MMD PAT SAM WWW) (*see also* L of C, SOR)

SOS course BrA (WWI) sniping, observation, and scouting course.

soul to be saved USN (19th c.) used in a kindly manner to refer to an officer who was kind and considerate toward his men; used harshly to refer to an officer who seemingly had no soul. (AST)

sound MM/BrN>USN (15th c.–present) to measure the depth of the water under a vessel by heaving the lead; to measure the depth of the contents of a vessel's water tanks or bilges. (OST SLA) (*see* heave the lead)

sound out MM (18th c.–present) to investigate or enquire. (NSB)

sound off USA/USMC (1930s–present) to speak up; to count off by squads while in formation; to a military band, to begin playing. (*see also* tell off) USMC (1980s) to yell, shout, or complain. (AFR AFS ASC GWD SAM)

soup USN/USAAF (WWII) bad weather,

such as a heavy cloud cover, rain, or fog, that created poor visibility. (AFR) (*see also* pea soup)

soupy USAF (1950s) said of cloudy, wet, and foggy weather. (AFS) (*see also* soup, pea soup)

sour oranges USAF (1950s) bad weather. (AFS) (*see* sweet oranges)

souvenir AusA (1915–18) to steal from an army supply depot; to search for battlefield mementos.

souvy *See* curio

sow belly USA/USMC (1860s) bacon, often ninety percent fat. (AFR EMP MMD)

space cadet USAF (1950s) a skilled pilot who enjoyed demonstrating his abilities. (1970s) one whose mind is not working with all gears in mesh, a confused, rambling, off-the-wall person. (AFS)

spar MM/BrN>USN (17th c.–present) a pole, vertical or horizontal, that supports the rigging of a ship. Masts, yards, and booms are all spars. (*see* rigging)

spearhead[1] Br>USA/USMC (1350s–20th c.) the pointed end of a spear. USA/USMC (1920s) the lead unit in an attack.

spearhead[2] USA/USMC (1920s) to lead an attack upon the enemy.

spec USA (1960s) specialist.

special duty USAF (1950s) duty outside one's regular area of responsibility. (AFS)

special feces USA (1960s) a nasty pun on "special forces."

special forces USA/USN/USMC (1960s) American forces trained in guerrilla warfare and known as Green Berets from the color of their uniform berets. They trained South Vietnamese troops and took part in many covert operations.

special services USA/USAF (1950s) entertainment and recreational events sponsored by personnel services for the benefit of Air Force personnel and their families. (AFS ASC)

speed artist USAAF (WWII) a radio operator who could operate his telegraph key at a high rate of speed. (AFR)

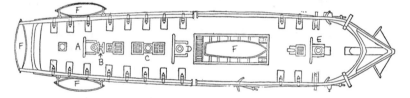

spar deck of a three-masted sailing ship. A=mizzenmast. B=wheel. C=capstan. D=main mast. E=foremast. F=boats.

spar deck BrN>USN (16th c.–present) the uppermost deck of a ship.

spark chaser USAF (1950s) electrical specialist.

Sparks USA/USMC/USN/USAF (20th c.) radio operator. (MMD TON)

sparrow's fart AusA (WWII, North Africa) dawn, the first rays of sunlight. (ADW)

SPARS USCG (WWII) women reservists of the United States Coast Guard Reserve, established November 22, 1942. The name was derived from the motto of the USCG: *Semper Paratus,* always prepared. (*see* United States Navy Volunteer Reserve, Classes V9 and W9)

spider hole USMC (WWII–present) concealed field position for a single man from which one could ambush unwary enemy soldiers.

spiff bar USA (WWII) local bar. (GWD)

spiggoty USA (WWII) a native of Central or South America who did not "spiggoty eenglish." (GWD)

spike a gun BrA>USA (16th–19th c.) to render an artillery piece useless by driving an iron spike into its vent or touchhole; to make authority null and void; in an argument, to render a point of view useless. (CWO)

spin a yarn USN (18th c.–present) to tell a tall tale. In the age of sail, sailors often told stories as they took old lines apart and spun the fibers into lighter lines, or yarn. (TON)

spin on USAAF (WWII) to fall down; to get excited. (AFR) (*see* in a spin)

spit and polish USA/USMC (WWII–present) strict attention to one's military appearance. (PAT)

spit kid USN (18th–19th c.) a spittoon. Spittoons were located in various places aboard ship to accommodate the many sailors who chewed tobacco, which, unlike smoking, was permitted any time and anywhere aboard ship. (20th c.) a brass spittoon; aka spit kit. (ANE RAS) (*see also* smoking lamp is lit, smoking lamp is out)

spit kit *See* spit kid

spit shine USMC/USN (1930s–present) a high polish on leather equipment achieved by combining water or spit and much elbow grease with the polish. (PAT SAM)

spittoon *See* spit kid

splice the main brace BrN>USN (18th–20th c.) to gather for the daily ration of beer or grog. Originally, to repair lines damaged in combat, often hard and dangerous work that was rewarded with a special ration of grog. USN (1960s) to drink hard liquor. (OST TON) (*see* grog)

Splinterville *See* Boomtown

split the blanket USA (1860s) among the cavalry, to share one's bedroll with a friend.

SPO USNA (WWII) squadron petty officer. (AFR) (*see* squadron, petty officer)

spoiled USN (18th–19th c.) said of one who was maimed or killed by the recoil of his gun or cannon.

Spook *See* Puff the Magic Dragon

Spooky *See* Puff the Magic Dragon

spoon USA (WWII) a hot date.

spoon up USA (WWII) to polish shoes and brass in preparation for a hot date or inspection. (SID) (*see* spoon)

spot promotion USA/USAF (1950s) temporary promotion, given "on the spot," of an officer to a higher rank to provide him with the legal authority required for his assignment. (AFS ASC) (*see also* brevet)

spree MM (18th–20th c.) a sailor's time ashore, usually a wild tear through port.

Ashore: a wild time of brief duration. (SLA)

spud coxswain USN (20th c.) one assigned to prepare vegetables for the ship's galley; also spelled spud coxs'n. (TON)

spun-in seagull USNA (WWII) government-issue chicken. (AFR) (*see also* buzzard)

squad It>Fr>Br>USA/USMC (16th c.–present) [French *escouade* or Italian *squadra*, square of four men] a group of soldiers. In the USA and USMC, the size of a squad has varied from four to twelve men. (DWO MCT) USA (1864) a small party of men. (WWII) a sergeant, corporal, and ten men (privates) who operate as a team; a group of men assigned to a specific task, such as a sanitary, weapons, or demolition squad. (1950s) a unit smaller than a section and commanded by an NCO. (ASC MDB MDC MMD) (*see* section)

squaddy BrA (WWII) a soldier or trooper. (DRA)

squadron BrA>USA (18th c.–present) BrA (1768) a small body of mounted horsemen consisting of three troops. USA (1860s) two companies, or troops, of cavalry. USAAF> USAF (WWII–present) two or three flights of aircraft. (ASC MD MDB MMD) (*see* troop^2)

squared away USN/USMC (18th c.–present) in the age of sail, said of a ship whose yards and sails were at right angles to the deck and directly before the wind; said of one who is neat and correctly dressed; said of a place or ship that is neat and trim; said of a person or ship ready for combat. (AFR PAT SAM SLA)

Squarefoot, Jimmy *See* Jimmy Squarefoot

square head BrA (WWI) a nickname for the Germans in general and the Prussians specifically, from the shape of their 1916 steel helmet; aka Johnny Squarehead. (WWW) (*see also* Jerry)

Squarehead, Johnny *See* square head

square the yards MM (18th–20th c.) to settle or balance an account; to repair. (SLA)

squawk sheet USAF (1950s) a list of problems and complaints about an aircraft compiled by its pilot and aircrew. (AFS)

squaw man USA (1860s–WWII) one who

lived with and/or married a Native American woman. (WWII) one who lived with and/or married a native of the Pacific islands. (ATK)

squeaker USA (WWII) carrier pigeon. (GWD)

squid *See* anchor clanker

squinter USA (WWII) the gunner, usually a corporal, who sighted the gun (squinted) through the range finder. (GWD SID)

squirt job USAF (1950s) a jet plane, which in operation appeared to squirt flame from its engines. (AFS)

SRD BrA (WWI) service rum diluted, stamped on government-issue rum jars. To a British soldier it meant "soon run dry." AusA (1915–18) acronym stamped on army-issue rum jars to indicate that they had come from the Supply Reserve Depot. To the men, who saw less rum than they would have liked, it meant "seldom reaches destination."

stable police USA (WWI) detail assigned to clean stables. (EMP)

stack arms *See* mark time

stacked USA/USMC/USN/USAF (WWII–present) descriptive of a well-endowed woman. USAF (1950s) said of an aircraft flying in a staggered formation with one thousand feet between each layer. The formation was used when many planes were attempting to land at the same field at the same time. (AFS)

stack pencils *See* mark time

staff CSA/USA (1860s) officers who supported and assisted an army commander. The term may have arisen from the ancient practice among such officers of carrying a staff as a symbol of authority. (MCT MMD)

staff officer USA/USMC/USN (WWII–present) one who serves on the staff of a headquarters unit or who works directly with a unit's commanding officer. (AFS)

Stamps USN (1960s) nickname for the mail clerk on a naval vessel.

standard Br>USA (12th c.–present) [Anglo-Norman *estaundart*, unfurled battle flag] a battle flag marking a rallying point in combat; a flag marking command point from which orders are issued. Br (1768) an eighteen-inch square flag carried at the head of a cavalry squadron. US (1814–61) a flag, colors, or banner captured from the enemy and placed on public display in places deemed proper by the president per Act of Congress, April 18, 1814. US (WWII) national, regimental, or state flag carried by mounted troops. US (WWII–1958) a flag carried by motorized and mounted troops. (ASC DWO EMP MD MMD TLL) (*see* colors)

stand a trick USN (19th c.–present) to stand watch, especially at a ship's wheel or lookout, in an efficient and proper manner. Ashore: to pay a woman for sex. (ANE) (*see also* trick)

stand by USA/USMC/USN/USAF (WWI–present) to prepare for some sort of action, to be ready. (AFS SAM)

stand by for a ram USN/USMC (mid-1860s) to prepare for the impact of an enemy ship. (WWII) to prepare for imminent serious or dangerous action; to brace for action or an event. (SAM)

stand down[1] Br>USA (WWI) to leave only a few men on watch by having most troops step down from the parapet of a trench; to take a brief rest from duty; to be at ease.

stand down[2] USA (1960s) a brief rest for troops on the march that left only a few men on security duty.

stand off USN (18th c.–present) to keep away; to keep one's distance.

stand tall USA (1960s) to be ready; to snap to attention.

stand to BrA (WWI) to man a post from dawn to full daylight.

starboard MM (13th c.–present) [Old English *steorbord*, steering board] the right side of a vessel when one's back is to the stern. Before the introduction of ship's wheels, the steering board was located on the right side of the ship near the stern. (OST TON)

star gaze USAF (1950s) the look of one who actively desired to become a general officer—the stars of a general's rank reflected in his eyes. (AFS)

star gazer USA (WWII) a general's orderly, who gazed all day at the stars on the general's shoulders. (GWD)

star rank USAF (1950s) a rank at or above that of brigadier general. (AFS)

stars and stripes USA (WWI–WWII) a dish consisting of baked beans (stars) with a layer of bacon strips (stripes) across the top. (MMD)

starter *See* colt

stateside USA/USMC/USN/USAF (1960s) in the United States.

static agitator USAAF (WWII) a student or trainee radio operator. (AFR)

static bender USAAF (WWII) a qualified radio operator. (AFR)

station USA (1950s) a fixed place or location to which personnel are assigned. (ASC)

station allowance USAF (1950s) special allowance of money to offset unusually high living expenses at a particular base. (AFS)

steam and cream USA (1960s) a massage parlor where sex was also available.

steam shovel USAAF (WWII) a potato peeler. (AFR)

steel helmet USA (WWII) a steel helmet, aka devil's bonnet; a hospital bedpan, aka submarine. (GWD)

steel helmet

steel pot USA/USN/USMC (WWII–1990s) standard WWII steel helmet. (*see also* tin pot)

steep tub BrN (1750s) a barrel of fresh water in which salted meat was soaked, or steeped, for at least twenty-four hours in an attempt to remove some of the salt.

steer clear MM (18th c.–present) to move aside in order to avoid collision; to avoid or shun. (NSB)

steersman USN (20th c.) the man who steers the vessel. (SEA) (*see also* helmsman)

Step out! USA/USAAF (WWII) hurry up! (AFR)

sterling silver MM (18th c.) coin silver; originally, Easterling Silver, from a tribe on the Baltic Sea that insisted on payment in silver.

With the passage of time, "Easterling" became "sterling," and coin silver became known as sterling silver. (OST)

stern MM (14th c.–present) [Old Norse *steer*, steering] the aft, or rear, section of a ship, where the wheel and rudder are found. (OST)

stern chase BrN>USN (18th–19th c.) a maneuver in which the pursued vessel turns her stern to the pursuer and attempts to outrun her. (TWW)

stern chaser BrN>USN (18th–19th c.) gun mounted in the stern of a vessel and used to keep a pursuing enemy at a safe distance. (TWW) (*see also* bow chaser)

stewburner USA (1960s) army cook.

S3 USA (WWII) the staff officer of a lower echelon headquarters' staff who is responsible for the unit's operational training. (ASC) (*see* G3)

stick actuator USAF (1980s) pilot.

stick-in-the-mud MM (17th c.) an English pirate who was hanged and buried in the mud of the Thames River at low tide. When the tide came in, all traces of the body were destroyed. (19th c.–present) a dull, boring person, one who lacks drive and ambition. (TON)

stick to your guns BrN>USN/USA (18th c.) an order to a ship's gun crews to remain at stations regardless of the situation. (1839) to maintain one's point of view, to keep one's resolve in the face of opposition. (CWO)

stiff *See* tar water

stinko USA (WWII) totally drunk. (GWD SID)

stir USA (WWII) jail. (MMD) (*see also* jail)

stir up a little hate BrA (WWI) to agitate Germans in a quiet sector with severe artillery bombardment. From a German song entitled the "Hymn of Hate." (*see also* hate)

stitched around USN (19th–early 20th c.) said of uniform cuffs and collars that were reinforced with decorative needlework to prevent fraying. Sailors were permitted to put fancy needlework on hats, shirts, frocks, trousers, and neckerchiefs, the designs varying from man to man and from ship to ship.

In 1910, the practice was banned, but it was revived with the appearance of liberty cuffs and collars during the WWII–Korean War era. (*see* liberty cuffs)

stockade USA (1833) a wall fashioned of pointed stakes driven into the ground; the enclosure that such a wall contained. (1861) a fortification made from heavy, upright logs set side by side; an enclosed area for confinement of animals or prisoners. (WWII–present) military jail. (AGE MD MMD TLL) (*see also* jail)

stockfish BrN (18th c.) dried codfish, used for soup stock. (TWW)

stocks and bonds USA (1929) toilet paper, from a comparison to the value of stocks and bonds after the 1929 stock market crash. (GWD) (*see also* six by four)

Stokes trench mortar BrA (WWI) a primitive, portable mortar that was transported to the frontlines in a small handcart; aka handcart artillery, mouth organ.

Stonewaller USA (1940) a member of the 116th Infantry, 29th Division. The 116th comprised mainly Virginians who took great pride in the legacy of Thomas J. "Stonewall" Jackson. Jackson earned his nickname at the first battle of Bull Run, when the steadfastness of his men caused Gen. Bernard Bee to call out, "There stands Jackson like a stone wall! Rally behind the Virginians!" The men of the 116th believed themselves to be made of the same mettle and proved that they were on D day at Normandy, France.

stooge USA (WWII) company clerk; aka company stooge. (ATK) (*see also* clerks and jerks)

storeship BrN (18th c.) a troop transport or cargo ship owned and operated by the navy. (TWW)

storm *See* assault

storm flag USA (19th c.–present) a national flag measuring nine feet by five feet which is flown in foul weather. (1950s–present) a national flag that drapes a coffin at a military funeral. (AFS ASC MMD)

storm trooper GrA (WWI) [German *Strum Truppen* and *Stoss Truppen*, storm troops or shock troops] a member of a volunteer company of one hundred bachelors or married men without children who were armed with machine guns, hand grenades, and flame throwers. They were expected to hit the enemy hard and break their resistance before the regular troops attacked. GrA>USA (1920s–30s) *Strum Abteilung,* or SA, Hitler's Brown Shirts. (WWII) name applied by Allied press to elite German assault troops; aka shock troops.

stovepipe USA (WWI–WWII) trench mortar, from its appearance. (GWD MMD) USAF (1950s) single-engine jet plane. (AFS)

stow MM (17th c.–present) [Dutch *stouwen*, to cram or pack] to put away in the proper place; to pack cargo in a vessel's hold; to quiet down, as in *Stow it!* (OST SLA)

strac USA (1960s) soldier trained and ready around the clock, an outstanding, efficient, proficient soldier.

strafe BrA (WWI) [German *strafen*, to punish] to punish or attack, especially with machine gun fire. USA (WWI–present) to attack with machine gun fire from an aircraft. (GWD MCT)

straggler CSA/USA (1833–present) one who strays from the main body of troops or falls behind during a march. (MD MMD TLL)

straight duty USA (WWI–WWII) duty with one's assigned unit. (EMP MMD)

straightfin *See* guppy

straight line USAF (1950s) to land a plane without the use of holding or approach patterns. (AFS)

Straits USN (WWII) strait of Gibraltar. (BCD)

stranger's fever *See* yellow fever

straphanger USA (1960s) one who did no useful work; that is, one whose presence provided a place to hang a pack, or straps, but otherwise did not contribute to the task at hand.

strategy Fr>Br>USA (17th c.–present) [French *strategie*, generalship>English *strategy*, to lead army] the overall plan of a military campaign, which generally does not include details of operations. (DWO MD MMD) (*see also* tactics)

strawberries USA (WWII) government-issue prunes. (GWD)

strawfoot USA (1860s) one recently off the farm, a hayseed; a new soldier. (IHA)

street monkeys USA (WWI–WWII) army band. (AFR MMD)

stretcher *See* litter

strike MM/USA/USN/USMC/USAF (18th c.–present) to hit or attack; to lower a flag or sail; to break camp. USA (1960s) to barhop. (ASC DWO MMD)

strike me blind BrN>USN (18th–19th c.) pudding or oatmeal dish to which pitifully few dried raisins were added. The joke was that one could go blind looking for the raisins. (TON)

striker USA/USN/USMC (WWI–1950s) an officer's orderly, who usually received extra pay for extra duty. USN (WWII) an enlisted man who attempted to qualify for petty officer's rating. USN (1980s) a sailor who was trained as a specialist; a trainee in a specialty area. (ASC ATK) (*see* dog robber)

strings USA (1960s) ropes approximately 120 feet in length, used to lower troops into (or to rescue them from) an area where the helicopter could not land.

stripes USN/USA (19th c.–1980s) a naval officer, from the stripes on his uniform cuffs; scars left from flogging.

stripes and lashes USA (1860s) army's version of a flogging. In 1861, desertion in time of war was the only crime that warranted flogging, a prescribed forty-eight lashes. (MD)

stripped saddle USA (1870s–WWII) cavalry term for a saddle with only a sabre and a rifle boot attached. (EMP)

stromboli BrA (1940, North Africa) a potent mixture of alcohol that was fifty percent wine, forty-five percent gin, and five percent peach juice. Described by veterans as a "lethal, volatile, persistent, corrosive, and explosive beverage." (DRA) (*see also* hooch, RSM's Milk)

Stuart *See* Honey

stuffed cloud USAAF (WWII) a mountain-top hidden by clouds. (SID)

Stuka USA (WWII) nickname for a large, hungry Georgia mosquito, after a German dive-bomber of the era. (GWD)

stump jumper *See* plow jockey

stunt AusA (1915–18) a military operation, most often a small-scale one.

stupidity stripes *See* hash marks

stupor juice BrA (WWII) an alcoholic beverage. (*see also* Anzac shandy, killdevil, lightning, panther blood, serum, stromboli, swill, tiger piss, white lightning)

S2 USA (WWII) the intelligence officer of a lower echelon headquarters' staff. The S2 is in charge of military information and security. (ASC) (*see* G2)

subaltern BrA (18th c.) a lieutenant, second lieutenant, cornet, or ensign. (MDB) BrA (mid-19th c.–present) a first or second lieutenant. (MMD) (*see* cornet, ensign, second lieutenant)

sub-caliber day USA (1900–WWI) the day on which soldiers were issued clothing. Some risked court-martial by selling the clothing to secondhand shops. (WWII–Korean War) the day on which the PX issued credit vouchers. (ATK) (*see also* jawbone payday, PX)

submarine USN>GrN/BrN (WWI–present) a warship designed for undersea operations. (*see* iron coffin, mousetrap, pallbearer, pig boat, steel helmet, tin can)

subsistence USAF (1950s) an allowance given to airmen in lieu of meals and/or other provisions.

suck a monkey USN (19th c.) to use a straw to drink alcohol from a jar or a barrel. The shore detail would drain off most of the paint from a five-gallon monkey, or barrel, replacing it with whiskey or other booze and a layer of olive oil. The monkey was then recaulked, marked, and stowed in the ship's paint locker. In a day or two the lead paint sank to the bottom and the oil rose to the top, leaving a neat cache of whiskey in between. The sailors tapped a hole in the lid of the keg and inserted a straw into the layer of alcohol to drink it. (ANE) (*see* monkey)

sucker list USA (WWII) duty roster. (GWD)

sugar report USA (WWII) letter to one's girlfriend. (AFR GWD)

sugar sugar BrA (WWII) a gung ho Nazi, usually one who was armed. (DRA)

suicide ditch BrA (WWI) jumping-off point in the frontline trenches.

suicide squad BrA (WWI) those most likely to be targets of German snipers, including runners, machine gunners, dispatch riders, bombers, and officers. On a rough day, such men had a twenty-three-minute life expectancy. (AGE) (*see* bomber)

Sunday soldier USA (WWII) a reservist, one who pulled duty only on weekends. (*see* parlor soldier)

Sunday togs *See* civilian clothes

sundowner USN (19th c.) a captain who insisted that all his men be back on board by sundown; a captain who did not allow his men ashore in their home port until the sun had set; one who did not drink alcohol until the day's work had been finished. (TON) USAF (1980s) a foul-up so incompetent that his wing commander had him removed from base before sundown.

sunfisher USA (1870s–WWII) a cavalry mount that jumped high, twisted, and kicked in an attempt to dismount its rider. (EMP)

sunshiner USA (1898–WWII) one who had been in the tropics so long that he complained about the slightest change in the weather. (MCT)

superintendent USAF (1950s) commander of the Air Force academy. (AFS)

superior USA/USMC/USN/USAF (19th–20th c.) one with higher rank. (AFS)

Superman drawers USA (WWII) long woolen underwear. (AFR)

Superthud *See* Thud

supreme commander USA (WWII) commander of an international military force. (AFS)

survey USMC (1930s–Korean War) to exchange or replace. USAF/USMC (1950s–present) to inspect government equipment to determine the cause of suspected damage or loss. USMC (1980s) to turn in worn out or unusable gear. USA (18th–20th c.) to gather the detailed information needed to make a map. (AFS ASC MMD SAM)

sutler BrA (1768) a merchant who sold provisions and other small items to soldiers from tents pitched behind the regiment, near the commanding officer's tent. USA (18th–19th c.) one who followed the army and sold all sorts of necessities as well as alcohol to soldiers. (MD MDB MMD TLL) (*see also* canteen, post exchange, PX)

Suzie USMC (1980s) girlfriend back at home; aka Suzie Robincrotch, Suzie Rottencrotch.

swab Br>USN/USMC (16th–20th c.) mop, made from rope yarn in early days. USN (18th–19th c.) fringed epaulette; a sailor's name for an officer who wore a fringed epaulette on his shoulders as an emblem of rank; aka swabbie. USMC (20th c.) Marine's mocking name for a sailor. (ANE OST PAT SAM WEA) (*see also* anchor clanker, bluejacket, gob, swab jockey)

swabbie *See* swab

swabbo! USN (19th c.) cry that went up from a gun crew when a target was missed. (TON)

swab jockey USMC (WWII–present) Marine's derogatory name for a sailor; aka deck ape, seaweed, squid, swab, swabbie. (SAM) (*see also* anchor clanker, flatfoot, Popeye)

swacked USAAF (WWII) long-winded; drunk; aka draped, swamped, wing-heavy. (AFR)

SWAK (swack) USA/USMC/USN/USAAF (WWII) sealed with a kiss.

SWALK (swalk) USMC/USA/USN/USAAF (WWII) sealed with a loving kiss.

swallow the anchor MM (19th c.) to leave the sea forever. (OST TON)

swampseed USA (WWII) government-issue rice. (SID)

swanks USAAF (WWII) one's best clothes. (AFR)

swamped *See* swacked

swear like a sailor BrN>USN (19th c.) to curse extensively. Ironically, common sailors generally were not as profane as landsmen since they were forbidden to swear under penalty of severe flogging.

Officers, who were expected to be gentlemen and therefore above the law and sin, were often noted for their profanity. (BMO)

swear like a trooper BrA>USA/CSA (17th c.–present) to use extensive profanity, probably from the notoriously colorful language of mounted troops. During the seventeenth century, variations appeared, such as swear like an abbot, swear like a tinker, and swear like a carter.

sweat it out USA (WWII) to await results or a solution to a problem; aka sweat. (AFR GWD)

sweat the glass BrN>USN (18th–19th c.) to tap an hourglass, which makes the sand fall faster, in order to end a watch a few minutes early. (TON) (*see also* flog the clock)

sweep BrN>USN (18th–19th c.) an oversized oar. (TWW)

sweet oranges USAF (1950s) good, fair weather. (AFS) (*see also* sour oranges)

swig MM (19th c.) a short pull on a line; a quick sip of booze. (AST)

swill USA/USAAF (WWII) beer. (AFR) (*see also* Anzac shandy, killdevil, lightning, panther blood, serum, stromboli, stupor juice, tiger piss, white lightning)

swinging dick USA/USN/USMC/USAF (1960s–present) any male in the service.

swing the lead USA (WWII) to tell a tall tale. (MMD)

swivel-eyed MM (19th c.) cross-eyed or squinty; said of a girl who flirted with many men. (AST)

swoop the platoon USMC (1980s) in boot camp, to question all members of a platoon in an effort to support charges filed by one of its members.

sword rattler USN (1940s–60s) one who extolled his own importance based on achievements and/or rank. (WEA)

sympathy check USA (WWII) well-meant advice from a chaplain. (GWD)

système D>FrA (WWI) the system; military or government regulations and rules. (WWW) (*see also* red tape)

T

tabard USA (1950s) a silk streamer attached to a trumpet or bugle. (ASC)

tabasco USA (1960s) napalm. Like tabasco sauce, it never stops burning.

TAC (tac) USAF (1950s) Tactical Air Command. (AFS)

TACAIR (tack·air) USAF (1960s) Tactical Air Support.

tactics Br>USA (17th c.–present) [Ancient Greek *tassein*, to arrange in battle] deliberate, orchestrated actions taken by troops on a field of battle. The word relates to the details of the action rather than the overall battle plan. (DWO MD MMD) (*see also* strategy)

TAD USA (1960s) temporary active duty.

taffy apple *See* toffee-apple

TAG USA (1950s) adjutant general of the army. (ASC) (*see* AG)

tag and bag USA (1960s–present) to affix an identification tag to a corpse and place it in a body bag. Often issued as an order: *tag 'em and bag 'em.* (AET)

tailor mades USA/USMC/USN (WWI–WWII) factory-made cigarettes. (AFR ATK EMP) (*see also* hand-rolled)

tail skids USAAF (WWII) pork chops, so named because the shape of their bones resembles the tail skid of an aircraft. (GWD)

take USA (1860s) to capture, as ground or prisoners; to accept a challenge; to write on paper. (MD)

take a dekko *See* dekko

take a hike USA/USMC/USN (19th c.) to go away, get lost; aka hike off. (ANE)

take a king's shilling BrA (18th c.–WWI) to enlist in the army. In the eighteenth century, enlistees commonly were paid a shilling in advance toward the purchase of necessary items. Frequently the money was spent instead on farewell drinks. (AGE)

take another blanket *See* take on

take a sight USN (19th c.) to thumb one's nose at someone, especially an officer, when he is not looking. (TON)

take down *See* take out

take fire USA (1960s) to be fired upon by the enemy.

take in the slack MM (18th c.–present) to haul on a line until it is taut; to render assistance with a task. (SLA)

taken aback BrN/USMM (18th c.–present) said of a ship running against the wind when the wind presses against the front of the sail, causing the ship to stop its forward movement and, in some cases, move backward. Ashore: surprised, astonished, dumbfounded. (SLA)

take off BrA/USAAF>USAF (1915–present) to get an aircraft airborne. USAAF (1930s) to leave; to move or run away. (IHA)

take on USA (1880s–WWII) to reenlist within three months of discharge; aka take another blanket. (AGE)

take out USA (1991) to kill; to eliminate or destroy an enemy position, vehicle, or unit; aka take down. (AET)

take the wind out of his sails BrA/USN (18th c.–present) to perform a sailing tactic in which one vessel closes to the windward of another, thereby blocking the wind from its sails and preventing it from maneuvering; to get the best of an opponent in an argument. (TON)

taksan (tak·sahn) USA (post-1945) many or much, used mainly by those who served with occupation forces in Japan or were stationed there during the Korean War. (MCT)

T and T USA (1960s) through and through, a wound caused by a projectile or shell fragment that passed through the body.

tangled in the soup USAAF (WWII) said of a pilot lost in the fog. (GWD) (*see also* soup)

tanker *See* tankman

tankerman *See* tankman

tankman USA (1960s–present) a member of an armored unit; aka tanker, tankerman, treadhead.

tank trap USA/USMC (WWI–present) an obstacle intended to slow or stop an armored assault. (IHA MMD)

taps MM/USA (17th c.–present) [Dutch *taptoe,* time to close pub taps] a bugle call signaling lights-out, often played at memorial services and funerals. The tune in use today was composed in 1861 by Gen. Daniel Butter-field with the help of bugler Oliver W. Norton to replace the Napoleonic bugle call for lights-out then being used by the Union army. It was first played at a military funeral early in the Civil War, during the Peninsular campaign, when the Confederates were too close for the traditional firing of an artillery piece. (ASC MCT TON) (*see also* tattoo)

taptoe *See* tattoo

tar MM (16th–20th c.) a sailor, who worked with tar and often got it on his skin and clothing. Naval tar was a mixture of pine pitch, lamp black, alcohol (often whiskey), and other ingredients used to waterproof everything aboard ship, from clothing and hats to line. USA (1960s) hashish.

tar baby USA (1960s) a soldier addicted to hashish. (*see* tar)

TARFU (tar·FU) USMC/USA (WWII–1960s) things are really fucked up.

tarheel CSA/USA (1860s) a North Carolinian. (IHA)

tarpaulin BrN>USA/USN/USMC/USAF (17th c.–present) a sheet made waterproof by an application of tar. (OST) (*see* tar)

tarpaulin muster USN (18th–19th c.) collection from the crew of financial aid for a shipmate who was down on his luck; a collection of money taken up to buy booze. Money was dropped or thrown onto a tarpaulin spread on the deck. (AST TON)

tartar USN (19th c.) crew's nickname for a ship's captain with a mean and evil temper. (ANE)

tar water CSA/USA (1860s) alcoholic beverage; aka nokum (KNOCK·um), stiff, joy juice, bark. (LRY)

TAS USAF (1950s) true air speed. (AFS)

task force USN (1942–present) an attack force with a specific misson. The term was first used in reference to the landings of Allied forces in North Africa. US Govt (1970s) a panel of politicians assigned to study a specific issue and make policy recommendations. (IHA)

tattoo BrA/USA/USMC (17th–19th c.) [Dutch *taptoe*, to close taps on kegs at pubs] a drumroll that signaled Dutch innkeepers to close their beer taps and order British soldiers out into the street during the English and Dutch wars of the early seventeenth century. The summons was issued by a drummer in the company of a sergeant and the officer of the day. During the early seventeenth century, British soldiers used the Dutch term taptoe; at some point later in the seventeenth century the word became tattoo. USA (1813–present) the 9 P.M. call for lights-out. In 1835, the tattoo was played on a bugle for the first time. From the 1860s to the present, the terms tattoo and taps have been used interchangeably. (ATK DWO MCT) (*see also* taps)

taxi up USAAF (WWII) to approach. (AFR)

taxpayer's pudding USA (WWII) a rich bread pudding made fancy by sauce and fruit. (MMD)

TB USA (WWI) a throwback, an officer removed from the frontlines for inefficiency. (WWW)

T–block USMC (1980s) a plastic stopper placed in the breech of a rifle to prevent accidental discharge.

TC USAAF (WWII) the training cadre, officers and NCOs who trained other personnel. (AFR)

TDY USAF (1950s) temporary duty. (AFS ASC)

tea cake USA (WWII) hardtack. (GWD) (*see* hardtack)

teamster USA (1770s–WWI) a wagon driver. (IHA) (*see also* mule skinner)

tear 'em out USAAF (WWII) to grind a vehicle's gears when shifting. (AFR)

tear gas GrA/BrA/FrA/USA (WWI) a non-poisonous gas that incapacitates the victim by attacking the mucous membranes of the nose, eyes, and throat. (IHA)

Ted BrA (1940, North Africa) [Italian *Tedesco*, a German] a German soldier; aka Tedeskee. (ADW DRA) (*see also* boche, Heine, hun, Jerry, Katzenjammer Kid, kraut, moffer)

teddy bear BrA (WWI) a shaggy fur or goatskin coat, sometimes sleeveless, issued to British troops in the winter of 1914–15.

Tedeskee *See* Ted

tee tee *See* titi

teeth dullers CSA/USA (1860s) hardtack; aka tea cakes.

tell it to the Marines USN (18th c.–present) an exclamation made when one doubts the truth of a statement, implying that the Marines are dumb enough to believe it. USMC (WWI–WWII) a slogan reflecting defiance and a challenge to the enemy that was used to entice recruits. (ANE)

tell off USN (19th c.) to count off or select men for a task. (ANE) (*see also* sound off)

tender[1] BrN>USN (17th–18th c.) [French *tendre*, delicate] a vessel that carried supplies, dispatches, and mail. (OST TWW)

tender[2] BrN>USN (18th c.) said of a vessel with poor stability. (OST TWW)

ten o'clock duty USA (WWII) an easy, cushy detail. (GWD) (*see* detail)

tent peg USA (1960s) a worthless individual.

tenué (TEN·ewe·ay) FrA (WWI) [French *tenué*, attire] uniform; getup; dress clothes. (WWW)

tenué de fantaisie (TEN·ewe·ay deh FAN·tah·see) FrA (WWI) [French *tenué de fantaisie*, fantasy uniform] a nonregulation military uniform. (WWW)

terrier *See* territorial soldier

territorial soldier BrA (WWI) a militiaman who trained on weekends; aka terrier, Saturday night soldier. The British regulars held these troops in utter contempt. (AGE)

tête du pont (tet dew pont) [French *tête du pont,* head of the bridge] USA (1860s) a field fortification built to protect a bridge; aka bridgehead. (MD) (*see also* bridgehead)

Teufelhund (TOY·ful·hoond) GrA/USMC (WWI) [German *Teufelhund*, devil dog] Devil Dogs, a nickname earned by the men of the Twenty-third U.S. Army Infantry Regiment, the First and Third Battalions of the Fifth U.S. Marine Regiment, and the Third Battalion of the Sixth U.S. Marine Regiment during the battle of Belleau Wood, France, on June 6, 1918. (IHA)

TF USN/USA (1960s) task force.

TFW USAF (1960s) tactical fighter wing.

that's the gear BrA (WWI) that's right, that's proper.

that's torn it BrA (WWI) an expression of surprise or disgust. (*see also* Carry me out, let me die!, Good night, nurse!)

theater of operations USA/USMC/USAF/USN (WWII) the active combat zone of a military theater. (IHA)

there are no days like that USA (1960s) a way of saying that a hoped-for event was very unlikely to occur.

there's a bullet with my name on it USA (WWII–Korean War) a fatalistic expression uttered by one who thought his odds of remaining uninjured or alive were slim. (PAT SAM)

thieves' cat MM (17th–20th c.) a cat-o'-nine-tails with lead shot or a metal piece sewn into each tail's end. The tails were soaked in brine to stiffen them, and the effect was comparable to being struck with a quarter-inch wire. The use of thieves' cats was outlawed by the British navy in the mid-1700s and by the United States in 1799, but it continued on slave ships and some blood ships in merchant services. (RAS) (*see* blood ships, blue Monday, black Monday, boy's cat, cat-o'-nine-tails, earn your stripes, flog, man's cat)

things on springs *See* junk on the bunk

third force USA (1960s) South Vietnamese neutrals.

third grader USA (WWII) staff sergeant who wore three stripes on his sleeves; aka three-striper. (AFR)

third hat USMC (1980s) the third of three assistant drill instructors, who was in charge of the platoon's administration and discipline.

third lieutenant USA (WWII) a sergeant, who wore three stripes on his sleeve; aka third grader, three-striper. (SID)

Thirty-three *See* Ba-moi-ba

thirty-year man USA/USMC (1930s–70s) a career military man; aka lifer dog. (SAM) (*see also* lifer, lifer dog)

three and a kick USA (WWI) punishment consisting of three months in the guardhouse and a dishonorable discharge. (EMP)

three hairs USA (1960s) a rude name for Vietnamese women, who were rumored to have little or no pubic hair.

three-point landing USAAF (WWII) a breakfast of ham and eggs. (GWD)

three-seventy USA (WWII) the army private's daily wage of three meals and seventy cents in cash (ninety meals and twenty-one dollars per month). (GWD)

three sheets to the wind and a fourth a-shakin' USN (1821) very drunk, with little or no control over one's actions. A sheet is a line that holds the corner of a sail in place. If the line is loosened, the sail flaps wildly. A ship with three sheets to the wind is nearly out of control. (ANE AST SLA)

three-star general USA (WWII) a lieutenant general. (ASC)

three-striper *See* third grader

throttle jockey USAF (1950s–70s) a fighter pilot. (AFS)

throttle twister USA (WWII) a motorcycle rider. (GWD)

through the mill *See* go through the mill

thrown off guard USA (WWI) said of a soldier removed from guard duty because his equipment was insufficiently clean. Soldiers thrown off guard were brought up on charges and given extra duty the next day. (EMP)

throws his weight around *See* chucks his weight around

throw the book at him USA (WWI–1960s) to punish a wrongdoer to the fullest extent of the law. (GWD)

Thud USA/USMC/USN/USAF (1960s–70s) an F105 Thunderchief, the U.S.-made fighter plane most commonly shot down by anti-aircraft fire during the Vietnam War; aka Superthud.

Thule coolie USA (1960s) one stationed at Thule, Greenland.

thumbs up BrA/USA (WWI–WWII) a hand signal or verbal expression indicating that everything is all right. (EMP)

thumper *See* M79 grenade launcher

thump gun *See* M79 grenade launcher

ticket BrN (1750s) a voucher issued to British sailors and deducted from wages due at final pay off. Tickets were used to buy shipboard necessities from the purser. (*see* pay off, purser) BrA>USA (WWI) an official military discharge. US/USN/USMC (1960s) a tag inscribed by a medic (USA) or corpsman (USN/USMC) with a description of wounds and secured to an injured serviceman.

ticking BrA (WWII, North Africa) extremely upset. (ADW) (*see also* brassed off, cheese off)

tiddley suits BrN (1750s) a sailor's best clothes, worn during his brief visits ashore.

tiffin BrA (1940s, North Africa) a cold lunch. (WID)

tiger USAF (1950s) an overeager combat pilot. (AFS)

Tiger Beer *See* Ba-moi-ba

tiger meat USA (WWII) canned beef. (AFR)

Tiger piss *See* Ba-moi-ba

tiger stripes USA (1960s) a uniform with a camouflage pattern resembling tiger stripes that was issued mainly to long-range reconnaissance patrols and special forces. (*see* special forces)

tight CSA/USA (1860s) intoxicated; aka wallpapered. (LRY) USA/USMC/USN/USAF (1960s) close, as a relationship with an especially good friend.

tiller MM/BrN>USN (15th c.–present) [Anglo-Norse>Middle English *telian,* a steering arm] a wooden steering beam attached to a vessel's rudder and used to steer the vessel. Since the late seventeenth century, large vessels have been steered by means of a ship's wheel. (OST SLA)

tin bender USAF (1980s) an aircraft structural repair specialist.

tin can USN (1910) a Ford automobile. (1914–18) a submarine. (WWII) a small naval destroyer with thin armor. (AFR IHA)

tinclads USN (1860s) lightly armored, steam-powered vessels. (IHA)

tin fish BrA>USN (WWI–WWII) a torpedo. During WWI, the term tin shark was more commonly used. (IHA) (*see also* torps)

tin hat BrA>USA/ USMC (WWI) Model 1916 metal helmet. (AGE)

tin hat

tin lizzie *See* Chauchat automatic assault rifle

tin pot USA/USN/USMC (WWII–1990s) a steel helmet; a steel pot.

TINS (tins) USN (1980s–present) this is no shit, the opening words of a tall tale.

tin school USA (1950s) a civilian military school, whose cadets were considered to be toy or tin soldiers. (MCT) (*see also* tin soldier)

tin shark *See* tin fish

tin soldier USN (19th c.) a U.S. Marine. USA (WWII) a former or current cadet at a civilian military school. (ATK) (*see also* tin school)

tin titty USA (WWII) canned milk; aka canned cow, city cow, galvanized Guernsey.

tire patch USA (WWII) an army pancake, which was as tough and durable as a rubber tire patch. (GWD)

titi (tee·tee) USA (1960s) [Vietnamese *titi,* small] very little; also spelled tee tee.

tits up USN (1980s–present) broken beyond repair; aka belly up, sneakers up.

TL USA (1960s) team leader.

TM BrA (WWI) trench mortar. USA (WWI) the town major, an officer (usually a second lieutenant) in charge of billeting the troops. (WWW) (*see* billet)

TNT BrA>USA/USN/USMC (WWI) trinitrotoluene, the explosive most commonly